S0-BOH-770

PERGAMON INTERNATIONAL LIBRARY
of Science, Technology, Engineering and Social Studies

*The 1000-volume original paperback library in aid of education,
industrial training and the enjoyment of leisure*

Publisher: Robert Maxwell, M.C.

SKILL TRAINING FOR COMMUNITY LIVING:
Applying Structured Learning Therapy

───────── Publisher's Notice to Educators ─────────

THE PERGAMON TEXTBOOK
INSPECTION COPY SERVICE

An inspection copy of any book published in the Pergamon
International Library will gladly be sent without obligation for
consideration for course adoption or recommendation. Copies may
be retained for a period of 60 days from receipt and returned if not
suitable. When a particular title is adopted or recommended for
adoption for class use and the recommendation results in a sale of
12 or more copies, the inspection copy may be retained with our
compliments. If after examination the lecturer decides that the
book is not suitable for adoption but would like to retain it for his
personal library, then our Educators' Discount of 10% is allowed on
the invoiced price. The Publishers will be pleased to receive
suggestions for revised editions and new titles to be published in this
important International Library.

OTHER STRUCTURED LEARNING MATERIALS AVAILABLE FROM PERGAMON PRESS

Skill Training for Community Living
   Basic Skills Program
   Application Skills Program
   Trainer Skills Program

Theodore Lownik Library
Illinois Benedictine College
Lisle, Illinois 60532

SKILL TRAINING FOR COMMUNITY LIVING:
Applying Structured Learning Therapy

ARNOLD P. GOLDSTEIN
Psychology Department
Syracuse University
Syracuse, New York

ROBERT P. SPRAFKIN
N. JANE GERSHAW
Syracuse Veterans Administration Hospital
Syracuse, New York
and
SUNY Upstate Medical Center

PERGAMON PRESS/STRUCTURED LEARNING ASSOCIATES
New York • Toronto • Oxford • Sydney • Frankfurt • Paris

362.21
G 624s

Pergamon Press Offices:

U.S.A.   Pergamon Press Inc., Maxwell House, Fairview Park,
                       Elmsford, New York 10523, U.S.A.

U.K.   Pergamon Press Ltd., Headington Hill Hall, Oxford OX3, OBW,
                       England

CANADA   Pergamon of Canada, Ltd., 207 Queen's Quay West,
                       Toronto 1, Canada

AUSTRALIA   Pergamon Press (Aust) Pty. Ltd., 19a Boundary Street,
                       Rushcutters Bay, N.S.W. 2011, Australia

FRANCE   Pergamon Press SARL, 24 rue des Ecoles,
                       75240 Paris, Cedex 05, France

WEST GERMANY   Pergamon Press GmbH, 6242 Kronberg/Taunus,
                       Frankfurt-am-Main, West Germany

Copyright © 1976 Pergamon Press, Inc. and Structured Learning Associates

Library of Congress Cataloging in Publication Data

Goldstein, Arnold P.
    Skill training for community living.

    Bibliography: p.
    1. Mentally ill--Rehabilitation.   2. Psycho-
therapy.   I. Sprafkin, Robert P., joint author.
II. Gershaw, N. Jane, joint author.   III. Title.
[DNLM: 1. Social adjustment.   2. Mental disorders
--Rehabilitation.   3. Community mental health.
services.   WM30 G624s]
RC576.G58   1976   362.2'1   76-16518
ISBN 0-08-021109-7
ISBN 0-08-021108-9 pbk.

*All Rights Reserved. No part of this publication may be
reproduced, stored in a retrieval system or transmitted
in any form or by any means: electronic, electrostatic,
magnetic tape, mechanical, photocopying, recording or
otherwise, without permission in writing from the publishers.*

The preparation of this book was supported in part
by PHS Research Grant MH 13669 from the National
Institute of Mental Health. This assistance is gratefully
acknowledged.

Printed in the United States of America

Dedicated with sincerest appreciation to the Structured Learning trainers of the Marcy Psychiatric Center, Marcy, N.Y.

Peggy Cerino
Cliff Ganey
Charlotte Gorsky
Jerry Kingsbury
Lorraine Krupp
Beth Moyer

Contents

1
Introduction

Frank spent 13 years at Summerville State Hospital before being discharged five months ago. He now lives in the Bates Hotel along with several dozen other persons, most of whom also resided in Summerville for many years. Life at the Bates is grim—deteriorating surroundings, very little social interaction, poor quality food, occasional bizarre behavior from a number of the residents, and, mostly, idle people doing little but passively watching time go by. In a great many ways, living on the back wards at Summerville and rooming at the Bates are not very different.

Helen is 2,000 miles away, but could be living down the hall from Frank. She spent six and a half years in a state hospital, the first time. There have been three readmissions since. Helen still has considerable difficulty relating to people or coping with daily stresses. Three weeks ago she was discharged to a halfway house.

There are literally thousands of Franks and Helens in the United States today, living in boarding houses, hotels, hostels, foster homes, group homes, proprietary homes, apartments, community residences, and a variety of health-related facilities. They are ex-mental hospital patients; many will soon be patients again—almost all of them living empty and unproductive lives, almost all of them markedly deficient in that broad array of coping and mastery skills needed by all of us to make our way in life.

In 1903, the first year that a national patient census was available, 144,000 persons resided in America's public mental hospitals. Their numbers grew steadily and inexorably, to a peak census of 559,000 in 1955. In that year the ataractic drugs were introduced in force around the nation. Largely because of the consequent reduction in disturbed and disturbing behaviors, as well as the continuing appeal of community treatment models, the census has decreased every year since then. In mid-1973, for example, the census figure was 248,562. These social statistics reflect the destinies of two types of persons, who might best be called "leavers" and "remainers." "Leavers" are people who are admitted to a mental hospital, stay in the hospital for a relatively short period of time (usually a few weeks or months), and are discharged. A large proportion of such persons will be readmitted, and often will go through a continuing sequence of admission-discharge cycles. Approximately one-third of all mental hospital patients are of this "revolving door" or "leaver" type. "Remainers," accounting for about two-thirds of all mental hospital residents, are those "chronic" patients who have been hospitalized for two or more continuous years. During this century, the probability of release for such patients has remained a static six percent.

It is the central notion of this book that both "leavers" and "remainers"—both the patient who is discharged and is unable to remain out of hospital, and the patient functioning too poorly to be discharged—would benefit greatly from intensive training in those coping and mastery skills necessary for satisfying and effective daily living in the community.

"Remainers" (those persons spending year after year in dependent roles requiring little initiative or assumption of adult responsibilities) become apathetic, withdrawn individuals, increasingly less well prepared to function autonomously or even semi-autonomously in the community. This pattern of "training" to be a good patient rather than an independent, community citizen has been described as the "Social Breakdown Syndrome" or a "colonization effect." Social, interpersonal, and intrapersonal coping and mastery skills wither from disuse and indifference. We urge that such persons be trained not (as they now are) in how to be compliantly passive but, instead, in the ability to make requests, give instructions, and respond with initiative to others' behaviors; not (as they now are) in sitting silently and noninteractively hour after hour but, instead, in how to start and carry on conversations and how to listen attentively to others; not (as they now are) to yield automatically to the directions of authority figures, however arbitrary, but, instead, in the use of appropriate assertiveness. We fully concur with Paul (1969), who observes that ". . . if the long-stay, Social Breakdown Syndrome patient is to have any chance of return to the community with tenure, with even a minimally independent existence, rehabilitation would necessarily focus upon: (a) *resocialization,* including the development of self-maintenance, interpersonal interaction, and communication skills. . . ." (p. 84)

A similar, skill-training prescription appears warranted for the "leavers," to both decrease the chances of readmission and increase the adequacy of their everyday functioning. Several investigations (e.g., Freeman & Simmons, 1963; Goldstein, 1973; Miller, 1967) have shown consistently that the ex-patient's social competency, interpersonal skill, and ability to deal effectively with daily stresses are among the major determinants of whether he remains out of the hospital. Thus, we would advocate that a systematic and intensive effort be made to teach such persons how to respond adequately to a rude waitress, a demanding employer, or a double-binding spouse; how to express both anger and affection; how to plan, organize, and conduct both leisure time and work activities; and how to do a great deal more.

In short, both the chronic, long-stay inpatient and the shorter-stay but often readmitted ex-patient are deficient in many of the skills necessary for leading satisfying and productive lives in the community. This book is about a skill-training approach we have developed to help such persons overcome these skill deficiencies. We call this approach Structured Learning Therapy. It consists of (1) modeling, (2) role playing, (3) social reinforcement, and (4) transfer training. The patient or ex-patient trainee is shown numerous specific and detailed examples (on audiotape, videotape, film, or live) of a person (the model) performing the skill behaviors we wish the trainee to learn (i.e., *modeling*); given considerable opportunity and encouragement to rehearse or practice the behaviors that have been modeled (i.e., *role playing*); provided with positive feedback, approval, or reward as his role-playing behavior becomes more and more like the behavior of the model (i.e., *social reinforcement*); and exposed to these three processes in such a manner that there will be maximum likelihood that the newly learned behaviors will in fact be applied in a stable manner on the job, on the ward, or elsewhere (i.e., *transfer training*). We shall devote a great deal of attention later in this book to helping the reader learn how to conduct Structured Learning Therapy groups. To better understand the background and development of Structured Learning Therapy, the remainder of the present chapter is devoted to a detailed description of its four major components.

MODELING

The study of modeling or imitation learning has a long history in psychological research. Imitation has been examined under many names: copying, empathic learning, observational learning, identification, vicarious learning, matched-dependent behavior, and, most frequently, modeling. This research has shown that modeling is an effective, reliable, and rapid technique for both the learning of new behaviors and the strengthening or weakening of behaviors learned earlier. Three types of learning by modeling have been identified:

1. Observational learning effects—the learning of new behaviors which the person has never performed before. For example, a long-time head attendant with a reputation for an authoritarian manner was transferred to a ward run by a democratically oriented supervising nurse. The supervising nurse treated the attendant with a great deal of respect for his knowledge and experience. At first, the attendant was uncomfortable in this new relationship because his previous supervisors, unlike his new one, had almost never seriously sought his opinion on important matters relating to ward operations. Now, the attendant is not only pleased that his opinions are valued and often put into effect, but he has begun to ask *his* subordinates for their ideas on a number of ward-related matters. As his supervisor relates to him, the attendant in like manner also makes it a point to thank his subordinates for their ideas and lets them know when he puts their suggestions into effect.

2. Inhibitory and disinhibitory effects—the strengthening or weakening of behaviors which previously were performed very rarely by the person, because to do so would lead to disapproval or other negative reactions. As an illustration of a disinhibitory effect of modeling, we once sought to investigate if the dislike of hospital staff members for certain types of chronic patients could be changed by use of modeling procedures (Goldstein, Cohen, Blake, and Walsh, 1971). Our first finding was that a large group of attendants expressed no bias against or dislike for the chronic alcoholic inpatient. However, after hearing a high status, experienced supervisory nurse (the model) express strong dislike for such patients, a majority of the attendants did also. It was as if hearing the negative attitudes of the supervisor served as a releaser, disinhibitor, or permission to express one's own negative attitudes.

3. Behavioral facilitation effects—the performance of previously learned behaviors which are neither new nor a source of potential negative reactions from others. For example, a social worker who

must frequently visit the homes of inner-city residents finds that the people she must interview provide fuller and more accurate information when they are relaxed. She has found that by acting relaxed and friendly herself, asking if she might sit down, explaining her purpose clearly in a soft and friendly manner, etc., she indeed is more frequently responded to in a relaxed and friendly manner by the persons she is interviewing.

The variety and number of different behaviors which research has shown are learned, strengthened, weakened, or facilitated through modeling are impressive indeed. These include acting aggressively, helping others, behaving independently, career planning, emotional arousal, social interaction, dependency, speech patterns, empathy, self-disclosure, and many more. It is clear from such research that modeling can be a reliable approach to the learning of behavior.

Yet it is also true that most people observe dozens and perhaps hundreds of behaviors by other people every day which they do not imitate. Many persons are exposed every day (by television, radio, magazines, and newspapers) to very polished, professional modeling displays of someone buying one product or another, but they do not later buy the product. And many persons observe expensively produced and expertly acted instructional films, but they remain uninstructed. Apparently, people learn by modeling under some circumstances but not others. Laboratory research on modeling has successfully identified a number of the circumstances that increase modeling, which we have called "modeling enhancers." These modeling enhancers are characteristics of the model, the modeling display, or the trainee (the observer), which have been shown to significantly affect the degree to which learning by imitation occurs.

Modeling Enhancers

Model characteristics. Greater modeling will occur when the model (the person to be imitated): (a) seems to be highly skilled or expert, (b) is of high status, (c) controls rewards desired by the trainee, (d) is of the same sex, approximate age, and race as the trainee, (e) is apparently friendly and helpful, and, of particular importance, (f) is rewarded for the given behaviors. That is, we are all more likely to imitate expert or powerful but pleasant people who receive rewards (reinforcement) for what they are doing, especially when the particular rewards involved are something that we, too, desire.

Modeling display characteristics. Greater modeling will occur when the modeling display shows the behaviors to be imitated: (a) in a clear and detailed manner, (b) in the order from least to most difficult behaviors, (c) with enough repetition to make overlearning likely, (d) with as little irrelevant (not to be learned) detail as possible, and (e) when several different models, rather than a single model, are used.

Trainee characteristics. Greater modeling will occur when the trainee is: (a) told to imitate the model, (b) similar to the model in background or in attitude toward the skill, (c) friendly toward or likes the model, and, most important, (d) rewarded for performing the modeled behaviors.

Our understanding of both the effects of these modeling enhancers, as well as modeling itself, can be made clearer by noting that learning by modeling involves three phases or stages.

Stages of Modeling

1. *Attention.* A trainee cannot learn from watching a model unless he pays attention to the modeling display and, in particular, to the specific model behaviors it is hoped that he will learn—i.e., the *learning points.** If the learning points are buried in a large number of other stimuli, the likelihood of his paying sufficient attention to them may decrease. Thus, as noted earlier, one important modeling enhancer is minimizing irrelevant stimuli in the modeling display. Attention to and learning of the display's learning points also will be made difficult if too many learning points are built into the display—i.e., we must concern ourselves with modeling enhancement by minimizing competing stimuli. Those few behaviors or learning points that actually make up a given skill, and thus are displayed, must be shown in a vivid, "real life," and repetitive manner to maximize the likelihood that the trainee actually pays attention to them. Similarly, the attention stage of modeling will be enhanced when the model is of high status, competent, of the same age, race, and sex as the trainee, and especially when the model is rewarded for performing the learning point behaviors.

2. *Retention.* In order to later reproduce the behaviors he has observed, the trainee must remember or retain them. Since the

---

*Chapter 4 is a presentation of the specific skills portrayed in the Structured Learning Therapy modeling tapes that we have developed, and the learning points constituting each skill.

learning points of the modeling display itself are no longer present, retention must occur by memory. Memory is aided if the behaviors displayed are classified or coded by the observer. Another name for such coding is "covert rehearsal"—i.e., reviewing in one's own mind the performance of the displayed behaviors. As research has shown, however, an even more important aid to retention is overt or behavioral rehearsal. Such practice of the specific learning point behaviors is most crucial for learning and, indeed, is the second major procedure of Structured Learning Therapy. We refer here to role playing, a procedure we shall examine in depth shortly. It should be noted at this point, however, that the likelihood of retention via either covert or overt rehearsal is greatly aided by reward provided to both the model and/or the trainee.

3. *Reproduction.* Researchers interested in human learning have typically distinguished between learning (acquiring or gaining knowledge about how to do something) and performance (doing it). Having paid attention to and remembered the learning points shown on the modeling display, we may say that the person has learned. Our main interest, however, is not so much in whether the person *can* reproduce the behaviors he has seen, but whether he *does* reproduce them. The likelihood that a person will actually perform behavior that he has learned will depend mostly on his expectation of reward for doing so. His expectation of reward has been shown to be determined by the amount, consistency, recency, and frequency of the reward he observes being provided the model for performing the desired behaviors. We shall examine further the crucial nature of reward for learning and performance later in this chapter, when we turn to the third major procedure of Structured Learning Therapy— namely, social reinforcement.

A final but most important part of Structured Learning goes beyond the issue of whether the trainee performs the modeled behaviors in the training setting and asks what will cause him to perform them in a consistent, stable, and enduring manner in his real-life environment (e.g., ward, home, etc.). We shall turn to this issue later also, in our consideration of the fourth component of Structured Learning Therapy—namely, transfer training.

Modeling in Everyday Life

A great deal of research has been done on the effectiveness of modeling in real-life settings. Lefkowitz, Blake, and Mouton (1954), for example, looked at the effect of a model upon the frequency of pedestrian traffic violations. They arranged to have an individual (the model) either cross a street or wait to cross during a 40-second period in which a "wait" pedestrian traffic signal was lit. This experiment was done in Austin, Texas, over a period of several hours, and at three separate locations in the city's central business district. The imitative behavior (crossing or waiting) of 2,103 pedestrians was observed. Their results indicated that significantly* more pedestrians crossed against the "wait" signals when the model crossed than (a) when the model waited or (b) when no model was present.

Like almost all the modeling studies we will look at in this chapter, Lefkowitz *et al.* (1954) not only successfully showed a modeling effect, but also reported information about one factor which increases such modeling. We noted earlier that it has been shown that high-status persons (or those that appear to be) are imitated more than persons of lower status. Lefkowitz *et al.* showed this to be true even when "status" was defined very simply in terms of how their model was dressed. Half the time he was dressed "in clothing intended to typify a high-status person, with a freshly pressed suit, shined shoes, white shirt, tie and straw hat." The other half of the time the same model was dressed in "well-worn scuffed shoes, soiled patched trousers and unpressed blue denim shirt." The results were that significantly more persons "followed the leader" and crossed against the wait signal when the model doing so was well dressed.

Research reported by Bryan and Test (1967) shows us that not only may negative real-life behavior (traffic violations) be modeled, but positive, helping behaviors as well. In their first research report, entitled "Lady in Distress," an automobile with a flat left-rear tire was parked on a busy Los Angeles street. A young woman was stationed by the car, and an inflated tire was leaned against the left side of the car. The car, the girl, the flat tire, and the spare were all easily seen by the passing traffic. The foregoing describes the no-model part of the experiment. Half the time during the eight hours which the experiment lasted, a second auto was parked on the same street one-quarter mile before the car described above. This car was raised by a jack under its left rear bumper, and a girl was watching a man (the model) changing a flat tire. This was the study's

---

*Significantly (or "statistically significant") will be used throughout this book in the technical sense—i.e., such a result is very likely a "real" result, one which would occur by chance less than five times in a hundred.

modeling procedure. Since no access roads entered the street on which the two cars were parked, any driver passing the first car (with model) also saw the second (no model) car. During the study, 4,000 vehicles passed the two cars. Significantly more drivers stopped at the second car and offered help to the stranded motorist when the model was present at the first car as compared to when the model and the car he was working on were not present.

A second, rather similar, study was conducted by the same researchers at a Princeton, New Jersey, shopping center. Here the procedure involved a model going up to a Salvation Army kettle, placing a donation in it, and walking away. Observers recorded the number of donations made by passersby during the 20 seconds immediately after each of 365 donations made by the model, and the number made during 365 other 20-second periods with no model present. Again, a modeling effect was shown—significantly more passersby made a donation when the model had just done so.

Modeling and the Interview

The research described above demonstrates the occurrence of modeling in certain everyday situations. A second group of research studies has examined the use of modeling to change the behavior of persons in various types of interviews. These studies ask whether we can increase interviewee self-disclosure, self-exploration, and progress toward interview goals by first showing him a model engaged in such activities. Marlatt, Jacobson, Johnson and Morrice (1970) reported a study in which 32 college students were each interviewed individually. They could talk in their interview about one or more problems out of three mentioned to them by the interviewer. Before their second interview, half of the interviewees listened to a tape-recorded interview in which the interviewee (model) revealed a great deal of information in that problem area which the listener had spoken about *least* in his own first interview. The other half of the interviewees heard no such model. Results indicated that interviewees exposed to the problem-revealing model discussed this area significantly more in their own second interview than either they themselves had before or than those interviewees who heard no model.

Liberman (1970) has reported similar results in a study involving alcoholic patients in a psychiatric hospital. Before being interviewed, each patient listened to a tape recording in which a patient (model) answered several personal questions about his family, his feelings, his drinking, etc. in either a highly self-disclosing manner or by revealing very little about himself. After hearing the tape, each patient was interviewed by a doctor who asked the same questions as had been put to the model on the tape. Patients who had heard a high self-disclosing model revealed significantly more about themselves in this interview than did not only those hearing a low disclosing model, but also as compared to other patients hearing either a neutral tape or no tape at all. Similar results have been reported by others (Lack, 1971; Truax and Wargo, 1969; Whalen, 1969).

Other interview behaviors have been shown to be affected by modeling. Friedenberg (1971) and Walsh (1971) are able to increase interviewee liking for the interviewer; Krumboltz and Thoresen (1964) and Krumboltz, Varenhorst and Thoresen (1967), working with career-planning interviews, were successful in increasing the degree to which interviewees sought out career information both during and after the interview; studies by Matarazzo, Wiens and Saslow (1965) made successful use of modeling to increase the sheer amount of interviewee talking.

Modeling to Decrease Fears

Several studies have tested the usefulness of modeling to reduce or eliminate strong fears or phobias. Kleinsasser (1968) reported success with this method in reducing anxiety about speaking before groups; Ritter (1969) was similarly successful in eliminating fear of heights; in perhaps one of the most dramatic examples of successful modeling, Bandura, Blanchard, and Ritter (1969) were successful in dealing with intense fear of snakes. This last study is worth a closer look. The researchers placed an advertisement in a newspaper for persons with a very strong fear of snakes. Forty-eight persons answered the ad and were given modeling or a comparison treatment. The researcher's description of how the modeling was done is of interest:

> In the initial procedure, subjects observed through a one-way mirror the experimenter [the model] perform a series of threatening activities with the king snake that provided striking demonstrations that close interaction with the snake does not have harmful consequences. During this period . . . the experimenter held the snake close to his face, allowed it to crawl over his body at will, and let it loose to slither about

the room. After returning the snake to its glass cage, the experimenter invited the subjects to join him in the room and to be seated in one of four chairs placed at various distances from the experimenter's chair. The experimenter then removed the snake from the cage and commenced treatment, beginning with relatively non-threatening performance tasks and proceeding through increasingly fear-provoking activities ... At each step the experimenter himself performed fearless behavior and gradually led subjects into touching, stroking, and then holding the midsection of the snake's body with gloved and then with bare hands while the experimenter held the snake securely by the head and tail ... After subjects no longer felt any apprehension about touching the snake under these secure conditions, anxieties about contact with the snake's head area and entwining tail were extinguished ... as subjects became less fearful the experimenter gradually reduced his participation and control over the snake until eventually subjects were able to hold the snake in their laps without assistance, to let the snake crawl freely over their bodies ... Treatment was terminated when subjects were able to execute all the snake interaction tasks independently. (Bandura *et al.,* 1969, p. 180)

Thus we see from this investigation that even a deeply held and persistent fear may be altered by means of modeling procedures.

Other Modeling Investigations

A number of additional studies of modeling have been conducted. Their variety and overall positive outcome is impressive indeed. Rosenbaum and Tucker (1962) showed that, in horse betting, more competent bettors are imitated significantly more than are less successful ones. Klinger (1970) demonstrated that persons will be more easily hypnotized if they first observe a model displaying hypnotic behavior. Aggression, both its increase (Feshback, 1964) and decrease (Chittenden, 1942), has been shown to be influenced by modeling procedures. Some of our own earlier research made successful use of modeling to change the behavior of hospital staff. In these studies we were able to demonstrate an increase in the empathy shown by a group of ministers (Perry, 1970) and a group of hospital aides (Sutton, 1970); the self-disclosure of nurse-interviewers (Lack, 1971); the friendliness of nurse-interviewers

(Goldstein *et al.,* 1971); and the assertive or independent behavior displayed by several groups of neurotic outpatients (Goldstein, Martens, Hubben, VonBelle, Schaaf, Wiersema, and Goodhart, 1973).

Modeling – Necessary but Insufficient

The positive outcome in these several modeling studies may make the reader wonder about the need for the other components of Structured Learning Therapy. If so many types of behavior have been successfully changed by watching a model, why are role playing, social reinforcement, and transfer training necessary? Our answer is clear. Modeling alone is not enough because its many positive effects are very often not lasting effects. For example, we have taught ministers (by modeling) to be more empathic when conducting interviews. They were more empathic *immediately* after training, but a very short time later their increased empathy had disappeared. We found exactly the same result in our modeling study of empathy with nurses and hospital aides (Sutton, 1970), and in yet other of our investigations in which we used modeling to change patient behavior (Friedenberg, 1971; Walsh, 1971). Others have reported similar results (e.g., Burrs and Kapche, 1969). We noted earlier that learning appears to be improved when the learner has opportunity and encouragement to practice, rehearse, or role play the behaviors he has seen performed by the model, and when he is rewarded for doing so. Stated otherwise, viewing the modeling display teaches the trainee *what* to do. He needs, in addition, enough practice to learn *how* to do it, and reward to motivate him or, in effect, to answer the question of *why* he should behave in certain ways. Let us now turn to the "how" question—that is to the second component of Structured Learning Therapy, role playing.

ROLE PLAYING

Role playing has been defined as ". . . a situation in which an individual is asked to take a role [behave in certain ways] not normally his own, or if his own in a place not normal for the enactment of the role." (Mann, 1956). The use of role playing, acting, behavioral rehearsal, and similar methods to help a person change his behavior or attitudes in the direction of the role he is playing has been a popular approach for many years. Recently, clinical psychologists have shown the value of role playing to increase assertive or independent behavior in unassertive and dependent patients, to reduce smoking, and to change the attitudes of hospitalized mental patients toward treatment staff.

Role playing has also been the target of much research by social psychologists. Perhaps as many as one hundred studies have been done, mostly aimed at discovering the effects of role playing on attitude change. In the typical experiment of this type, the research subjects are first given some sort of attitude questionnaire. One of the attitude dimensions on this questionnaire is selected for the study. The subjects are then placed in one of three experimental groups. Those assigned to the role-play group are requested to make a speech or other public statement on the attitude dimension, in support of attitudes which are *opposite* to those they really believe. That is, they must actively defend a viewpoint which is opposed to their own views. Subjects in the second group, the exposure group, hold the same private attitudes as the role-play subjects but are not requested to make such a speech opposite to their real attitudes. They simply are required to listen to one of the speeches made by a role-play subject. Control group subjects neither make nor hear such a speech. All subjects are then given the attitude questionnaire a second time. This type of experiment has consistently shown that role-playing subjects change in their attitudes (away from what they privately believed, toward what they publicly said) significantly more than either exposure or control subjects.

Role playing has also been used a great deal in industry. These industrial applications of role playing include management, supervisor, and foreman training; salesman training; reducing labor-management conflict; selection; overcoming resistance to change; handling grievance procedures; developing communication skills; reduction of anticipatory anxiety; and increasing creativity.

Studies such as these, in clinical, social, or industrial settings, combine to form an impressive demonstration of the value of role playing for behavior and attitude change. However, we also noted earlier that modeling procedures have been shown to lead to substantial behavior change, but that such change is quite likely to disappear unless sufficient attention is given in developing and using the modeling procedures to a broad selection of modeling enhancers, unless sufficient opportunity for practice or rehearsal is provided, and unless sufficient incentive or reinforcement is delivered. Likewise with role playing. Behavior or attitude change through role playing either will not occur or will not be lasting if the role player does not have enough information about the content of the role to enact it (or if he is not shown such information by a model) and if insufficient attention has been paid to what may be called role-play enhancers.

Role-play enhancers, like modeling enhancers, are procedures which increase the likelihood of lasting behavior change. Specifically, behavior change from role playing will be greater and more lasting, the greater is the role player's:

1. *choice* regarding whether to take part in the role playing;
2. *commitment* to the behavior or attitude he is role playing, in the sense that his enactment is public rather than private, or otherwise difficult to disown;
3. *improvisation* in enacting the role-play behaviors; and
4. reward, approval, or *reinforcement* for enacting the role-play behaviors.

Research on Role Playing

One rather dramatic use of role playing is a study conducted by Janis and Mann (1965) aimed at decreasing smoking. Their research subjects were 26 young women who were all smokers. Their attitudes toward stopping smoking and the number of cigarettes each smoked per day were recorded at the beginning of the study. They were asked to assume that they were medical patients who had just undergone a series of diagnostic tests and were awaiting the results. The experimenter took the part of a physician. Half of the women were asked to play the role of patient (role players) and the other 13 "patients" (listeners) listened to tape recordings of the role players. The role players then individually acted five scenes with the "physician," all of which were designed to arouse fear. Scene one involved role playing being in a waiting room. The role player was encouraged to express fear regarding the outcome of the diagnosis. The second scene involved a conversation with the "physician" at which time she learned that she had lung cancer and that surgery was necessary. During the third scene, she expressed her concern about the diagnosis; during the fourth scene, she discussed the hospital arrangements and the moderate likelihood of a successful outcome. The fifth scene involved a conversation with the "physician" about the relationship between smoking and lung cancer. Attitude measurement and number of cigarettes smoked per day were recorded again. Results indicated that the role players' attitudes about the smoking-lung cancer relationship and willingness to try to stop smoking changed significantly more than did the listeners' attitudes. Furthermore, and certainly of greater importance from a behavioral viewpoint, the role players were actually smoking significantly fewer cigarettes per day.

A second impressive demonstration of the effects of role playing has been reported by McFall and Marston (1970). They worked with 42 people who felt that they were too unassertive and dependent. The purpose of the role playing was to increase assertive and independent behavior. The researchers developed 24 situations which the subject was asked to listen to and then respond to by role playing what an assertive person might say and do. For example, in one situation he heard:

> **Narrator:** Imagine that this morning you took your car to a local Standard station, and you explicitly told the mechanic to give you a simple tune-up. The bill should have been about $20. It is now later in the afternoon and you're at the station to pick up your car. The mechanic is walking over to you.

> **Mechanic:** 'Okay, let me make out a ticket for you. The tune-up was $12 for parts and $8 for labor. Uh, grease and oil job was $6. Antifreeze was $5. Uh, $4 for a new oil filter, and uh, $5 for rotating the tires. That's $40 in all. Will this be cash or charge?'

Subjects were encouraged and helped to role play assertive responses to the situations. They were given coaching on their directness, tone of voice, inflection, communication of feeling, and so forth. After completion of these procedures, role players were compared on several measures of assertiveness with other subjects who had discussed, but not role played being more assertive, and others who had neither role played nor discussed assertiveness. The role players were not only significantly more assertive on these measures, but also were significantly less anxious about being assertive. McFall and Marston, furthermore, tried to find out if the role-play training had any effect on the assertiveness of subjects in their real-life behavior. Two weeks after their role play participation, each subject was telephoned by another experimenter posing as a magazine salesman. Working from a prepared script, the "salesman" delivered a hard-sell pitch for magazine subscriptions. The telephone call was terminated only (1) after the subject agreed to buy, (2) after five minutes had passed without a sale, (3) after all sales gambits had been used without success, or (4) after the subject had hung up on the "salesman." Analysis of these telephone conversations revealed that the subjects who had undergone the role playing showed strong sales resistance at a significantly earlier point in the telephone call than did both other groups of subjects.

The two investigations we have just described—of smoking and of assertiveness—are similar to our use of role playing in Structured Learning Therapy since they both had clearly *behavioral* targets. Most research on role playing, however, has focused upon *attitude*—not behavior change. Culbertson (1957) sought to learn if attitudes toward integration in housing could be changed by role playing. Her research subjects were 95 adults whose attitudes toward integration she measured, and whom she then divided into three groups.

1. Role players. These subjects were required to act three roles in favor of the use of educational programs to prevent or reduce tensions and antagonisms in a community about to be integrated.

2. Observers. These subjects listened to the role play, but did not role play themselves.

3. Controls. These subjects completed the attitude measures (pre and post), as did role players and observers, but neither role played nor observed any role playing. Results of this investigation indicated significantly greater attitude change in a pro-integration direction among role players than either observers or controls.

Using the same or very similar experimental procedures, role players have shown significantly more attitude change than observers or controls on such other attitude dimensions as admission of the Peoples Republic of China to the United Nations (Zimbardo, 1965), the sale and use of alcohol (Harvey and Beverly, 1961), attitudes toward another person (Davis and Jones, 1960), the value of compulsory religious education (Cohen and Latane, 1962), the need to increase college tuition (Brock and Blackwood, 1962), attitudes toward the police (Brehm and Cohen, 1962), and attitudes toward an experiment and its procedures (Carlsmith, Collins, and Helmreich, 1966).

Thus, we see from this small sample of research on role playing that role playing can lead to decreased smoking, increased assertiveness, and many types of attitude change.

Role Playing — Necessary but Insufficient

Thus far we have presented considerable evidence for the value of role-playing procedures in a variety of settings. We said earlier that modeling appears to be a necessary but not sufficient procedure for bringing about *durable* behavior change. We would now propose that role playing also may be seen as a necessary but insufficient behavior change technique. Its effects, as seems true for modeling used alone, often do not appear to be lasting ones. Three investigations reported by Lichtenstein, Keutzer, and Himes (1969) on the effects of role playing on smoking failed to demonstrate any lasting behavioral change. Furthermore, a very careful study reported by Hollander (1970) found no behavior change due to role playing, even though choice, commitment, improvisation, and reward were all reflected in her procedures. Thus, in most attempts to help a person change his behavior, neither modeling alone nor role playing alone is enough. Combining the two is an improvement, for then the trainee knows *what* to do and *how* to do it. But even this combination is insufficient, for the trainee still needs to know *why* he should behave in new ways. That is, a motivational or incentive component *must* also be added to the "training package." It is for this purpose that we now turn to consideration of social reinforcement.

SOCIAL REINFORCEMENT

The nature and effects of reinforcement have received more study than any other aspect of the learning process.* Reinforcement has typically been defined as any event that serves to increase the likelihood that a given behavior will occur. Three types of reinforcement have been described: (1) material reinforcement, such as food or money, (2) social reinforcement, such as praise or approval from others, and (3) self-reinforcement, which is a person's positive evaluation of his own behavior. Effective training must give proper

---

*In our earlier discussion of the reproduction phase of modeling, we briefly mentioned the difference between learning and performance. Learning refers to acquiring knowledge, to coming to know how to do something, to the perception and storage of stimulus-response relationships. Learning defined this way is an internal process and, as such, cannot be directly observed. Performance refers to action, to doing what was learned. Many researchers are taking the position that the main effects of reinforcement are on performance—i.e., on the occurrence and nature of how and when what is learned is actually enacted.

attention to all three types of reinforcement. Material reinforcement may be viewed as a necessary base, without which the "higher" levels of reinforcement (social and self) may not function. For many patients, especially a number of long-term or chronic inpatients, material reinforcement may be the only class of reinforcement to which they will respond at first, a notion underlying the development of token economies in mental hospital settings. But there is considerable evidence that, although patient behaviors change as a function of token rewards, such changed behavior typically disappears (or extinguishes) when the tokens are no longer forthcoming. It is for this reason that an effort is usually made on token economy wards to pair social reinforcement with material reinforcement and, eventually, to have the former substitute for the latter. In real-life settings, a job well done (if it receives any reward at all) receives a verbal "nice job" more often than a tangible reward, and helping a friend with a chore elicits "thanks" or approval, not money or objects. Stated otherwise, it is important that a skill-training effort not rely too heavily or too long upon material reinforcers.

Even though social reinforcers may be more likely and hence more valuable than material reinforcers in the real-life sense described above, it is also true that many valuable real-life behaviors go unnoticed, uncommented upon, and unappreciated by others. Therefore, social reinforcement, too, may be an unreliable ally in the skill-training enterprise. For their own needs and reasons, such potential social reinforcement suppliers as hospital staff, relatives, and friends may often be either nonrewarding or simply unavailable. If, however, we can aid trainees in becoming their own reinforcement suppliers, if we can help them evaluate their own skill behaviors and silently praise or approve effective performance, we have made a very major stride toward increasing the chances that newly learned skills will be performed in a reliable and enduring way where they count—in their homes, work sites, or other real-life settings.

We have so far defined reinforcement, indicated the nature and consequences of different types of reinforcement, and emphasized its importance for human performance. In looking for effective training methods, it is insufficient to simply acknowledge that reinforcement is a crucial ingredient in the training process, for how effective and enduring the influence of reinforcement is on performance will depend upon several characteristics of the reinforcements that are used. It is these characteristics or reinforcement enhancers that we now wish to examine.

Reinforcement Enhancers

1. *Type of reinforcement.* As McGehee and Thayer (1961) have observed, "What one person regards as a rewarding experience may be regarded by another as neutral or non-rewarding, or even punishing" (p. 140). While it is obviously true that certain types of reinforcers, such as approval, food, affection and money, have a high likelihood of serving as effective reinforcers for most people most of the time, this will not always be the case. Both the individual's own reinforcement history and his needs at the time will affect whether the intended reinforcer is in fact reinforcing. It is desirable, therefore, that *all* training procedures take account of and respond to the individual reinforcement histories and current needs of the participating trainees. This means choosing not only between given material, social, and self-reinforcers when necessary, but making changes in these choices in a continuing and sensitive manner.

2. *Delay of reinforcement.* Laboratory research on learning has consistently shown that behavior change occurs most effectively when the reinforcement follows immediately after the desired behavior. Reinforcement strengthens the behavior which was going on just before the reinforcement took place and makes it likely that the behavior will occur again. Thus, it is possible that delayed reinforcement can lead to the strengthening of inappropriate or ineffective behaviors should such behaviors occur between the desired behavior and the onset of reinforcement. This may, however, be less of a danger than it seems, since people usually remember why they are being reinforced or rewarded. As Bandura (1969) has noted: "A person who is paid on a piecework basis is likely to maintain a high performance level, although he receives his total payment at the end of the month rather than in small amounts immediately after each unit of work has been completed" (pp. 231-232).

3. *Response-contingent reinforcement.* Related to the issue of immediate versus delayed reinforcement are other matters of timing which aid or inhibit the effects of reinforcement on performance. Bandura (1969) has commented:

> In many instances considerable rewards are bestowed, but they are not made conditional upon the behavior that change agents wish to promote . . . special privileges, activities, and rewards are generally furnished according to fixed time schedules rather than performance requirements, and, in many cases, positive reinforcers are inadvertently made contingent upon the wrong types of behavior (pp. 229-230).

Thus, it is clear that the contingent relationship or linkage between performance and reinforcement must be reflected in training procedures and made sufficiently clear to the trainee.

4. *Amount and quality of reinforcement.* In addition to considerations noted above—concerning type, timing, and contingency of the reinforcement provided—the amount and quality of reinforcement will be a major source of its effect upon performance. With certain important exceptions, the greater the amount of reinforcement, the greater the positive effect upon performance. One limitation on this principle is that increases in certain types of reinforcement do increase performance, but in smaller and smaller amounts. Research on amount of reinforcement serves as further illustration of the difference between learning and performance. In the laboratory at least, subjects appear to learn (acquire new knowledge) no more rapidly for large rewards than for small ones. Once learning has taken place, however, performance will often be more dependable if larger rewards are provided.

5. *Opportunity for reinforcement.* A further requirement for successful and consistent performance is that the behavior to be reinforced must occur with sufficient frequency that reinforcement can be provided. If such behaviors are too infrequent, insufficient opportunity will exist to influence them through contingent reinforcement. We may note here that beyond its several types of practice effects noted earlier, role playing provides excellent opportunities to offer appropriate contingent reinforcement.

6. *Partial (intermittent) reinforcement.* Partial reinforcement refers to the reinforcement of only some of the person's correct responses by reinforcing at fixed times (e.g., once every five minutes), at a fixed number of responses (e.g., every fifth correct response), on a variable time or response schedule (e.g., randomly choosing—within limits—the time or correct response to reward), and on other schedules. In all instances, it has been consistently shown that responses acquired under conditions of partial reinforcement are exceedingly resistant to extinction. That is, they continue to occur even when they are not reinforced at all.

In summary of our discussion of reinforcement thus far, research evidence combines to indicate that high levels of performance are likely to occur if the trainee is given enough opportunity to receive immediate reinforcements of a kind that is right for *him,* in sufficiently large amounts, and offered in a response-contingent manner on an intermittent schedule. We wish at this point in our discussion to highlight the importance of reinforcement in training a variety of behaviors by presenting a small sample of the research investigations supporting these conclusions.

Research on Reinforcement

Verbal behavior—how much a person speaks, what he says, and when and how he says it—has been the target of much research on human reinforcement, especially social reinforcement. Verplanck (1955) proposed that when two people are having a conversation, and one person agrees with or paraphrases the opinions stated by the other person, such agreement or paraphrasing should serve as a reinforcement. If this is the case, the rate of stating opinions by the first person should increase. To test this hypothesis, Verplanck had 17 experimenters conduct half-hour conversations with a total of 24 other subjects. During the first ten minutes of each half-hour conversation, the experimenter did not agree with or paraphrase any opinion statements offered by the subject. During the second ten minutes, every opinion statement by the subject was responded to by the experimenter who either agreed with it ("Yes," "You're right," "That's so," nodding, smiling, etc.) or paraphrased it. During the last ten minutes of each conversation, agreement and paraphrasing were again withheld. If Verplanck's prediction was correct, if agreement and paraphrasing are indeed social reinforcers, subjects should have clearly increased in opinion statements during the second phase of each conversations, and decreased in such statements during the third phase, when the supposed reinforcements were withheld. Analysis of the 24 conversations, which were held in public and private places and covered a broad range of topics, revealed significant support for the predictions. Every reinforced subject increased in his rate of offering opinions, while 21 of the 24 decreased in rate with nonreinforcement.

Related findings, also showing the ability of reinforcement to alter verbal behavior, are reported by Hildum and Brown (1956). In an attitude survey conducted by telephone, they predicted that the use of the word "good" by the interviewer would serve as a reinforcer and, therefore, change the interviewee's statements. During half of the calls made, the interviewer answered with "good" to interviewee statements which agreed with the attitude issue; during the other calls, he responded the same way to disagreeing statements. A significant difference emerged between the two groups. Those reinforced for agreeing became more agreeable; those reinforced for disagreeing increased in disagreement. This study was later repeated successfully by other researchers. Other investigators have reported closely related results. Cohen, Kalish, Thurston, and Cohen (1954) and Taffel (1955) have each shown that responses such as "mm-hmm" serve as reinforcers and increase the frequency of different types of speech. McNair (1957) and Sidowski (1954) used similar reinforcement procedures to successfully increase the sheer amount of subject talking. Oakes and his co-workers have also demonstrated reinforcement effects in their research on verbal behavior in groups of individuals (Oakes, Droge, and August, 1961).

Many other investigations have shown that reinforcement can increase, decrease, or otherwise change what subjects say, their opinions, their attitudes, and a wide range of other behaviors. More specifically, behaviors shown to be changed by reinforcement include remembering personal experiences (Quay, 1959), expressions of feeling (Salzinger and Pisoni, 1957), evaluations of other people (Gelfand and Singer, 1968), acceptance of self (Nuthman, 1957), attitudes toward capital punishment (Ekman, 1958), test-taking behavior (Fahmy, 1953), hostility (Binder, McConnell, and Sjoholm, 1957; Phillips, 1968), social interaction (Milby, 1970), undesirable classroom behavior (Wasik, Senn, Welch, and Cooper, 1969), and many, many more. In studies such as these, the words or actions shown to serve as effective social reinforcers have included "good," "mm-hmm," "fine," "all right," "that's accurate," "I see," head-nod, smile, and leaning forward.

We have presented considerable evidence supporting the behavior change impact of modeling, role playing, and reinforcement. We have held that neither modeling alone nor role playing alone yields results nearly as effective as the two combined. We now wish to take a similar position regarding reinforcement. While it is true that reinforcement alone is more likely to lead to lasting behavior change than either modeling or role playing alone, it is also true that the behaviors to be reinforced must occur with sufficient correctness and sufficient frequency for reinforcement to have its intended effect.* Modeling can provide the correctness, role playing can provide the frequency.

Yet there is one further component of Structured Learning Therapy to consider, a component responsive to the massive failure of both training program gains and psychotherapeutic gains to

---

*See our earlier discussion of response-contingent reinforcement, p. 19.

transfer from the training site to real-life settings. Thus, we now turn to transfer of training.

TRANSFER OF TRAINING

The main interest of any training program (and where most training programs fail) is not in the trainee's performance at the training site but, instead, in how well he performs in his real-life setting. If satisfactory performance has been developed at the time of training, what procedures are available to maximize the chances that such performance will continue in a durable manner on the job, on the ward, at home, or at other places or times where it is appropriate? Stated otherwise, how can we encourage transfer of training?

Research has identified five different principles of transfer enhancement. While it may prove difficult to implement all of these principles in any given training program, their combined impact is to greatly increase the likelihood of satisfactory, positive transfer. We wish to describe these principles below and, in the chapter which follows, we shall examine their implementation in Structured Learning Therapy.

1. *General principles.* Transfer of training has been increased by giving the trainee general principles which cover satisfactory performance in both the training and real-life settings. We refer here to giving the trainee, in a clear and complete manner, the organizing concepts, principles, or rationales that explain or account for the stimulus-response relationships in both places. We are urging that both the "big picture" and the reasons why be provided.

2. *Response availability.* Transfer of training has been increased by procedures that maximize response availability. It has been well established by research that, other things being equal, the response or behavior that has occurred most frequently in the past will be more likely to occur on later occasions. This principle of transfer originates from research on overlearning, which demonstrates that the higher the degree of original learning, the greater the probable level of later transfer. Overlearning may not only increase the likelihood of positive transfer, it may also decrease the chances that negative transfer will occur. When more than one skill is being taught, *negative* transfer (interference rather than facilitation) is likely to occur if training on the second skill is begun while the first is still only partially learned, an unlikely event if enough practice to ensure overlearning had been provided.

A second aspect of the effects of overlearning on transfer, noted by McGehee and Thayer (1961), concerns the effects on the trainer's reinforcement-giving behavior as the trainee shows continued quality performance. They note:

> In striving for overlearning, however, the trainer must be alert to the fact that he will tend to discontinue reinforcement as the trainee becomes more skilled. He will be tempted to assume that the trainee knows what he is supposed to do now so he needs no attention. If this occurs, motivation may drop, and the lack of reinforcement can lead to extinction. The decline in motivation may be offset in a number of ways, such as by an indication that less close supervision by the trainer is a sign of real progress on the trainee's part. Reinforcement cannot be eliminated completely, but must be reduced gradually and supplanted by intrinsic task reinforcement. (p. 177)

3. *Identical elements.* In the earliest experimental work with transfer of training, it was demonstrated that the greater the number of identical elements or characteristics shared by the training and application settings, the greater the later transfer from training to application. Over the years, this finding has been repeatedly reaffirmed. Ideally what would be identical, or as similar as possible, would include *both* the interpersonal and physical characteristics of the training and application settings. Thus, if possible, the trainee would be trained along with those persons with whom he lives, works, or otherwise interacts regularly; training would take place to the extent feasible at home, at work, or at other real-life settings (stores, cars, bars, etc.) rather than at a therapy or training center; the furnishings, materials, and other physical characteristics of the two settings, as well as the nature and scheduling of reinforcements would be as similar as possible.

4. *Stimulus variability.* Several investigators have demonstrated that positive transfer is greater when a variety of training stimuli are employed (Callantine and Warren, 1955; Duncan, 1958; Shore and Sechrest, 1961). As will be seen in Chapter 2, the broad array of interpersonal stimuli represented by the several models, trainers, and role play co-actors utilized in Structured Learning Therapy readily provides an example of this principle of transfer enhancement. The diverse styles and behaviors of these several persons all have the potential of serving in application settings as stimuli or cues for the

desirable skill behaviors acquired during the Structured Learning Therapy sessions.

5. *Performance feedback.* As noted above, in our discussion of response availability, the training needs of the trainee are all too likely to be forgotten once he "graduates" from being a trainee and leaves the training site for his real-life setting. Our efforts until "graduation day" may have been educationally perfect. By whatever training techniques, we may have brought the trainee to an exceedingly high level of performance excellence. We may also have sought to maximize transfer by providing him with general principles, high levels of response availability, maximum identical elements in the training and application settings, and considerable stimulus variability. And yet, given all of these successful efforts, our training may fail if we stop at this point. Training provides skills, information, knowledge, and the *potential* for their successful application. It is primarily reinforcement that will decide what happens at the application site, that determines whether the learning acquired finds enduring expression in successful performance. Performance feedback to maximize such transfer must include not only corrective feedback for poor quality performance, but full attention to continued reinforcement for satisfactory performance. Such reinforcement must take account of all the dimensions of reinforcement (scheduling, source, nature, amount, etc.) noted earlier as crucial aspects of the training process.

We have underscored several times in this chapter the importance of *continued* (if intermittent) reinforcement for *lasting* behavior change. Are the new behaviors ignored? Or, as is perhaps more common, are they reinforced at first and then ignored? Continued, if periodic, reinforcement is clearly a very necessary enhancer of enduring transfer of training. Our belief in this principle is sufficiently strong that, when implementing Structured Learning Therapy for patient training purposes, we have (whenever possible) sought to teach relatives, friends, parents, and other real-life reinforcement dispensors for the patient-trainees the value of and procedures for providing the patient or ex-patient with *continued* performance feedback. To the extent that these efforts have proven successful, a benevolent learning cycle is established whereby the likelihood of continued performance feedback, and thus maximal transfer, is increased.

REVIEW

We have examined in detail four particularly effective procedures for skill training purposes—modeling, role playing, social reinforcement, and transfer training. The nature of each, techniques which maximize their impact, a sample of the wide variety of learning targets to which each has been successfully applied, and samples of supporting research have been presented. Yet, in discussing each procedure, our enthusiasm was lessened by one or more cautionary notes. For example, while modeling does indeed result in the learning of new behaviors, without sufficient practice old ways of acting very clearly tend to recur. Practice or role playing is also an important aid to new learning, but one must practice *correct* behaviors, and without prior modeling or similar demonstration, the trainee's performance is advanced very little. Given both modeling and role playing, the newly learned behaviors have greater likelihood of persisting, but will not do so unless the trainee sees his use of these behaviors to be a rewarding experience. Thus, the crucial necessity for reinforcement. Yet, while reinforcement is indeed crucial, and while evidence supporting its impact on behavior change is very impressive, we have held that willingness to offer reinforcement is also frequently not enough for effective human learning. The behaviors to be reinforced must be enacted by the trainee correctly and with sufficient frequency that adequate opportunity for reinforcement occurs. It is procedures such as modeling and role playing which lead to such sufficient frequency of correct enactment. Without such procedures, the new behaviors—even if reinforced—may occur too seldom for stable learning to occur. Combining these three procedures would, it appears, bring us much closer to an effective and widely applicable approach to human learning, whether the learner be a supervisor, a staff member, a patient, or other. Yet, a truly effective approach to learning must also demonstrate such learning beyond the training setting and must prove to be powerful, broadly applicable, and reliably enduring in the learner's *real-life setting*. Thus we turned in our presentation to transfer training. Five principles were described, as were some examples of their use in Structured Learning Therapy. Having covered this ground, we wish, in our next chapter, to describe and illustrate our use of these procedures for training patients and ex-patients.

2

Trainer Preparation and Training Procedures

Leading a Structured Learning Therapy session involves the effective use of a variety of skills. Some of these are general leadership skills, or those skills which almost any type of group leader needs in order to communicate his message clearly. The competent Structured Learning Therapy trainer must also possess certain clinical skills. These skills involve the ability to understand, empathize with, and influence trainees or patients, whether they are state hospital residents, boarding house tenants, or clients at a community clinic. Yet a third set of necessary skills are those specific to Structured Learning Therapy. They involve a clear understanding of the learning principles discussed in Chapter 1, and the ability to use a specific series of training procedures based on these learning principles. It is the nature and effective use of these specific modeling, role playing, social reinforcement, and transfer training procedures that are the major focus of the present chapter. First, however, let us examine who may effectively serve as a Structured Learning Therapy trainer.

TRAINERS – WHO ARE THEY?

In 1955, The National Institute of Mental Health appointed the Joint Commission on Mental Illness and Health. The task of this Commission was to assess the available resources of the United States in the mental health field as well as the country's current and predicted needs in this area. In their summary of manpower needs in the mental health field, the Commission recommended that:

> In the absence of more specific and definitive scientific evidence of the causes of mental illnesses, psychiatry and the allied mental health professions should adopt and practice a broad, liberal philosophy of what constitutes and who can do treatment within the framework of their hospitals, clinics, or other professional service agencies, particularly in relation to persons with psychoses or severe personality or character disorders that incapacitate them for work, family life, and every day activity. (*Action for Mental Health,* 1961, p. 248-249)

With regard to treatment goals, the Commission recommended that we seek to enable the mentally ill to live and function within the community—that is, that steps be taken to deal with the effects of long-term institutionalization which had kept many patients from being able to return to the community. It was further recommended that community facilities be established for the treatment of mental illness, thus in many instances avoiding the need for hospitalization altogether. Should hospitalization be required, it should be brief, with the patient returned to community treatment facilities as soon as possible. The Commission's decision to recommend a broadened definition of who should be permitted to treat patients was intended to serve the purpose of facilitating such community-based treatment.

The Community Mental Health Movement was essentially born out of this NIMH document. Its thrust, then and today, is community-based treatment, and its manpower resources include psychiatrists, psychologists, social workers, mental health workers, occupational therapists, nurses, therapy aides, psychiatric technicians, and a host of other professional and paraprofessional helpers.

As the community mental health movement has grown, the roles of such workers in the field have undergone considerable change. No longer does only the psychiatrist conduct the psychotherapy; no longer does the attendant only supervise or stand guard over the patients; no longer does the social worker alone talk to the patient's family members and the recreation worker change the records at the ward dance. Instead, the roles of each of these people have tended to blend. Therapy aides as well as occupational therapists have begun to wear the more general hat of therapist, whose task it is to work on the problem of maintaining a patient within the community or returning a hospitalized patient to the community from which he came. Their goal is to help the individual function well enough so that he can live independently with a minimal need for institutional care. Certainly, areas of specialty within the mental health field have not totally lost their meaning. Clearly, it is still recognized that particular training in techniques of family therapy, for instance, gives the social worker, psychiatrist, or psychologist certain expertise in the field. Where the blending of roles occurs is in the recent recognition that the psychiatric technician or other mental health worker might also function as a family therapist if given sufficient opportunity to develop skills in this area through apprenticeship or in-service training by a specialist in the field.

Between 1966 and 1968 a survey of NIMH-sponsored mental health projects on the use of nonprofessional manpower was undertaken (Sobey, 1970). The results of this survey demonstrated that in almost 90 percent of the mental health projects reporting, nonprofessionals were functioning in a therapeutic capacity by providing individual and group counseling as well as socialization, activity, and milieu therapy. In nearly 70 percent of the projects surveyed, nonprofessionals were making use of special skills aimed at tutoring and retraining of patients. In nearly 55 percent of the projects, nonprofessional workers functioned in the area of community adjustment, which involved helping patients make the transition to and maintain themselves in the community. Those workers who were considered nonprofessionals included tutors, teacher aides, recreational workers, nursing and ward personnel, vocational rehabilitation workers, and mental health aides. Sobey (1970) found that one way in which the work of nonprofessionals was distinguished from that of professionals was that nonprofessionals tended to spend more of their work time in direct patient contact than did professionals. Professionals tended to have, in addition to direct service obligations to patients, obligations to train and supervise nonprofessional staff as well as a variety of administrative responsibilities.

The results of Sobey's survey demonstrate the blurring of roles in the field of mental health. In this chapter, addressed to the issue of training in Structured Learning Therapy, we do not presuppose that only certain professionals can become Structured Learning Therapy trainers. We hold, instead, to the notion that adequate training and experience in general leadership skills, clinical skills, and specific Structured Learning Therapy skills are necessary in order to function well in this therapeutic role.

TRAINER SKILLS – LEADERSHIP AND CLINICAL SKILLS

The success of any therapeutic or training endeavor is clearly dependent in large part upon the skills and personal characteristics of the therapist or trainer. The nature of the skills and/or qualities needed to be an effective therapist has been the subject of much theoretical speculation as well as experimental research. One essential general leadership skill is the ability to communicate effectively. Janis and Hovland (1959) have described three processes in the listener which bear upon whether he will learn the material being presented by a speaker. These involve: (1) attention to the communications being presented, (2) comprehension of the message conveyed, and (3) acceptance of the message. They suggest that without any one of these three listener processes, the speaker will not convey the intended message and the listener will not learn what was meant to be taught.

How can the trainer's communication skills affect these processes in the listener or trainee? At the most basic level, a group trainer needs to be able to speak the language of his trainees. He needs to communicate at their language level and with sufficient clarity of thought that his ideas can be comprehended. This requires a good knowledge of the group with which he is working. Most clinicians agree that there is no better teacher of this skill than experience. As a trainer begins to talk with his trainees and asks for their comments or questions regarding what he has said, he can soon learn whether he has been too complex or difficult for them or whether he has spent too much time explaining a concept which his trainees find easily understandable.

Research conducted by Hovland, Janis, and Kelley (1953) has demonstrated that listener attention, comprehension, and, in particular, acceptance of a communication will be affected strongly by how trustworthy and how expert the listener views the communicator to be. The effectiveness of Structured Learning Therapy, therefore, is likely to be enhanced to the degree that the trainers are able to conduct themselves in a proficient or expert manner, and do so in ways that generate a sense of trustworthiness in the eyes of the trainees. Similar views about the importance of leader trustworthiness and expertise in group psychotherapy have been offered by Yalom (1970) and Grotjahn (1971).

Yalom (1970) suggests that the group therapist serves in two basic therapeutic roles. The therapist or trainer is the group's technical expert who establishes group norms or rules, utilizes specialized therapy techniques, gives information, and provides reinforcement. The therapist also functions as an example of such behaviors as forthrightness, honesty, and nondefensiveness.

Grotjahn (1971), in an examination of the qualities of the competent group therapist, writes:

> A psychotherapist must be a man for all seasons. He must be reliable; he must invite trust and confidence. In order to do so he must have trust and confidence in himself in the first place and in other people in the second. He does not need to be superior in his knowledge, not even in his intelligence, and any one of his patients may be superior in some respect—but none should be superior in honesty and sincerity. He must be an expert in the mastery of communication, whether it be the therapist's communication with himself or with the people he tries to understand. (pp. 757-758)

The descriptions provided by Yalom (1970) and Grotjahn (1971) are good examples of the clinical and interpersonal skills which most practitioners would agree are needed by a group therapist.

Clinical description has its limits, however, and Truax and Carkhuff (1967) have gone beyond descriptive statements in their research, seeking to identify those therapeutic, facilitative conditions provided by a therapist which appear to promote therapeutic change. Those therapist-provided conditions shown by their research to facilitate such change in patients include:

> 1. Empathic understanding—a therapist's ability to accurately understand the feelings of his client, and to clearly communicate this understanding to the client. At optimal levels of empathic understanding, the therapist's responses add deeper feeling and meaning to the communications of the client.

> 2. Warmth—a therapist's ability to communicate a sense of caring and basic respect for his client's feelings, experiences, and worth as a human being.

> 3. Genuineness—a congruence between what the therapist feels and thinks and what he communicates to his client. The therapist's communications to his client are real and at the same time therapeutically constructive.

Before turning to necessary trainer skills which are specific to Structured Learning Therapy, we wish to note briefly one final, important trainer skill relevant to trainee motivation in all types of training activities. Poser (1966) has shown that therapeutic change was related to the enthusiasm and spontaneity of the therapist. He compared the therapeutic effectiveness of untrained college student volunteers with that of highly trained professionals in their work with chronic schizophrenic patients. Among his conclusions was the suggestion that:

> It seems likely that the naive enthusiasm they [untrained therapists] brought to the therapeutic enterprise, as well as their lack of "professional stance" permitted them to respond more freely to their patients' mood swings from day to day. Certainly, the activities in which they engaged their patients had a less stereotyped character than that offered by their professional counterparts. (p. 288)

Although Poser's remarks are speculative, they suggest that spontaneity, enthusiasm, and flexibility on the part of the therapist may well help to motivate the chronic patient.

TRAINER SKILLS – STRUCTURED LEARNING THERAPY SKILLS

Overview

In each training session, a group of six to 12 patients (1) are presented with a brief audiotape or live portrayal of specific skill behaviors shown to be helpful in dealing with common problems of daily living (**Modeling**), (2) are given extensive opportunity, encouragement, and training to behaviorally rehearse or practice the effective behaviors they have heard (**Role Playing**), (3) are provided corrective feedback and approval or praise as their role playing of the behaviors becomes more and more similar to the tape model's behavior (**Social Reinforcement**); and most important, (4) each of these procedures is carried out in such a way that transfer of the newly learned behaviors from the training setting to the patient's real-life setting will be highly likely (**Transfer Training**).

Generally, the task of the Structured Learning therapist or trainer is to apply these learning principles and procedures. First, however, the trainer needs to define the skills in which the trainees are deficient. In Chapter 4, we provide the reader with a comprehensive list of interpersonal and planning skills along with the learning points or behavioral steps which make up these skills. How a trainer goes about selecting appropriate skills for and with a given patient is discussed in Chapter 3.

The next task of the trainer is to provide modeling displays or examples of the skill in use, according to the behavioral steps or learning points. These displays should encompass a broad range of content areas, with a strong emphasis upon content relevant to the lives of the trainee group. The modeling vignettes can be presented live or on audiotape, videotape, or film.

Following trainee exposure to the modeling displays, the trainer conducts role playing in which the trainees enact the previously modeled skill according to its learning points and using content which relates to the trainee's personal life experiences. In the role playing or behavioral rehearsal, trainees are provided an opportunity to rehearse for present and future difficulties using the given skill.

In the next phase of the group, the trainer provides opportunities for social reinforcement via activities in which the role-playing trainee receives feedback from other trainees as well as the trainers on how well he executed the role play. The purpose of these activities is to provide social reward for following the learning points as well as corrective feedback for skill enactment which the trainee might improve. Reinforcement is provided on a highly individualized basis, with improvement rather than absolute performance often the criterion for praise.

As a last step, the trainer provides opportunity for transfer training or the use of the practiced skill in the trainee's real-life environment. This is accomplished through a number of procedures, including the assignment of homework in which the trainee is asked to use the skill in a particular real-life setting with a particular person and to report back to the group on his accomplishment at the outset of the next session.

The above description is an overview of the major procedures which constitute the Structured Learning Therapy session. The implementation of these components is illustrated in the remainder of this chapter, which includes an example of a Structured Learning Therapy session.* For purposes of illustration, we have chosen to use

---

*A somewhat more appreviated description than this chapter of the procedures which constitute Structured Learning Therapy, and the major considerations involved in the use of these procedures, are presented in Supplement A: *Trainer's Manual for Structured Learning.*

an initial session run by two Structured Learning Therapy trainers.**
Note that the trainers' roles in the initial session are highly active as
they explictly instruct the trainees in the ground rules for this and
future sessions.

Structured Learning Therapy Session

Preparation

> Our two Structured Learning therapists are Ann and Robert.
> Ann is a social worker and Robert is a psychiatric nurse.
> They have been working together on the team of an Exit
> Unit at Arborville State Hospital. The Unit was set up to
> house 40 chronic patients who were about to make the
> transition from hospital to community. The team was given
> the job of preparing patients for, and facilitating, this
> transition. Ann and Robert have decided to run a series of
> Structured Learning Therapy sessions in order to work on a
> variety of interpersonal communication and planning skills
> which they have observed are lacking or infrequently used in
> their patient population.
>
> From their Unit, Ann and Robert have selected six patients
> who have been observed by staff members to be quiet and
> withdrawn. All of them have demonstrated an ability to
> communicate verbally when they are experiencing an imme-
> diate need or problem. Steven Fuller asks for cigarettes
> loudly and clearly, and Patty Barr has no difficulty asking for
> second helpings in the cafeteria. None of the group members,
> however, appears to seek out social stimulation. Most spend
> their time quietly alone. They do little or nothing of a social

Therapy. We have used this manual in a number of inpatient and outpatient centers. It is
useful as a trainer's guide especially for those personnel for whom the present text may
prove to be too detailed. For example, there are clinical settings which function in such a
way that the present book should be mastered by supervisory personnel, but in which the
Trainer's Manual may prove sufficient (as far as relevant written materials are concerned) for
trainers working solely at the implementation level.

**The role playing and feedback activities which constitute most of each Structured
Learning Therapy session are a series of "action-reaction" sequences in which effective skill
behaviors are first rehearsed (role playing) and then critiqued (feedback). As such, the
trainer must both lead and observe. We have found that one trainer is very hard pressed to
do both of these tasks well at the same time, and thus we strongly recommend that each
session be led by two trainers.

nature in the hospital, and they remain on the hospital grounds despite the fact that they all have town passes.

Once the group members have been selected on the basis of shared deficits in given skill areas, the next task for the trainer is to determine which specific skills to teach. In starting a new group, we suggest selection of a skill which is easy enough that it can be successfully learned and practiced by the majority of group members without great difficulty. (Subsequent relevant skills should be chosen and utilized in rough order of graduated difficulty.) A successful first experience with Structured Learning Therapy helps to provide trainees with sufficient reinforcement so that they will be more motivated to participate actively in future sessions. Also important in beginning group sessions is laying a groundwork of basic skills upon which later skills can be built.

> In discussing the first skill to be taught to their group, Ann and Robert have decided that the basic conversational skills need to be taught. They agree that *Starting a Conversation* is a skill which their trainees are likely to be able to learn and practice with some measure of success. Practicing this skill will enable trainees to take an important initial step in functioning socially within the group as well as on the ward.

If modeling tapes are available, the trainers' preparation for this initial session, as well as future sessions, is made considerably easier. Each of our modeling tapes consists of ten vignettes or skits which demonstrate the skill to be taught in a variety of inpatient and outpatient application settings. In each vignette the actors demonstrate the skill according to its particular learning points. If modeling tapes are not available, the trainers can serve as live models for their group. Trainers can enact a series of prearranged skits portraying the learning points for a given skill.* We suggest that five to ten skits be used for modeling purposes and that the content of the skits be both varied and representative of application settings which the trainees are likely to encounter in their lives. It is important that the general content or outline for each of these skits be worked out in advance of the group session in order to keep the pace of this part of the

---

*Should a live modeling procedure be employed, we advocate that trainers adhere strictly to the learning points in their portrayals. Any departure from the learning points tends to defeat the purpose of the vignettes as demonstration of the skill in use.

Structured Learning Therapy session flowing smoothly.

Having established who should be included and what to teach initially, the trainers need to make some procedural decisions regarding time and place to meet. We have found that sessions scheduled between one and three times per week tend to foster continuity and promote rapid learning. Spacing of sessions is most desirable, with a minimum of one free day between sessions. Trainees are thus given some opportunity to try out on the ward, at home, or in some other application setting what was learned in the session itself. Sessions can be as short as half an hour and as long as two hours depending upon the attention span and level of verbal interaction and discussion in the group. The largest proportion of group time should be spent in role playing. We have found that individual role plays can be as brief as 30 seconds or as long as 15 minutes.

The setting in which a Structured Learning Therapy group is conducted can be of particular importance in enhancing transfer of training. In Chapter 1 we described the principle of identical elements, which states that the more similar the training setting is to the real-life setting in which the skills are to be utilized, the greater the likely transfer. With regard to the physical aspects of the Structured Learning Therapy group room, we suggest that the group be conducted in a setting in which the atmosphere and furnishings resemble as closely as possible the real-life setting of the trainees.

Depending upon the real-life application settings in which the new skills are to be utilized, various props can make the role playing more realistic. A telephone and a table and chairs (for restaurant and kitchen scenes) are some of the props which trainers will often find useful. If more elaborate furnishings are available, such as livingroom or bedroom furniture and office and other work-site props for the enactment of scenes which will eventually be applied in such settings, they can be used most beneficially. When elaborate props are not readily available, the trainer can frequently use substitute or imaginary props. A chair, for example, can easily serve as a television set if it is labeled as such.

In order to maximize trainee attention to relevant stimuli in the group room, we advocate that furniture be arranged so that each trainee has a clear view of the instructors and the role players. One example of a functional arrangement of furniture for a Structured Learning Therapy group room is illustrated in Fig. 1. With this arrangement, trainees sit at desks or tables arranged in a horseshoe. Two chairs in the front of the room are used for role playing. A chalkboard in the front of the room behind and to one side of the role players is used by the trainers to write the learning points of the skill being taught during that session.

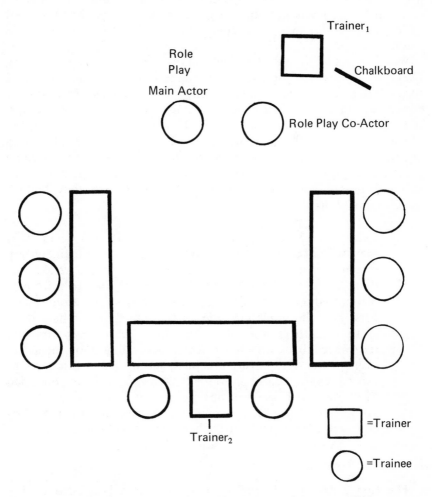

Fig. 1. A Functional Room Arrangement for Structured Learning Therapy

All trainees in the group should be supplied with a card or sheet of paper containing the learning points of the skill being taught. This card serves several teaching purposes: (1) trainees can follow the learning points during the modeling tape; (2) trainees who are role playing can look at the learning points during their enactment;

(3) trainees who are observing the role playing can follow the learning points in preparation for the feedback discussion; and (4) trainees can compile a collection of skills with learning points which they can review and use outside of the training session. In addition to the learning point cards, each trainee should be provided with pencil and paper to enable him to take notes on the role playing.

We have found it useful in the majority of Structured Learning Therapy groups to provide each trainee with a simplified and structured guide which explains group procedures and is useful for taking certain types of notes during and between training sessions. This guide, the *Trainee's Notebook for Structured Learning Therapy** outlines the procedural details for Structured Learning Therapy and provides note pages for the trainee to write learning points, role play notes, and homework assignments. The *Notebook* also serves as a convenient reference for trainees as they build a repertoire of skills.

> Returning to our two trainers, Ann and Robert decide that they will set aside one and one-half hours for their first group meeting. They will hold group meetings once a week. The hour and a half will give them sufficient time to introduce Structured Learning Therapy procedures to the group members, play the modeling tape for the first skill, and have most group members role play the skill's learning points and receive feedback on their efforts. Depending upon the attention span and responsiveness of the group, the future sessions can be lengthened or shortened accordingly. Having obtained cards on which the learning points for "Starting a Conversation" are printed, and having made sure that the modeling tape is available, Ann and Robert are ready to begin.

The Group Begins

The first Structured Learning Therapy session is opened by the trainers who first introduce themselves and then encourage each trainee to give his name and some information about himself. Name tags are filled out and worn by each group member to help trainees get to know the leaders as well as other trainees. Following this, the trainers provide the group with basic information about the group

*See Supplement B.

and its purpose. The intent here is to familiarize trainees with the notion of skill training for improved interpersonal relationships and as an aid to functioning more effectively in the hospital and/or the community.

Ann and Robert open their group as follows:

Robert: Well, maybe we can get started now; if you'll all sit down. That's fine. I don't know all of you and you don't know me. I'm Robert Allen. I work here on the Exit Unit.

Ann: And I'm Ann Carter. I'm working on the Unit also. We're going to be the two trainers who will be with you in this group. And before we get into chatting with you about what we might be doing in here, it probably would be a good idea if we all introduce ourselves. Would you like to begin?

Trainee 1: My name is Steven Fuller.

Robert: Would you, Mr. Fuller, put on your name tag so that we can all begin to learn one another's names. Would you all do that. That's fine, good! Do you want to tell us anything about yourself, Mr. Fuller, how long you've been here or . . . what you did before you came, or anything like that?

Trainee 1: I worked on a farm. I've been here ten years.

Ann: Thank you Mr. Fuller. How about you, can you tell us about yourself?

Trainee 2: Well, I'm Virginia Daley. Um, I've been here this time for four years and before for three years.

Trainee 3: I'm Patty Barr and I hope that this is going to be interesting because so many times we get sent to these classes and we really don't do anything here.

Robert: Mmh, mmh. O.K.

Trainee 4: I'm Mr. Jordan, and uh, I don't know . . . uh, I've been in the hospital only about five years and, um, I don't know. . . .

Trainee 5: I'm Ann Cappellini and, um, I raised six children and, I . . . um . . . don't have anything to do anymore, so I signed myself in.

Trainee 6: I'm Gretchen Krause. I . . . I've been here a long time.

Robert: Uh, huh . . .

Ann: I think that's everybody.

Robert: Maybe we could start by telling you a little bit about what we might do here. I noticed when we were introducing ourselves, Mrs. Barr said something about this being a class. In certain ways, it is going to be a little bit like a class, because we will be learning certain skills that will be useful to each of us—here in the hospital, but especially outside of the hospital. The kinds of skills that we will be trying to help you learn are the things that we all have to do everyday, things like getting along with people, talking with people, listening to people, making certain kinds of plans; dealing with our feelings when we're angry or when we're upset. Things that everybody has to do, but that some of us sometimes have trouble doing. I noticed as we were introducing ourselves, a couple of you mentioned that this is your second stay in this hospital. We know that people sometimes wind up coming back to hospitals like this because they have difficulty with just the kinds of skills I've mentioned.

Trainee 2: Yeah, but you know, I get self-conscious, you know, everybody's going to be listening to one another and I get embarrassed, you know, if I do the wrong thing or say the wrong thing.

Robert: Well, that's a feeling that many people have, so I understand what you're saying. But we'll all go along here at our own pace and no one will be forcing anyone to say or do anything when they don't feel like it.

Trainee 4: I don't know why I'm here. You're talking about these as things you're going to use outside the hospital. I've been here five years and I'll probably stay another five.

Ann: These are skills that you can use in the hospital, too. We've found that people have trouble getting along in the hospital as well as outside the hospital. They have difficulty getting along with people on their ward, or with staff people, or with families that come to visit. So the kinds of skills that we're talking about are things that can help you in here as well as out.

Robert: I was wondering what thoughts any of you might have about what we've said. I mentioned the kinds of things that this group deals with as helping people learn to do the things that help them get along with other people— starting conversations, expressing anger, expressing appreciation, dealing with other kinds of feelings. Does that ring a bell with anyone, as something that they might find useful or something that they might need?

Trainee 2: Well . . . I think my doctor told me that that's one of my problems.

Ann: Which one of those is a problem for you, Mrs. Daley?

Trainee 2: Well, um, sometimes I have trouble talking with other people.

Ann: Mh, hmm. What kind of trouble?

Trainee 2: Well, I don't know . . . expressing myself, maybe.

Robert: O.K. That is the kind of thing that this group can perhaps be helpful with.

Trainee 2: Well, I hope so.

Ann: How about anybody else?

Trainee 3: I don't know if I really need this. I don't have any trouble talking to people.

Trainee 5: You know, my husband used to say when we went out that I was kind of boring to be with, you know, I didn't know what to talk about. I . . . I . . . is that why you've invited me here?

Robert: Well, we invited you here because we felt that you were among the people on the Unit who might benefit from not only training in conversations, but some of the other things we may get into. And I would say to you and Mrs. Barr, let's give it a try. It may be the case that you don't have trouble starting a conversation, but there may be some other skills that may be useful to you. Let's just wait and see.

Following the general introduction, the trainers then explain the Structured Learning Therapy procedures—including learning points, modeling, role playing, and feedback—with a brief discussion of the rationale for each procedure. We have found it useful for trainers to describe Structured Learning Therapy procedures in the context of the first skill to be taught. Trainers hand out the Skill Cards to the trainees and begin by describing the skill as a series of behavioral steps, then go on to explain how modeling, role playing, and feedback facilitate the learning of these steps.

Ann and Robert introduce Structured Learning Therapy procedures in the following way:

Ann: The next thing we will be doing is telling you about what you can expect when you come to group meetings.

Robert: O.K. The procedures that we use here go something like this. We're going to try to take one skill at a time. We thought that a good skill to start with would be "Starting a Conversation." We know that each of you has had some difficulty starting a conversation at some time, either because you've had some reluctance to actually talk to other people or because you have had conversations with other people but somehow the conversations haven't actually turned out the way you wanted. So, as a way of illustrating or showing each of you how we like to run these classes, let's start by discussing the skill of "Starting a Conversation." Let me first give you each a Skill Card that has certain sentences on it. You'll notice at the top of the card it says "Starting a Conversation" and then there are five sentences. We call these sentences learning points. Each sentence describes what someone does when trying to start a conversation successfully. Let me just read along. You'll notice, by the way, that we've written the learning points on the board also, if you want to look there. The first thing we do when we want to start a conversation with somebody is choose the right place and time. The second, we greet the other person with words. We say hello, how are you, or something like that. As the third step in starting a successful conversation, we make small talk. People frequently talk about the weather, sports, or things like that. Now, we're getting close to the main purpose of the conversation, so in the fourth step, we have to judge if the other person is listening and if he or she wants to talk to us. And the last step or the last thing we do, is to open the topic we want to talk about. So, here's a skill called "Starting a Conversation" and here are the steps that we want to teach. Now the question is how do we do this teaching?

Ann: What you're going to hear right now is a demonstration or modeling tape that has on it a number of good examples of starting a conversation according to these learning points or steps that you have on your Skill Cards in front of you. On the tape will be about ten examples of how people in different situations start a conversation and do it well. After we listen to the modeling tape, we will be practicing doing that ourselves. And you'll have your card right in front of you and you'll be able to take it over to the chair over there and practice starting a conversation with somebody.

Robert: Some people call this role playing or practice, but another good thing to call it is rehearsal. We would like, for example, for Mrs. Daley to come up and try these learning points as a way of starting a conversation. We would like you to have in mind someone with whom you would actually like to talk, here at the hospital or at home. So that what you will be doing is rehearsing this skill for when you might really start a conversation with someone. After you try it, we will have what we call feedback discussion, in which we will be able to tell you how you did.

The final part of the trainer's introductory remarks focus on the ground rules or structure of the group. Trainees are instructed as to meeting times, place, attendance requirements, etc. They are encouraged to participate actively and speak up when they feel they have something to say.

Ann and Robert, our two trainers, explain the ground rules as follows:

Robert: I did want to say that we will be meeting in this room and at this time each week, for a one and a half hour meeting. We will be trying in these skill-training meeting to build on what happened in the previous meetings. For example, after we talk about "Starting a Conversation" today, next week we might be discussing "Carrying on a Conversation," or something like that. So we want to be sure that you try not to miss meetings or come late to meetings.

Ann: I see that almost everybody seems comfortable talking here already, and that's something we'd like to encourage you to do. Also, if you have questions, or have comments to make about what someone else has said, do feel free to express yourself.

Modeling

In introducing the particular skill to be taught, we have found that trainers can maximize the group's attention to the task by writing the name of the skill and the learning points on the chalkboard as well as distributing Skill Cards containing the same information to the trainees. Immediately before playing the modeling tape, a brief comment on the meaning of the skill and its usefulness in the lives of the trainee can help serve to motivate the trainees to attend closely to material that will follow. Furthermore, trainees should be instructed to follow each modeling vignette carefully, and note how each portrays the learning points in proper sequence. We suggest strongly that the modeling tape be completed before any discussion of it by the trainees. As we discussed in Chapter 1, the larger the number of trials to which a trainee is exposed, the more likely the material will be learned. Although this phase of Structured Learning Therapy may at times seem tedious or overly drawn out to the trainers, the trainers should remember that the skill is one in which the trainee group is deficient.

Ann and Robert introduce the modeling tape as follows:

Robert: Well, O.K., why don't we get started and see how it goes. We have a tape here called "Starting a Conversation." Listen carefully, as I know that learning this skill will help you to talk with people in a way which will make them want to listen to you and want to talk with you again. You have the Skill Cards out in front of you and you're going to hear several examples of these steps, these learning points. As you listen, follow on the card or on the board, so you can see and hear each step as it unfolds. O.K.?

Ann: As you listen to the tape, I'm going to be up at the board pointing out each step as it occurs. So, if you get lost, just look up at the board and you'll see where we are in the learning points.

Role Playing

Once the playing of the modeling tape has been completed, the trainer's task is to engage the trainees in a discussion of the skill in question as it relates to their own lives. A good way to initiate this discussion is to ask the trainees whether any of the vignettes or problems which have been modeled seem familiar to them. As the discussion gets under way, the trainers should listen for and focus on any examples which the trainees present of use of the modeled skill in their own lives. Of particular interest is any comment about how the skill has been a problem for the trainee. Once this information has been gathered, the trainer has a meaningful basis for engaging the trainee in role playing.

When a Structured Learning Therapy group meets for the first time, the idea of role playing can be a rather frightening prospect for trainees. Acting out a problem in front of a group of people is surely a new experience. We advise that trainers do not ask for volunteers until the trainee whose problem is being discussed has practically volunteered himself. By this we mean that prior to the structuring of the group's role playing, the trainer should elicit from the trainee all relevant details about his use and misuse of the skill in question. These details include where the skill is used, how the trainee has found the skill to be a problem, and how the learning points differ from the method the trainee has used in the past. Once all of this information has been obtained, the trainee is then encouraged to role play the skill in a new way—that is, according to the learning points he has heard modeled.

> Ann and Robert initiate the following discussion following the modeling tape:
>
> **Robert:** O.K., you've heard the tape, with a number of examples of these learning points. What's your reaction? Do any of the examples sound familiar to anyone?
> **Trainee 3:** I don't know if I can do that.
> **Robert:** Think it might be tough?
> **Trainee 3:** Yeah, I do.
> **Robert:** What about that seems tough?
> **Trainee 3:** Oh, I don't know. I can't think of things to say just like that.
> **Ann:** Is it different than the way you usually start a conversation, Mrs. Barr?
> **Trainee 3:** I never really thought about how I start a conversation.
> **Ann:** Um, hmm.
> **Robert:** You just do it automatically?
> **Trainee 3:** Yeah, you just do it.

Trainee 2: That's how I get into trouble.

Ann: What do you mean, Mrs. Daley?

Trainee 2: Well, my husband used to complain about my starting things at the wrong time.

Ann: Uh huh.

Trainee 2: I try to talk to him when he's trying to read the newspaper or . . .

Ann: So, you have something to ask him when he's in the middle of doing something else?

Trainee 2: Well, I just like to talk with him. You know . . . he thinks that's very inconsiderate. Because I don't choose the right time, I guess.

Ann: So that's that first learning point, to choose the right time and place. You sometimes seem to forget to do that when you start a conversation with him.

Trainee 2: That's funny. Because that's what I immediately thought of when we first saw the cards.

Trainee 3: You know, a lot of times the attendants on our ward—they seem to brush you off all the time, they . . . or maybe I'm starting at the wrong time or something. I don't know—a lot of times they say: "later . . . later . . . I'll talk to you later."

Ann: Well, why don't we stay with Mrs. Daley for now and use your experience as our first role play.

Robert: What do you think, Mrs. Daley? Would you, uh . . . .

Trainee 2: I've gotta get up there and . . .

Robert: Well, why don't you give it a try. We'll try to be as helpful as we can. O.K.?

Ann: We'll be telling you exactly how to do the role playing.

Trainee 2: O.K. Alright.

In setting the stage for role playing, the trainee is asked to select someone in the group who reminds him of the person with whom he is likely to have the skill-relevant interaction in his real life. This second trainee is designated as the co-actor. After describing all relevant information about the significant other person so that the co-actor can portray this character in a realistic fashion, the trainee is asked to provide any missing data about the real skill problem situation. The final aspect of setting the stage involves creating an atmosphere similar to that of the application setting. If the scene takes place on a street corner, the main actor and co-actor should role-play the scene standing at an improvised or imagined street corner. As discussed earlier in this chapter, we advocate the use of any props or equipment to help simulate the application setting.

Just prior to starting the role play:

1. The main actor is reminded to stay in role and to follow the learning points.
2. The co-actor is reminded to respond to the main actor as though he were the significant other person.
3. The rest of the trainees in the group are instructed to attend closely to the role playing, paying particular attention to whether the learning points are being followed, and to note this on paper so that they can later provide the role players with feedback.

Frequently, new role players will step out of role between learning points to ask the trainer for some feedback on their performance. When this happens, the trainer should advise the role player to get back into role and complete the enactment. Should the trainer notice any significant procedural errors which would indicate that the instructions have been misunderstood or misinterpreted, the trainer would do well to stop the role playing, provide the needed instruction, and then ask the role players to begin again.

In order to exemplify the role-playing procedures, let us return to our two trainers:

Robert: Why don't you pick the other person to role-play with you. Someone who resembles your husband as much as possible. Who might that be?

Trainee 2: Well . . . let's see. I think maybe Mr. Fuller.

Robert: O.K. Mr. Fuller, would you mind taking the role of the husband here?

Trainee 1: I don't think I can do it.

Robert: Mrs. Daley will be trying to start a conversation with you. We would not be asking you to follow learning points, just respond to her comments and questions. Want to just give it a try?

Trainee 1: Yeah . . . but I don't talk good to people.

Robert: I'm glad you'll try. If you have any difficulty, we'll try to help you out. Alright?

Trainee 1: Yeah.

Ann: We're going to need a little bit of information from you, Mrs. Daley. Mr. Fuller, how about if you listen very carefully because we'll have to find out about the part you will be playing. Mrs. Daley, what's your husband's name?

Trainee 2: Uh, John.

Ann: And you call him John?

Trainee 2: Yeah.

Ann: And what does he call you?

Trainee 2: Virginia.

Ann: Can you tell us a little bit about what John is like?

Trainee 2: Well, he's very quiet. That's one of the reasons why I chose Mr. Fuller. He's a very nice man. But he likes time to himself. Like I said before, when he's doing something else, he doesn't like to be interrupted.

Ann: And, when you talk with him, what's his manner like? How does he react?

Trainee 2: Well, again, if he's not involved in something else he pays attention to me.

Ann: Then he will listen to you?

Trainee 2: Oh, yes; oh, yes. He's a very understanding man.

Ann: Mr. Fuller, do you have some picture of what you're supposed to be like as John?

Trainee 1: Yeah, I guess so. I don't know what I'm supposed to say, though.

Ann: I guess that's going to depend on what Mrs. Daley asks you, or what she wants to talk with you about.

Ann: Where might you be having a conversation with your husband, Mrs. Daley?

Trainee 2: Well, ... most often I guess it would be in the evening, after supper.

Ann: And where would that be? Where would you be sitting?

Trainee 2: Well, probably in front of the T.V. set. Probably I would be sitting in a chair and he would be lying on the couch.

Ann: He'd be lying on the couch? O.K., well, let's make this chair here your chair, Mrs. Daley. Mr. Fuller, we're going to use this chair here as the couch. Can you make it feel like a couch a little bit? See how comfortable you can get in that chair and pretend that you're relaxing on the couch. See that chair over there? That's the television set. And, what might be on the T.V.?

Trainee 2: We always watch the news.

Ann: O.K. What might you be wanting to talk to John about the next time you see him, or the next time you get into that kind of setting at home?

Trainee 2: Gee . . . I don't know. Oh, money maybe. That's always something we have to talk over.

Ann: Is that a problem for you and John right now?

Trainee 2: It sure is.

Ann: So that's the main topic that you want to talk with John about. And when is the next time that you will be home, Mrs. Daley?

Trainee 2: Well, I don't know. The doctor said I could go home for a weekend in a couple of weeks.

Robert: Well, then why don't we begin. I'd like to give the rest of you an assignment while Mrs. Daley, Virginia, starts a conversation with John. I'd like each of you in the group to listen very carefully and follow the learning points either on the Skill Card or on the board, because when she's through, I want each of you to tell her how well she did. We will be focusing on which learning points she did well and which ones she missed. In that way, we can each help each other. John, after we're through I'm going to ask you how your wife made you feel when she was trying to start a conversation with you. Ann and I will also give you our impressions.

Ann: Mrs. Daley, some of the steps on the card are things you normally say to yourself, things that you do in your head. For now, we'd like you to say those things out loud to the group. O.K.?

Trainee 2: I'll try to do what you want.

Ann: You are now at home, Virginia, sitting in front of the television set and John is lying on the couch alongside you over there. The T.V. is on, and the news has just finished, and the ads are coming on and . . .

Trainee 2: So this would be the time.

Ann: Go ahead.

Trainee 2: So, I would wait for the station break before I try to start talking to my husband so I wouldn't interrupt him. 'John?'

Trainee 1: 'Yeah?'

Trainee 2: 'How was your day today?' That's right; I'm supposed to make small talk, right?

Ann: Yes, Try to stay there.

Trainee 2: Oh, yeah. Gee, I'm sorry . . . .

Robert: That's alright. Just keep going.

Trainee 2: I don't know what to say.

Robert: Whatever comes to mind.

Trainee 2: 'Say, John, did you have a good day today?'

Trainee 1: 'Yeah.'

Trainee 2: 'Everything went alright?'

Trainee 1: 'O.K.'

Trainee 2: Well, he is listening to me and he does look like he wants to talk with me. 'John, I think we ought to talk about the budget here in the house again. I . . . I don't have enough money.' Is that enough?

Ann: Yes, that's fine.

Feedback and Social Reinforcement

Upon completion of each role play, the trainers should turn the group's attention to providing the trainee who has role-played the skill with feedback on his performance. The goals of this activity are to let the main actor know how well he performed in following the learning points as well as any other useful information on how he might effectively use the skill in his real life. Particular emphasis is placed on encouraging the main actor to try out the new behaviors in the application setting.

In order to implement the feedback process, the recommended feedback sequence is:

1. The *co-actor* is asked: "How did the other person (main actor) make you feel?" "What were your reactions to him?"
2. Each trainee in the *audience* is asked, in turn: "How well were learning points followed?" "What specific behaviors did you like or dislike?" "How was the co-actor helpful?"
3. The *trainers* should comment on how well the learning points were followed and provide social reinforcement for close approximations. Effective reinforcement from the trainers should include the following:
   a) reinforcement provided at the earliest appropriate opportunity after role plays which follow the learning points,
   b) variation in specific content of reinforcement offered,
   c) reinforcement in an amount consistent with the quality of the role play,

d) no reinforcement when the role play departs significantly from the learning points, aside from encouragement for "trying" in the first session or two,
e) reinforcement on an intermittent basis in later sessions.
4. The *main actor* is asked: "What did you think of how you
did?" "How might you use this skill in your real life?"
"What did you think of the feedback you got from the rest
of the group?"

In all aspects of the feedback segment of the session, it is
important that the trainers seek to maintain a behavioral focus.
Broad generalities and sweeping evaluative comments are of little use
to the trainee in developing more effective skill usage in real-life
settings. Comments should be directed toward specific concrete
behaviors and their presence or absence. Certainly, feedback can be
positive or negative. An effort should be made, however, to comment
on some positive quality of even the poorest performance. Frequently, the comment, "good try," will provide the trainee with the
encouragement he needs and enable him to accept criticism of his
performance less despairingly.

Sometimes the discussion following the role play will provide the
main actor with some new approach to the problem he has role
played. For instance, the co-actor may suggest that the main actor
would do better if he did not shout or if he talked more slowly. At
such a time, or at a time when the main actor discovers that he has
not quite followed the learning points as instructed, it is frequently
useful to role-play the scene again.

Since a primary goal of Structured Learning Therapy is that of
skill flexibility, trainers should be aware that a role play which
departs markedly from the learning points may not be "wrong."
Other methods of performing the same skill may be useful in some
situations. Trainers should stress the fact that the learning points as
they are taught are one good alternative way of enacting a skill or
solving a particular problem, and that the trainee would do well to
learn the method being taught as a way of increasing his behavioral
repertoire.

In Ann and Robert's group the feedback discussion after the
first role play proceeds as follows:

Robert: That's fine. That's fine. Let's ... let's get some
reactions to that now. As your wife in the role playing was

talking to you, how . . . how did you feel, John?

Trainee 1: Well . . . I don't know. It was kind of confusing, that's all. It was kind of hard to think about being somebody else.

Ann: Role playing is difficult.

Robert: Let's get some reactions from some of the rest of the group. I noticed you were looking at the cards and listening. Any reactions to how well the learning points were followed?

Ann: What did Mrs. Daley do correctly?

Trainee 3: She chose the right time.

Ann: In what way did she do that, Mrs. Barr?

Trainee 3: Well, she waited until after dinner, and he could listen to her.

Ann: What was important about that?

Trainee 3: They couldn't have done any of the rest of those things unless she did that first thing right.

Robert: Let's go over these in order. You mentioned, Mrs. Barr, that she did the first learning point well. And I'm glad you noticed, because you mentioned earlier today that that was something you had trouble with.

Trainee 3: This has been a problem . . . yes.

Robert: How about the second learning point. "Greet the other person with words." Do you remember what she did about that?

Trainee 3: I don't really remember what she did . . .

Trainee 4: She said, "Hello."

Trainee 2: No, I didn't.

Trainee 4: You didn't?

Trainee 2: No. I spoke his name and I asked him what kind of a day he had.

Robert: That got us into the third learning point, which was to make small talk. Do the rest of you remember what she did then?

Trainee 5: She did that one just right, she asked him if he had a good day.

Robert: That's right.

Ann: How about the fourth learning point? Did she follow that?

Trainee 4: Yeah, yeah, we just said that.

Trainee 2: This made me feel silly, saying out loud what you are supposed to be thinking.

Robert: It is kind of artificial, but it does help us to learn.

Trainee 3: That small talk part bothers me, too. Sometimes it's not easy.

Robert: Uh, huh. Any reactions about the last learning point? "Open the main topic you want to talk about." Remember how that went?

Trainee 4: She started talking about the budget.

Trainee 3: I still don't understand how she knew he was listening.

Robert: What's your answer to that, Mrs. Daley? What made you think he was listening?

Trainee 2: He answered my question.

Robert: O.K. That was very good. Would you two like to go back to your seats now? And we'll give someone else a try.

Ann: That was really very good, Mrs. Daley. You followed all the learning points and you worked on a problem that you really have at home. Mr. Fuller, you did a good job too.

Trainee 4: Right, right . . . um . . . we didn't do bad either.

Robert: You're right, Mr. Jordan. The comments were very helpful.

Ann: Everybody seemed to be listening.

Following the feedback discussion for the first role play, all other group members in turn are given the opportunity to role-play and receive feedback. For each skill being taught, all trainees should be encouraged to take the role of the main actor at least once. Should time prohibit this from occurring in any given session, the role-playing segment of the following session should begin at the point where the last session left off. Depending upon the observed level of skill acquisition in the group, it may be advisable to replay the modeling tape in order to start this process.

Homework

In an effort to insure that transfer of training will occur, that the behaviors which are learned and practiced in the role playing are applied in their relevant real-life settings, a technique of assigning homework is employed. Homework assignments are decided upon at the end of the Structured Learning session just prior to the trainer's summary statement. Each trainee who has role-played a skill in the group during that session is asked to complete the top portion of a

Homework Report form (see Supplement B) on which he indicates where and when he plans to apply the skill outside of the session, and the learning points he intends to follow.* Whenever possible, the trainee should be asked to try out the exact scene he has role-played in the group. After engaging in the behavior in the real-life setting, the trainee completes the remainder of the form, which helps to evaluate how well he did in his attempt at transfer. His reactions are then discussed at the start of the next session, and the trainees and trainers provide him with corrective feedback and additional practice if necessary. Trainees who have not role played a particular skill in the group should be specifically advised against trying out the learning points before they have had a chance to practice in the group. This is to insure that the trainee does not apply the skill in an inappropriate or ineffective manner, with the possible consequence of receiving a negative response from people in his real-life environment. As a relevant homework assignment for trainees who have not role played a particular skill, it is often useful to ask them to think about possible material for role playing in the next session. It is in regard to the homework or transfer training that the assistance of persons outside of the group may be employed. As was mentioned in Chapter 1, unless there is some real-life reward to the trainee—unless at least some of the persons with whom he tries out his new skill respond in a positive, reinforcing way—it is unlikely that the new behavior will be sustained. If the trainee practices using a skill for an interaction with a family member, and is rebuffed when he actually tries using the skill, the likelihood of his trying again is reduced. Therefore, it is often helpful to enlist the aid of outside people— family members, ward personnel, employers—and to instruct them in how to respond when the trainee initiates the new behavior in the real-life situation.

We have found it useful to implement several supplemental programs outside of the Structured Learning Therapy setting which can help to provide the rewards or reinforcements trainees need so that their new behaviors are more likely to be maintained. These programs provide a mechanism through which the levels of external, social reward by people in the trainee's real-life environment can be maximized. For example, in several hospitals and agencies, we have

---

*As in other aspects of Structured Learning Therapy, the lower the ability of the trainees, the more structured and guided the group's activities should be. For instance, lower level groups may be asked to do less writing, or no writing, in completing their homework assignments.

actively sought to identify and develop environmental or external support by holding orientation meetings for hospital staff and for relatives and friends of trainees—i.e., their real-life reward and punishment givers. These meetings serve to acquaint significant others in the trainee's life with Structured Learning Therapy skill targets and, most important, with procedures whereby staff, relatives, and friends can encourage and reward trainees as they practice their newly learned skills. If a trainee does his homework, experiences the real-life interaction in a positive way, and then receives positive feedback and encouragement when he reports back to the group, he will be more likely to employ the new behaviors on a continuing basis in the future.

In assigning homework to their group, Ann and Robert find that Mrs. Daley cannot practice exactly what she has role played in class. They do, however, find a relevant assignment for her to practice. The homework segment of the session proceeds as follows:

Robert: We want to be of whatever help we can to all of you, not just in learning these skills here in the group, but in helping you to do them where they count—back on the ward, back at home—outside of the group. Now, I want to give out a form that I'd like you to look at. You'll notice it's called the "Homework Report." Only two of you have had a chance to try the learning points for "Starting a Conversation." We'd like those two of you to fill out this homework report. We would like you to think about who you can try these learning points with. If you have an opportunity out of the hospital, fine. But in the hospital would be fine also. You see where it says "fill in during this class." Would you write in "Starting a Conversation."

Ann: O.K. and let's get a little bit more specific than that so that you can plan your assignment a bit. Mrs. Daley, can you think of somebody that you might be able to start a conversation with between now and our next class meeting? Somebody with whom you may have a problem starting a conversation?

Trainee 2: It . . . it could be anybody?

Ann: Anybody.

Trainee 2: Could it be the doctor?

Ann: Absolutely.

Robert: Fine.

Ann: Is there a specific doctor with whom you are having a problem starting a conversation?

Trainee 2: Dr. George.

Robert: O.K. Would you write that in. Your assignment, then, is starting a conversation with Dr. George. When do you expect to see him?

Trainee 2: Well, I ... I have an appointment with him tomorrow.

Ann: You know, we'll be meeting again next Thursday.

Robert: O.K. Why don't you write in "on Friday." O.K.?

Trainee 2: Um, hmm.

Robert: And now write in the learning points you are to follow.

Trainee 2: O.K.

Robert: For those of you who haven't had a chance to role play today, I'd like you to go over the learning points in your head, and think about how you might try them. Next week you'll each have an opportunity to role play. I'd like to mention one other thing to the two of you who are going to do homework. Look at the bottom half of the sheet for a minute. We'd like you to fill that in after you try starting the conversation. That's so you'll be sure to remember what happened.

Robert: I think we've made a fine start today. Ann and I have enjoyed working with you and I think things will continue to go well.

Ann: Next week we'll be able to finish up this skill and give the rest of you a chance to do some role playing. Then we'll go on to another skill, maybe something a bit more complicated. It was nice meeting all of you.

Later Sessions

Once Structured Learning procedures are familiar to a trainee, group sessions tend to proceed rather smoothly. Experienced trainees require somewhat less instruction prior to role playing, while feedback and homework discussions take on a lively, animated quality. We have found that discussions in advanced groups tend to be longer, franker, and with increased emphasis on transfer issues. The content of role playing also tends to change in advanced groups.

As trainees receive social reinforcement from the trainers and from other group members, they tend to utilize the group setting as a place where they can work on increasingly complex and difficult skill-enactment problems.

Although Structured Learning Therapy procedures in early sessions rely heavily on the use of social reinforcement to build and maintain new behaviors, such environmental support is frequently insufficient to maintain newly learned skills. It is also the case that many real-life environments in which trainees work and live will actively resist a trainee's efforts at behavior change. For these reasons, we have found it useful to include in later transfer efforts a method through which trainees can learn to be their own independent rewarders. Once a trainee has practiced a new skill through role playing, made his first homework effort at it, and gotten group feedback, we recommend that the trainee continue to practice his new skill as frequently as possible. It is at this time that a program of self-reinforcement can and should be instituted. Trainees can be instructed in the nature of self-reinforcement and encouraged to "say something and do something nice for yourself" if they practice their new skill well. Homework Report 2 (see Supplement B) will aid both trainers and trainees in this effort. On this form, trainees can specify potential rewards and indicate how they rewarded themselves for a job well done. Trainees' notes can be collected by the trainer to provide a means for the trainer to keep abreast of independent progress being made by trainees without the necessity of consuming group time.

ADVANCED STRUCTURED LEARNING THERAPY –
APPLICATION GROUPS

Once trainees have achieved a reasonable level of competence in the various Basic Skills of Structured Learning Therapy, the task of the group becomes that of solving complex daily living problems by employing various skills in combination. For instance, finding a place to live may entail a Basic Skill sequence of: (1) Asking for Help, (2) Gathering Information, (3) Responding to Persuasion, (4) Negotiation, and finally (5) Decision Making. We have developed an extended series of Application Modeling Tapes portraying daily living problems for which various combinations of Basic Skills can be employed. The reader will find this series described and illustrated in Chapter 4. The Application Modeling Tapes are examples of the way particular people might solve various daily living problems. After playing an appropriate Application Modeling Tape, it is the task of the trainer to: (1) develop through discussion with an individual trainee a list of Basic Skills which meets his specific needs in solving the application problem at hand, (2) have the trainee role play the Basic Skills in sequence, (3) hold feedback discussion, and (4) assign homework relevant to the application problem. An example of the way in which an outpatient application group works is illustrated in a transcript of an Advanced Structured Learning Therapy session in Supplement C.

PROBLEM TRAINEES

The behavior of some trainees during Structured Learning Therapy sessions can frequently interfere with the training or therapeutic process. In this section we wish to identify several types of trainee resistance and a variety of methods by which such resistance can be reduced or eliminated.

One type of resistance that a trainer may encounter is that of *active refusal to participate as instructed.* In this category we include such trainee behaviors as refusal to role play or to participate in other aspects of the session, lateness, missing sessions, and walking out of sessions. Also included here is the problem of participation in a manner that is not in accordance with the instructions given by the trainer.

Another problem encountered in Structured Learning Therapy sessions is *inappropriate trainee behavior,* frequently related to the trainee's psychiatric condition. Included here are such behaviors as inattention to relevant material, excessive restlessness, bizarre behavior, and inability to remember material presented.

A third form of trainee resistance, perhaps the most common, is that of *trainee inactivity.* Here we have such trainee behaviors as falling asleep in class, minimal participation, minimal ability to understand the material presented, and apathy.

A fourth class of trainee behaviors which tends to interfere with the training process is that of *overactivity.* Included here are such trainee behaviors as frequent interruption of ongoing activity, monopolizing of the session, digression from the topic being discussed, and jumping out of role. Also in this category is the problem of the "therapist's-helper," the trainee who is constantly trying to participate in the leadership of the group, often as a means of either dominating other trainees or avoiding participation as a trainee himself.

There are a number of methods described in the psychotherapy literature for reducing patient resistance. We have adapted these methods and described them below as they apply to the Structured Learning Therapy group. Many of the methods are described as ways of dealing with resistance to role playing. They can also be useful in coping with resistance to other aspects of the Structured Learning Therapy session.

The first method of reducing trainee resistance is one we call *empathic encouragement.* It is a method we have found to be useful in dealing with *active resistance to participation* as well as *over-activity.* In using this technique, the trainer follows six steps:

1. Offer the resistant trainee the opportunity to explain, in greater detail, his reluctance to role play and listen nondefensively.
2. Clearly express your understanding of the resistant trainee's feelings.
3. If appropriate, respond that the trainee's view is a viable alternative.
4. Present your own view in greater detail, with both supporting reasons and probable outcomes.
5. Express the appropriateness of delaying a resolution of the trainer-trainee difference.
6. Urge the trainee to tentatively try to role play the given learning points.

Another general category of techniques for coping with resistance is one we call *simplification.* It involves shortening or simplifying a task which may be too complex or confusing to a trainee. It is particularly useful in instances of inappropriate trainee behavior. Methods of simplification include: reinforcement of minimal trainee accomplishment; shortening of role play; providing the trainee with a script to role play; having the trainee play a passive role (the co-actor) in role playing; having the trainee follow only one learning point; and telling the trainee the words to use in the role playing.

A third method of reducing trainee resistance is one which we call *threat reduction.* Threat reduction is generally useful with all types of trainee resistance and involves such techniques as: live modeling by the trainer to make role playing or other activities less threatening; reassurance of the trainee; and clarifying any aspects of the trainee's task which may be unclear.

When resistance occurs in the group in the form of inactivity, the trainer will frequently find it useful to employ a group of methods we have termed *elicitation of responses.* The goal of these techniques is to step up the activity level of the group. The techniques include: calling for volunteers; introducing topics for discussion; and asking specific trainees to participate, preferably choosing someone who has indicated (by eye contact or otherwise) some willingness to participate.

In coping with overactivity, or inappropriate behavior, trainers can employ a group of methods which may be described as *termination of responses.* The purpose of these methods is to minimize the occurrence and possible reinforcement of trainee behavior which conflicts with appropriate Structured Learning Therapy group behavior. These methods are: interruption of ongoing behavior; extinction of responses through inattention; terminating contact with the trainee and asking others to participate; and urging the trainee to get back on the right track.

A final method to deal with the resistive trainee is that of *instruction.* Instruction involves coaching, prompting, and elaboration of specific procedures. These methods tend to be useful when trainees are underactive, inappropriate, or actively refusing participation.

These several types of trainee resistance, and the various methods described above for reducing or eliminating such resistance, are illustrated in detail in Supplement D.

REVIEW

We began this chapter by identifying the types of persons who might serve as Structured Learning Therapy trainers, and by describing the leadership, clinical, and specific trainer skills necessary to do so effectively. The sequence of procedures which constitute Structured Learning Therapy were then presented and illustrated in considerable detail. Since a number of trainee behaviors may occur in Structured Learning Therapy sessions which serve to interfere with satisfactory skill learning, procedures for reducing and eliminating such trainee resistance were also described. Beyond the issue of trainee resistance or participation, there exists a wide array of additional trainee considerations which may facilitate or inhibit trainee skill development. These trainee considerations are the focus of the chapter which follows.

3
Inpatient and Outpatient Trainees

Who are the patients and former patients who are likely to benefit from Structured Learning Therapy? In the first chapter we met Frank, who had recently been discharged after 13 years in a state hospital, and Helen, who had experienced the "revolving door" of psychiatric admissions, discharges, and readmissions. What else do we know about such persons, their backgrounds, and the daily lives in and outside of hospitals? How did they get to be the way they are—people whose only stable identity is likely to be that of "psychiatric patient"? How can we attempt to help them, to stop the revolving door? In trying to answer this latter question, it is important to remember that our attempts to offer effective treatment must be responsive to the needs, values, lifestyles, and specific problems of our clients.

Most current, popular views of psychiatric or psychological treatment evoke images of highly verbal and abstract individual or group psychotherapy which is oriented toward helping the patient gain insight into the nature and causes of his problems. The likely patients in these verbal, insight-seeking psychotherapies also seem to fit into a stereotype—bright, motivated, middle- or upper-class individuals who are likely to gain the insight sought. They typically seek treatment voluntarily for problems which they view as internally caused. These are the people Schofield (1964) calls the YAVIS patients—young, attractive, verbal, intelligent, and successful. It is these people whom the majority of present-day psychotherapists prefer as patients, and with whom verbal, insight-oriented psycho-therapies are likely to be most successful.

Frank and Helen are not YAVIS patients. Rather, they are more apt to be lower- or working-class, middle-aged or elderly, physically ordinary or unattractive, verbally reticent, intellectually unexceptional or dull, and vocationally unsuccessful or marginal. They come (or are referred to treatment) in search of help with some concrete problem or crisis which they are unable to handle. They are likely to want the therapist to *actively* solve their problems for them—to tell them what to do, because that is their expectation of what doctors do.

Thus, non-YAVIS patients are not preferred candidates for traditional, verbal, insight-oriented psychotherapy. This is true both in terms of the patients' own expectational preference for an active, problem-oriented, advice-giving therapist, and in terms of the (middle-class) therapist's likely preference for working with people more like himself. Indeed, the non-YAVIS, lower- or working-class patient, when compared with patients from higher social classes is significantly more likely to:

1. be found unacceptable for treatment,
2. spend considerable time on the clinic's waiting list,
3. drop out (or be dropped out) after initial screening,
4. receive a socially less desirable formal diagnosis,
5. be assigned to the least experienced staff members,
6. hold prognostic and role expectations incongruent with those held by his therapist,
7. form a poor-quality relationship with his psychotherapist,
8. terminate or be terminated earlier, and
9. improve significantly less from either his own or his therapist's perspective.

In deciding which treatment is most appropriate for particular individuals, it is important to identify the factors which may contribute to a person's likelihood of success with one or another approach. This suggests the advantages of a prescriptive orientation to psychotherapy, rather than to assume, as many psychotherapists still do, that a particular therapy is equally applicable to most or all types of individuals with all types of problems.

A useful place to begin to examine differences which may predispose given individuals to both prefer and be more responsive to different types of treatment is with the individual's pattern of development through childhood. It is important to look at early environments and climates within the home because they may have a strong influence on the types of environments and social relationships that the child may come to both prefer and expect in later life. In the professional literature dealing with early home environments, one frequent focus of study is on the effects of permissiveness versus conformity to external, authoritarian discipline in child-rearing practices. Evidence suggests that these differences are related to social class. It has been demonstrated that there is a major emphasis in lower-class child-rearing on conformity to externally imposed authority and concrete standards, on the consequences of one's behavior more than one's intentions, and more concern with what the child *does* rather than what he feels or thinks (e.g., Dolger and Ginandes, 1946; Pearlin and Kohn, 1969; Tuma and Livson, 1960). Duval (1946) and others, on the other hand, characterize middle-class child-rearing practices as emphasizing self-direction, sharing and cooperation, confiding with parents, self-control, and, in general, much more concern with feelings, intentions, and inner dynamics.

These differences have clear implications for psychotherapeutic attempts to help an individual. If early life experiences train a person for self-reliance, self-control, and a concern for inner dynamics and one's own feelings and motivations, the type of treatment best prescribed is likely to be different than for a person who is taught to behave by conforming to externally imposed authority and to be more concerned for what one does than for one's feelings or motivations. The former—the customary early life experiences and values of middle- or upper-class, YAVIS individuals—is excellent preparation for verbal, abstract, insight-oriented psychotherapy. The latter—more likely to characterize the childhood experiences of lower- or working-class, non-YAVIS persons—does not adequately prepare one for traditional, introspective psychotherapy. Rather, such individuals are better prepared for a treatment approach which emphasizes learning and performing overt behaviors; requires conformity to clear, concrete examples; and whose procedures are authoritatively determined and administered.

LANGUAGE USAGE

In the previous section we discussed differences in childhood experiences as they relate to one's social class. These social class differences also appear to be related to the way one uses language.

While we would not question the fact that persons speaking different languages (Spanish and German, for example) would have difficulty understanding each other, we may be more surprised that persons apparently speaking the same language (English, for example) may be using it differently enough that they suffer from a communication gap. There is evidence that these differences are often linked to one's social class.

One type of social class difference in the use of language has to do with the *perspective* typically assumed by the speaker. Lower-class persons tend to describe events from their own perspective—events are described as the speaker sees and experiences them directly. Middle-class individuals, on the other hand, tend to describe events from a variety of perspectives, and appear more able to imagine and describe how other people experience events (Schatzman and Strauss, 1955). Middle-class persons appear to be more sensitive to the differences in perspective that are likely to exist between speakers (as in an interview situation), while lower-class respondents seem less sensitive to these possible differences. Persons from lower-class backgrounds tend to describe events in concrete terms, and make references to particular individuals rather than classes or categories of people. Persons from middle-class backgrounds, in contrast, more frequently use generalizations and abstractions to describe broader classes of events or people.

Bernstein (1961), who has contributed much to our knowledge in this area, draws a distinction between *elaborate* versus *restricted* verbal codes. The latter has been found to be typical of people from lower- and working-class backgrounds, while the elaborate code is more characteristic of middle-class persons. In the restricted code there is a major emphasis placed on concrete, global descriptions of events rather than on detailed accounts of the inner states of the speaker. Sentences tend to be short and grammatically simple. There is little expressed in the way of "inner" self-references, and little apparent interest in motivational processes. Users of the elaborate code, on the other hand, place considerable emphasis on the expression of inner states and subjective experiences, abstract concepts, accurate grammar and syntax, and shifts in perspective. These coding styles emphasize differences in the ways persons from different social class backgrounds communicate within their respective groups. While their communication styles may be effective *within* each group, they are sufficiently different so as to often interfere with effective communication *between* members of different social classes.

Thus, one can well imagine the frustration frequently encountered by both the (middle-class) therapist and the (lower- or working-class) patient in attempting to communicate about thoughts, feelings, symptoms, or behaviors. With the importance of verbal communication as great as it is in traditional psychotherapies, this communication gap is of critical interest. One could attempt to deal with this problem by training therapists to use language in the manner employed by their clients or by utilizing therapists who already use language in that way because of their own lower- or working-class backgrounds. Or one could try to train lower-class patients to speak in the language system of the middle-class therapist. The therapy approach we are advocating depends on none of the above-mentioned possibilities. Rather, we suggest the use of therapeutic methods that are not dependent upon abstract, complex conceptualizations or verbalizations on the part of either the patient or therapist; that do not focus on the inner dynamics, intentions, or feelings of the patient. Indeed, the action-oriented techniques of Structured Learning Therapy emphasize concrete examples, behavioral rehearsal, and social reward, and make very little use of the types of verbal interchanges that are used in traditional psychotherapies.

CONCRETENESS

As we mentioned in the previous section, one characteristic which differentiates the way in which language may be used is its degree of concreteness or abstractness. Many writers and researchers have suggested that this dimension of language usage is but one example of a broader orientation held by people which may be reflected in much of the person's perceptions and behaviors. For example, some of the characteristics of persons who can be described as highly concrete in their orientations are:

1. An inability to assume an "as if" attitude or set—i.e., an inability to go beyond the boundaries of present reality as they perceive it;
2. stereotyped or stimulus-bound behavior—i.e., responding in a fixed way to stimuli, rather than using insight or flexibility to solve problems;
3. an inability to understand and describe one's own behavior as someone else might view it, or difficulty "taking the role of the other";

4. difficulty in shifting one's own behavior from one aspect of a situation or task to another;
5. difficulty in keeping in mind several aspects of a task at the same time;
6. difficulty in planning ahead, in conceptualizing the future.

In short, persons who are especially concrete in their basic styles or orientations tend to perceive and act in rather simple, present-related, stereotyped ways. These qualities associated with concreteness accurately describe many of the trainees for whom Structured Learning Therapy is designed.

Some writers consider this concrete style as characteristic of lower-class persons in general, and view it as a defining attribute of "the culturally deprived child" (Riessman, 1962). Hunt and Dopyera (1966), on the other hand, while finding significant differences between lower- and middle-class youths on this conceptual dimension, also found considerable variation *within* their lower-class sample. Thus, while differences were found between the lower- and middle-class youths, there was still a wide range of differences found within the lower-class group, suggesting the need to be sensitive to *degrees* of concreteness.

Another important aspect of concreteness has to do with a person's ability to deal with threat or stress. As Harvey, Hunt, and Schroder (1961) and Kohn (1970) suggest, the highly concrete individual may be ill-equipped, because of his narrow range of available responses and problem-solving behaviors, to cope with the threats or stresses he is forced to confront on a day-to-day basis. Because of his limited resources and concrete responses, this individual may be highly vulnerable in the face of environmental stress and especially in the face of stress involving complex, ambiguous, or novel situations. He is likely to have difficulty in accurately interpreting the complexities of social reality and in coping in ways other than by the rather rigid, concrete means he has learned.

One way of helping the concrete individual cope more effectively with his environment is to make the environment as clear, direct, unambiguous, and structured as possible. Within this clearer, more unambiguous environment, the individual can then be encouraged to learn new ways of functioning. The potential role of Structured Learning Therapy in this context is to teach the specific social, personal, and interpersonal skills that are necessary in managing stress in a complex society, and to do so in a way that is consistent with the needs, values, and lifestyles of our likely trainee population.

That is, our treatment approach is congruent with the non-YAVIS trainees' expectations stemming from childhood experiences, language system, and level of concreteness. It is responsive to their deficiency in the skills that would enable them to cope with and master the many stresses and demands of their environments. We are not suggesting that Structured Learning Therapy is appropriate *only* for persons coming from lower- or working-class backgrounds. Nor are we suggesting that lower- or working-class origins *inevitably* predispose people toward particular disorders or preferences for treatment. We are suggesting, however, that these patterns of stress do exist, that some people prefer and do better with certain types of treatment. Perhaps most important, it is clear that certain individuals are deficient in many of the coping and mastery skills necessary for effective and satisfying living. These skill deficits often become the most salient characteristics of our patient and ex-patient clients. Furthermore, their continual patient status and hospital tenure is likely to increase the severity of their behavioral deficiencies (Paul, 1969; Zusman, 1967). Our task, then, is to identify and teach these skills in the most efficient and effective manner.

TYPES OF TRAINEES

In the first chapter we discussed "leavers" (who tend to stay in mental hospitals for short periods of time before discharge but who also are frequently readmitted) and "remainers" (whose hospital tenures are longer). As we mentioned then, the central purpose of this book is to describe and illustrate intensive training techniques potentially helpful for both of these types of individuals. For the "leavers," the techniques would be aimed at teaching skills that would enable them to remain out of the hospital and lead satisfying, effective lives in the community. For the "remainer," the training would focus on breaking the pattern of apathy, withdrawal, and "colonization," and would move them closer to eventual discharge from the hospital. While the trainees in which we are interested may accurately be described as "leavers" and "remainers" in terms of their histories of hospitalization, their training needs suggest the appropriateness of a three-way division:

> 1. *inpatients* — those long-term, chronic patients who could be trained to be more active, communicative, and self-directed for both within-hospital satisfaction and in prepa-

ration for their eventual movement out of the hospital;

2. *transitional patients* — those persons who will be discharged from the hospital in the foreseeable future, and need training and preparation in those interpersonal, personal, and planning skills that will enable them to get out and stay out of the hospital and become reintegrated into the community; and,

3. *outpatients* — those individuals (some of whom have been hospitalized) who are already living in the community and who need training in the skills necessary to enhance their personal lives.

Structured Learning Therapy, then, is likely to take place in hospitals, in transitional facilities (day- or night-hospitals, halfway houses, group homes, and so forth), or in community-based outpatient clinics. The specific skills to be taught must be determined by the immediate and longer term needs of the persons being trained. Clearly, the person who has been hospitalized, withdrawn, and noncommunicative for several years will have different skill-training needs (e.g., basic conversational skills) than the person who has been living in the community and needs help in learning how to relate more effectively to his wife and children. Just as the *methods* of training should be prescriptively appropriate to differences among trainees, so, too, should the *content* of what is being taught.

A trainee may be deficient in a given skill because he has never learned it. For example, some people may never have learned such skills as expressing anger effectively or understanding the feelings of others. Or, as is likely to be the case with many individuals who have spent considerable lengths of time in hospitals, the person may have learned the skill much earlier in time but no longer uses it and may well have forgotten how to do so, because its use has not proven rewarding for him. Many "chronic" patients, earlier in their lives, learned the skills involved in personal grooming or in carrying on conversations, but these skills have too often been left unpracticed, unrewarded, and hence unused on the back wards of too many mental hospitals (Murray and Cohen, 1959; Paul, 1969; Zusman, 1967). The crucial issue in terms of the person's training is whether or not he *currently* uses the skill effectively in appropriate situations.

BEHAVIORAL ASSESSMENT

Our emphasis is on *skill deficits*—on whether or not the person is able to carry out given skill-related behaviors—rather than on the diagnostic label that he carries with him. We are more interested in how a person actually behaves in various types of situations than in whether he has been diagnosed schizophrenic. Our main reason for avoiding a reliance on diagnostic labels as criteria for judging the usefulness of particular types of training is that the use of such labels often results in generalizations about patients which are not helpful in correcting or remediating specific skill deficits. For example, if we describe someone as "depressed" or "asocial," we still do not know *what* he does or does not do, *when* he performs or fails to perform certain behaviors, or *where* he acts in certain ways. When we call someone "asocial," do we mean that he never talks with anyone, that he talks with fewer people than we would expect, or that he has refused an invitation to a party? Because these diagnostic labels or broad descriptive categories do not tell us the *what, when,* and *where* of particular behaviors, we do not know what type of training, if any, would be appropriate.

In order to avoid the pitfalls that often result from the use of broad diagnostic categories, and in an effort to identify the specific skill deficits we wish to help the trainee work on, our pre-training assessment focuses on direct observation of behaviors. We are interested primarily in what the person does or does not do. Only then can we judge whether behavioral deficits (or excesses) exist: do the behaviors occur often enough (or too often), strongly enough (or too strongly), or in the appropriate situations? We can answer these questions only by actually observing behaviors and by recording them in concrete terms. So, while we cannot document "depression" (although we can infer that the person is depressed), we can *observe, count,* and *record* such behaviors as "sitting alone" or "crying." Thus, by employing behavioral observations and behavioral criteria, rather than broad diagnostic categories and inferences about symptoms or likely causes, we are in a far better position to identify the skill deficits for which we may then provide training.

TRAINER SELECTION OF TRAINEES FOR STRUCTURED LEARNING THERAPY

In most instances it will be the task of the trainer to directly select, or arrange for the selection of, trainees to participate in Structured Learning Therapy. As was mentioned previously, the skills to be taught must be responsive to the needs of the persons to be trained. We have described these needs primarily as behavioral or skill deficits—those areas of social, personal, or interpersonal functioning in which the person has not learned or does not employ appropriate behaviors in appropriate situations.*

After the trainer becomes familiar with the skills that might be taught, he must then identify which patients are deficient in which skills. This information can be best obtained from those persons who have the most direct and ongoing contact with the patient in various settings—ward personnel (nurses, doctors, aides), therapists, instructors, family members, or work supervisors. The settings might include wards, therapy groups, day rooms, classes, or work settings within a hospital or transitional facility, and/or homes, jobs, schools, or clinics outside of the hospital. It is important that the trainer get an assessment of how a person behaves in a *variety* of situations, since the presence or absence of a skill is likely to be partially a function of situational demands and expectations. A patient may be able to carry on conversations with other patients on a ward in a hospital, for example, but be found to be noncommunicative with persons in positions of authority or with family members when he is at home on a visit.

The SLT Skill Checklist (FORM S) (see Supplement E) has proven quite useful in identifying whether or not potential trainees use various skills. Using this Checklist, someone familiar with the patient can indicate whether, and how adequately, the patient employs the various skills described. The trainer who is selecting trainees can administer these checklists to relevant observers, and then begin to constitute a group or groups of trainees who are deficient in the same skills.

Another useful technique for identifying and recording behaviors to be taught is known as behavioral charting. With this method, which may be used along with the SLT Skill Checklist (FORM S), the frequency of occurrence of observed behaviors can be recorded so that persons showing low levels of performance of the skill(s) being observed may be considered for Structured Learning Therapy. On a behavioral chart, the specific behaviors to be observed and counted are identified and listed. Time periods (hours or days of the week) are designated. The behaviors to be observed—the "target behaviors"—are selected. The observer records how many times during each time period the specified behavior is observed. For example, if the behavior to be observed were "conversing at meal-

*These basic skill areas, which we have identified from (1) research on Structured Learning Therapy, (2) relevant professional literature, (3) surveys of patients and staff, and (4) our own clinical experiences, are described and illustrated in the following chapter.

times," the observer would observe and record how many times the particular patient is observed talking at meals. It is important to begin to record behaviors before any treatment has begun in order to be able later to evaluate the effectiveness of the treatment. This is known as the *baseline* or *base rate* of the behavior. Baseline data should be collected for at least a few days or a week or more prior to the beginning of training. Observing and charting of the behaviors should continue throughout the training period and also for a post-training observation period. Charting is continued after the training has been completed to see if any changes in behaviors (e.g., conversations at mealtimes) are maintained, increased, or decreased.

Behavioral charts can be completed by anyone who has an opportunity to regularly observe the patient in the situations under consideration. The person making the observations can also comment on any particular circumstances involved before, during, or after the performance of a target behavior. For example, in charting the target behavior "conversing at mealtimes," we observe a particular meal at which the person sits with other people he knows well, speaks frequently, and is rewarded for speaking; these observations should all be noted on the chart. If the person is then observed at a different meal, is not seen speaking, and it is noted that he is sitting with strangers who do not respond or reward his attempts to speak, then these bits of information can help clarify some of the situational factors that may facilitate or inhibit his conversing at mealtimes.

We have discussed Structured Learning Therapy as being particularly well-suited for many of those persons for whom traditional, verbal, insight-oriented psychotherapy appears to be inappropriate. We emphasized that Structured Learning Therapy is behavioral and action-oriented. Nevertheless, Structured Learning Therapy does involve a certain amount of verbal behavior and does involve group interaction. It also requires concentration over at least short periods of time. Thus, some patients who are unable to hear or comprehend verbal instructions or who cannot maintain attention or refrain from being disruptive in a group for at least short periods of time (perhaps as short as fifteen minutes) would probably not benefit from Structured Learning Therapy. It may be possible to work on such behaviors as verbal comprehension, attention span, or disruptiveness as preliminary preparation for Structured Learning Therapy. Some encouraging work in these areas has been done using various behavioral techniques (Ayllon and Azrin, 1968; Davison, 1969; Schaefer and Martin, 1969). However, until these minimal criteria are met, the patient will not be an appropriate candidate for a Structured Learning Therapy group. It may be possible, however, to use Structured Learning Therapy techniques on an individual basis, with a patient whose behavior would otherwise not meet minimal selection criteria for Structured Learning Therapy groups, as preparation for eventual inclusion in a group. For instance, if a patient has been observed to be too disruptive to be included in a Structured Learning Therapy group (e.g., "cannot sit quietly for more than five minutes without yelling"), a trainer might work with him on an individual basis, using Structured Learning Therapy techniques to develop alternatives to the disruptive behaviors. The decision as to whether or not a patient meets the minimum criteria for selection can be ascertained by using direct behavioral observation and behavioral charting, as discussed in the previous section.

TRAINEE SELF-SELECTION

Trainers, as was mentioned previously, will carry the major responsibility for organizing and running Structured Learning Therapy groups, for deciding which skills are to be taught, and for selecting or arranging for the selection of patients to participate. This is not to suggest, however, that all or even most patients are unable to decide whether or not they wish to participate in Structured Learning Therapy groups, or are unable to decide which skills they feel deficient in and in which they wish to receive training. Indeed, the potential trainee himself is in the best position to determine whether he *feels* deficient in a particular skill. Clinical experience has shown that if the patient himself does not acknowledge the deficiency, or if too great a gap exists between the trainer's perceptions and trainee's perceptions of training needs and specific skill deficiencies, then training will not be successful. Unless the trainee views the type or level of a given skill as relevant to his needs, he is unlikely to be motivated to participate in any active way. Also, the shift of responsibility for therapy participation and skill selection from the trainer alone to the trainer and trainee together increases the trainee's behavioral commitment and effort, which themselves may facilitate greater attraction to and motivation for the training experience (Goldstein, Heller, and Sechrest, 1966).

The method we suggest for patient self-selection parallels our earlier recommendation for selection by trainers. The patients should be provided with clear descriptions of the skill areas for which training might be offered, and then be given an opportunity to indicate whether they feel they are deficient in the particular skills. This information can be obtained most efficiently by using the SLT Skill Checklist (FORM T) (see Supplement E). Their responses can then be compared with observers' responses and used in constituting training groups. For example, if several patients indicate that they are having difficulty with such skills as "Expressing Anger" or "Self-Control," then a group might be formed to deal with these felt deficits. Observers' responses might suggest other skills that ought to be practiced either before or after those indicated by the patients.

The SLT Skill Checklist (FORM T) may be self-administered, so that groups of patients can respond to them. Some patients, however, may need to be aided in their self-selection via a structured interview. That is, some people who might benefit from Structured Learning Therapy may be unable to read or understand a written checklist, or they may be hesitant to complete it for a variety of other reasons. In these cases we suggest that the trainer interview the person individually, explain the Structured Learning Therapy procedures, and discuss the various skill areas mentioned on the Checklist. Such a structured interview also provides the trainer with an opportunity to answer any questions about Structured Learning Therapy that the person may have, offer support and reassurance, and make suggestions as to which specific skill areas seem appropriate for training. The structured interview format for selection offers an opportunity for the trainer to *negotiate* with the patient which skill areas might be the most useful ones in which to provide training. As with the example given previously, the patient might indicate that he needs training in "Expressing Anger." The trainer might acknowledge this, and suggest that before the patient begins working on that skill it would be helpful to concentrate on "Starting a Conversation," since he (the trainer) had observed some deficiencies in the latter skill area. The results of the interview negotiation should be an agreement regarding which skill areas both trainer and patient feel need to be worked on.

FORMING STRUCTURED LEARNING THERAPY GROUPS

While there is much debate in the professional literature over whether (therapy) groups should be homogeneously or heterogeneously constituted (e.g., should patients be similar or dissimilar to one another in terms of age, sex, problems, diagnoses, I.Q., background, etc.), the position we advocate for Structured Learning

Therapy groups is quite straightforward; trainees who are deficient in similar skills at similar levels should be grouped together. While this criterion seems simple and unambiguous, arriving at a method for grouping trainees homogeneously involves a number of considerations. As mentioned above, our selection and grouping of trainees is based primarily on assessments of their behaviors. In addition to the reasons previously stated in support of behavioral criteria and descriptions, another important consideration is relevant. Attempts at predicting therapy group performance based on other criteria, such as psychological tests or psychiatric diagnosis, have been largely unsuccessful (Yalom, 1970). Groupings based on observations of behavior have been somewhat more successful (Goldstein, Heller, and Sechrest, 1966). Hence, we recommend reliance on behavioral observations for grouping purposes. These observations of behaviors might be based on the type of observational techniques described above or they might be based on observations of behaviors in previous Structured Learning Therapy or other groups. Short-term "trial groups" might be constituted for the purpose of seeing how particular trainees perform, as a predictor of success of later, more involved Structured Learning Therapy groups. Thus, we are in a sense advocating relatively homogeneous groups of trainees, with such grouping based on a common need for training in similar skill areas at similar levels of deficiency.

When we mention level or degree of skill deficiency, we are referring to the complexity of the interpersonal tasks in which the skills might be employed. For example, in starting a conversation with one person, a simple "hello" is a less complex conversational skill than "Persuading Others." Both involve the expressive aspects of conversation, but the former is a prerequisite for the latter. Thus, two Structured Learning Therapy groups dealing with conversational skills might be formed; one involving trainees who are observed having difficulty in starting and carrying on even the most basic conversations, while the other might include trainees who are able to start and carry on conversations, but have difficulty in expressing anger, expressing complaints, expressing affection, or expressing other relatively complex feelings or ideas. The general type of skill deficits of both groups might be the same ("Conversational Skills"), but the level or degree of deficiency would differ. Once the skills of the former, more basic level are mastered, the group can then progress to the more advanced level.

One of the variables that appears to affect level or degree of skill deficiency—a variable important to consider in grouping trainees—has to do with the trainee's degree of concreteness or abstractness. The extremely concrete individual is likely to be confused if placed in a group of people who function at a more abstract level, and the more abstract functioning person will probably be bored if included in a group of especially concrete people. If the trainee tends to be quite concrete and limited as to the amount or complexity of the information he can process, he should be placed in a group with similarly concrete trainees so that the Structured Learning Therapy procedures can be structured and paced to meet his needs. How rapidly material is covered, how many role plays will be conducted, how simple the role playing needs to be, how abstractly or concretely the discussion and feedback are expressed, may all be affected by trainee concreteness. While the degree of the trainee's concreteness or abstractness is clearly important in determining group composition, it is not always easy to assess. Some indications of concreteness or abstractness may be inferred from the behavioral assessments described previously (e.g., a reliance on simple communication skills, as might be revealed by the SLT Skill Checklists, or other indications of fixed, stereotyped behaviors, as might be brought to light by the behavioral charting).

Another criterion for grouping trainees has to do with techniques for facilitating transfer of training from the therapy session to real-life situations. One of the primary methods for facilitating transfer of training, it will be recalled, is maximizing identical elements in the training and application settings. For grouping purposes, this may mean grouping people who have potential for resembling those in each other's real interpersonal environments. Specifically, if trainees are preparing to return to family situations, they should have training experiences (via role playing) with persons who resemble those persons with whom they will be living. If trainees are working on skills related to interpersonal relationships in marriage, then both males and females, in the same general age range, should be used to constitute the group. If the trainees are preparing to reenter gainful employment, then there should be people in the group who resemble likely co-workers. One important basis for grouping, then, is dependent largely on opportunities for relevant role playing aimed at transfer training rather than on more abstract principles which might dictate age, sex, or other demographic or diagnostic grouping considerations. Will the composition of the group reflect common skill deficits and allow for adequate behavioral rehearsal toward the goal of transfer of training to real-life situations? If these two general criteria can be met, then a potentially therapeutic Structured Learning Therapy group has been constituted.

GROUP SIZE AND LENGTH OF SESSIONS

The decision about how many trainees should be included in a Structured Learning Therapy group should be based on the effect of group size on opportunity to participate in the session. Structured Learning Therapy depends primarily upon active, role play participation for its effectiveness in teaching people skills.

To a lesser extent, trainees may be expected to learn via observation of other trainees, and through being provided with feedback from the trainers and other trainees. Thus, decisions as to group size must be made in response to the central question of, "Will the trainee have an opportunity to actively participate in the group?"

There is no magic number for optimal group size that will guarantee sufficient participation. In addition to trainee characteristics discussed earlier, optimal group size is influenced by the fact that some skills are more complex than others and require more time to role play. In general, we have found that groups that range in size from six to 12 trainees (plus two trainers) allow for productive training sessions. Most of the group's trainees are generally able to role play during the allotted time and not suffer from fatigue or boredom. If the initial grouping proves to be too large so that some of the trainees are not actively participating, then the group may be reduced in size. Likewise, if the group appears to be too small, without a wide enough array of role play opportunities to facilitate transfer training, then more trainees may be added.

What is optimal size for a given group is obviously also influenced by the length of the training sessions. While most sessions will be about one and one-half hours in length, this may not allow for enough time for all trainees to role play, and the session may be rescheduled for up to two hours. Or, because of limited attention span of some trainees in some groups, sessions may be scheduled for one hour or even one-half hour (or slightly less). If sessions are shortened to one-half hour or less, it is advisable to schedule several separate meetings a week, rather than the usual one or two. Participation can then be assured by providing more sessions rather than by extending the length of the individual session.

TRAINEES' REACTIONS TO GROUP

The outcome of the grouping procedures described above should be the formation of productive Structured Learning Therapy groups

—that is, groups in which trainees are able to comprehend the material as it is presented and engage in appropriate role playing, discussion, feedback, and transfer training exercises, and thus learn the skills being taught. This desired outcome may not always be the case, however. Despite efforts at appropriate grouping, trainees may be misplaced. Trainers generally get their first indication of possible misgrouping when trainees manifest some of the behaviors described as "resistive" in Chapter 2—cutting class, lateness, responding inappropriately, apathy, and so forth. These behaviors can be dealt with first by using the techniques for overcoming resistance described in Chapter 2. If these attempts are unsuccessful, then the trainee can be rescheduled into another group more appropriate to his level of functioning and his specific training needs. Indeed, knowledge of a trainee's inability to function appropriately in a particular group provides valuable assessment data for placing him in a group more appropriate to his type and degree of skill deficiences.

REVIEW

In this chapter we have discussed some of the defining characteristics of our trainees—their early home environments, the ways they typically use language, their levels of concreteness, their encounters with life stresses—as a way of developing an approach to treatment that is prescriptively appropriate to their needs, values, learning styles, expectations, and problems. We discussed the where and how of trainee selection and grouping, emphasizing the formation of Structured Learning Therapy groups primarily on the basis of degree and type of skill deficiencies. We described the skills that might be taught and some techniques for assessing skill deficits. The procedures and considerations involved in the actual formation of training groups to facilitate effective mastery of these skills were presented. We hope that careful examination and utilization of these considerations will help the reader plan, organize, and conduct effective Structured Learning Therapy groups.

4
Modeling Tapes

In Chapter 1 we examined several types of modeling effects; model, trainee, and display characteristics that enhance such effects; supporting modeling research of diverse types; and limitations on the endurance of modeling effects. In the present chapter we wish to acquaint the reader with the Structured Learning Therapy modeling audiotapes that we have developed.

Each of our modeling tapes is organized in the following format:

I. *Narrator's Introduction*
1. Introduction of self
   a) Name and title
   b) High status position — e.g., Hospital Director
2. Introduction of skill
   a) Name
   b) General (descriptive) definition
   c) Behavioral (learning points) definition
3. Incentive statement — How and why skill-presence may be rewarding
4. Discrimination statement — Examples of skill-absence, and how and why skill-absence may be unrewarding
5. Repeat statement of learning points and request for attention to what follows

II. *Modeling Displays*
Ten brief vignettes of the learning point behaviors, each vignette

portraying the complete set of learning points which constitute the given skill. A variety of actors (models) and situations are used. Situations portray a mix of in-hospital and community settings and events. Model characteristics (age, sex, apparent socio-economic level, etc.) are similar to typical trainee characteristics. The displays portray both overt model behaviors, as well as ideational and self-instructional learning points. Models are provided social reinforcement for skill enactment.

   III. *Narrator's Summary*

1. Repeat statement of learning points
2. Description of rewards to both models and actual trainees for skill usage
3. Urging of trainees to enact the learning points in the Structured Learning Therapy session which follows and, subsequently, in their real-life environments

This tape format fully reflects the array of modeling and transfer enhancers examined in Chapter 1, including attention-increasing material (e.g., narrator status and instructions); reward to both model and, potentially, trainee; sufficient repetition for both initial learning and overlearning; model-trainee similarity; use of a variety of models; portrayal of both overt and covert behaviors; and transfer training relevant statements to provide general principles (skill definitions), stimulus variability (diverse models), identical elements (representative skill content), and response availability (learning point repetition).

As is clear by now, our overall training goal is to aid trainees in learning those coping and mastery skills that are prerequisites for effective and satisfying daily lives. Based upon the several sources of information described in the preceding chapter, we have developed modeling tapes for the basic skills listed in Table 1 below.

Table 1. Modeling Tapes for Structured Learning

Series I. Conversation: Beginning Skills

   Skill   1. Starting a Conversation — talking to someone about light topics and then leading into more serious topics.

   Skill   2. Carrying on a Conversation — opening a main topic, elaborating on it, and responding to the reactions of the person you are talking to.

   Skill   3. Ending a Conversation — letting the other person know that you have been paying attention, and then closing the conversation appropriately.

Skill 4. Listening — paying attention to people, trying to understand them, and letting them know you are trying.

Series II. Conversations: Expressing Oneself
Skill 5. Expressing a Compliment — telling someone that you like something about him or about his actions.
Skill 6. Expressing Appreciation — letting another person know that you are grateful for something he has done for you.
Skill 7. Expressing Encouragement — telling someone that he should try to do something which he is not sure that he can do.
Skill 8. Asking for Help — requesting that someone aid you in handling a difficult situation which you have not been able to manage by yourself.
Skill 9. Giving Instructions — clearly explaining to someone how you would like a specific task done.
Skill 10. Expressing Affection — letting someone know that you care about him or her.
Skill 11. Expressing a Complaint — telling someone that he is responsible for creating a particular problem for you, and attempting to find a solution for the problem.
Skill 12. Persuading Others — attempting to convince another person that your ideas are better and will be more useful than his.
Skill 13. Expressing Anger — presenting your angry feelings in a direct and honest manner.

Series III. Conversations: Responding to Others
Skill 14. Responding to Praise — letting a person know that you are pleased with his praise and that you appreciate it.
Skill 15. Responding to the Feelings of Others (Empathy) — trying to understand what the other person is feeling and communicating your understanding to him.
Skill 16. Apologizing — telling someone sincerely that you are sorry for something you have done to cause him discomfort.
Skill 17. Following Instructions — carrying out one's directions to you in a competent manner.
Skill 18. Responding to Persuasion — considering another person's ideas, weighing them against your own, and then deciding which course of action will be best for you in the long run.
Skill 19. Responding to Failure — figuring out what went wrong and what you can do about it so that you can be more successful in the future.

Skill 20. Responding to Contradictory Messages — recognizing and dealing with the confusion that results when a person tells you one thing, but says or does things which indicate that he means something else.

Skill 21. Responding to a Complaint — dealing fairly with another person's dissatisfaction with a situation attributed to you.

Skill 22. Responding to Anger — trying to understand another person's anger and letting him know that you are trying.

Series IV. Planning Skills

Skill 23. Setting a Goal — deciding on what you would like to accomplish and judging whether your plan is realistic.

Skill 24. Gathering Information — deciding what specific information you need and asking the appropriate people for that information.

Skill 25. Concentrating on a Task — making those preparations that will enable you to get a job done efficiently.

Skill 26. Evaluating Your Abilities — examining your accomplishments fairly and honestly in order to decide how competent you are in a particular skill.

Skill 27. Preparing for a Stressful Conversation — planning ahead of time to present your point of view in a conversation which may be difficult.

Skill 28. Setting Problem Priorities — deciding which of several current problems is most urgent and should be worked on first.

Skill 29. Decision Making — deciding on a realistic course of action which you believe will be in your best interest.

Series V. Alternatives to Aggression

Skill 30. Identifying and Labeling Your Emotions — recognizing which emotion you are feeling.

Skill 31. Determining Responsibility — finding out whether your actions or the actions of others have caused an event to occur.

Skill 32. Making Requests — asking the appropriate person for what you need or want.

Skill 33. Relaxation — learning to calm down and relax when you are tense.

Skill 34. Self-control — controlling your temper before things get out of hand.

Skill 35. Negotiation — arriving at an agreement which is satisfactory to you and to another person who has taken a different position.

Skill 36. Helping Others — aiding others who are having difficulty handling a situation by themselves.

Skill 37. Assertiveness — standing up for yourself by letting other people know what you want, how you feel, or what you think about something.

We have documented elsewhere (Goldstein, 1973) that one of the major problems of all contemporary treatment and training approaches is the failure of the new knowledge, self-attitudes, or behaviors learned in the hospital, clinic, or training center to transfer to the trainee's real-life functioning. In Chapter 1 we described several principles for increasing the chances that positive transfer will occur. Yet, given the successful implementation of these transfer-enhancement principles, trainees may still find the leap from training to real-life application to be too great. To help bridge this gap, to further decrease the likelihood of a failure to transfer basic skills acquired during Structured Learning Therapy participation to real-life settings, we have developed an additional series of modeling tapes. We call these Application Tapes. Each one portrays a model enacting a sequence of three to eight basic skills, that sequential combination of skills necessary to deal effectively and in a satisfying way with a real-life problem, event, or situation. These Application Tapes are listed in Table 2.

Table 2. Modeling Tapes for Structured Learning

Skill 38. Finding a Place to Live
Skill 39. Moving In (typical)
Skill 40. Moving In (difficult)
Skill 41. Managing Money
Skill 42. Neighboring (apartment house)
Skill 43. Job Seeking (typical)
Skill 44. Job Seeking (difficult)
Skill 45. Job Keeping (average day's work)
Skill 46. Job Keeping (strict boss)
Skill 47. Receiving Telephone Calls (difficult)
Skill 48. Restaurant Eating (typical)
Skill 49. Organizing Time (typical)
Skill 50. Using Leisure Time (learning something new)
Skill 51. Using Leisure Time (interpersonal activity)
Skill 52. Social (party)
Skill 53. Social (church supper)

Skill 54. Marital (positive interaction)
Skill 55. Marital (negative interaction)
Skill 56. Using Community Resources (seeking money)
Skill 57. Using Community Resources (avoiding red tape)
Skill 58. Dealing with Crises (inpatient to nonpatient transition)
Skill 59. Dealing with Crises (loss)

Effective use of Structured Learning Therapy requires a satisfactory level of trainer skills (see Chapter 2), appropriate choice and grouping of trainees (see Chapter 3), and a proper selection of the skills to be taught. To aid the reader in this skill-selection task, the remainder of this chapter presents further information about the content of each modeling tape. For each Basic Skill (1-37), the sequence of behaviors which make up the skill (the learning points) is presented, along with one of the tape's ten vignettes in which a model portrays behaviors illustrating these learning points. For skills 38-59, the Application Tapes, we have indicated the specific Basic Skills which constitute each tape and, to further familiarize the reader with these materials, the Application Tapes for Job Seeking (difficult) and Using Community Resources (avoiding red tape) are transcribed in full.

BASIC SKILL TAPES

Skill 1. Starting a Conversation

Learning points
1. Choose the right place and time.
2. Greet the other person.
3. Make small talk.
4. Judge if the other person is listening and wants to talk with you.
5. Open the main topic you want to talk about.

Modeling vignette example
Person 1: *There's Peggy over there by the coffee bar. I've been meaning to get a hold of her to get that $10 back that she owes me. Now's the time to see her — there's no one else around.* *
Hi, Peg, how are you?

*In the sample vignettes in this chapter, all ideational content (i.e., material which the model thinks or "says" to himself) appears in italics.

Person 2: Uh, fine. How are you?

Person 1: Fine, thank you. Nice day.

Person 2: It's beautiful out. I was just out for a walk.

Person 1: What's been happening?

Person 2: Oh, not too much. Not really too much. I had a cup of coffee with a couple of the girls and that was about it for today. What have you been doing?

Person 1: Oh, I just came back from a shopping trip and I bought some clothes I'm gonna need for going away to college, and, uh, . . . uh . . . .

Person 2: Oh, I'd like to see your new clothes.

Person 1: Oh, apparently you've got some time to talk now. Could we perhaps get a cup of coffee and go sit down at a table?

Person 2: Sure can.

Person 1: Well, now that we've sat down with our coffee, I think that . . . if you don't mind I'd like to ask you . . . have you got that $10 that I borrowed . . . uh, that you borrowed from me about a month ago?

Skill 2. Carrying on a Conversation

Learning points
  1. Open the main topic you want to talk about.
  2. Present your thoughts and feelings on the topic.
  3. Ask for the other person's reactions.
  4. Respond to the other person's reactions.

Modeling vignette example

Person 1: Hi, Jean, I heard you're getting out the same day I am.

Person 2: Yes, next Tuesday.

Person 1: You know, I don't mind going out, but I . . . I don't have anybody to talk to. I don't know anybody downtown. They told me I have to find an apartment. I found one; it's really nice; it's very big and, uh, it's got two beds in it, and, um . . . I was wondering what you would think about, you know, moving in with me, you know, at least we'd be . . . you know . . . know somebody in town — have somebody to shop with. What do you think about that?

Person 2: That sounds like a good idea because I don't have a place. I've looked, but they're either too expensive or in a bad neighborhood; something's always wrong, so I'd like that.

Person 1: Well, this is in a real nice neighborhood. I know we'd get along, we've been in the same groups together and we kinda feel the same about things and . . .

Person 2: How much is the rent?

Person 1: Well, it's not too bad. You know, I'm getting extra money. Uh, I really think it'd be nice if we did live together.

Skill 3. Ending a Conversation

Learning points
1. Summarize your's and the other person's main points.
2. Draw a conclusion.
3. Ask for the other person's reaction.
4. Respond to the other person's reaction.
5. Make a closing remark.

Modeling vignette example

Person 1: So, it's alright with you if we room together. I'd really like it too, so let's do it. O.K.?

Person 2: Yes, I think it's a good idea.

Person 1: Alright, shall we go talk to the social worker now about our future plans? I'm sure she's free to see us now.

Skill 4. Listening

Learning points
1. Look at the other person.
2. Show your interest in the other's statement — e.g., nod your head, etc.
3. Ask questions on the same topic.
4. Add your thoughts and feelings on the topic.

Modeling vignette example

Person 1: *Gee, this is my first day on the unit and some of the other girls have told me that the supervisor always comes around and talks with you about your schedule. I understand that you're really made kinda responsible for getting where you're supposed to go on your own. So I really have to listen carefully. It also . . . it also seems that when you look at somebody when they're talking to you, you understand better what they're saying, and if you nod your head and look interested this also makes the other person aware that you understand.*

Person 2: Hi, Marcia, how are you?

Person 1: Good morning.

Person 2: Today's your first day on the unit with us. I thought I'd take a few minutes and sit down and talk with you if you have the time.

Person 1: Yes, I do.

Person 2: O.K. Seeing it's the first day on the unit, I want to explain that for the first two or three days you probably won't be assigned to any special therapies or have a fixed schedule.

Person 1: O.K.

Person 2: Uh, we use this time to ... for you to get to know the staff a little better and for the staff to get to know you. The, uh ... free time that you will have between meals or medication time, if you have medication, are on ...

Person 1: Medications?

Person 2: Yes. If the doctor has prescribed any medicine for you. He saw you . . . .

Person 1: Did he?

Person 2: I ... I'm not sure. I haven't seen your chart yet. But I could check on it.

Person 1: Where do ... where do you go ... like ... uh, to get your medication?

Person 2: Well, the head nurse of your ward will ... will explain that. But, for the first two or three days I think that I would like to ask you to go around and meet the staff and the other people that you will be living with and, uh, if ... there's some table games that you can perhaps participate in.

Person 1: You can play with those any time that you want?

Person 2: Anytime you want. And just familiarize yourself with the setting here.

Person 1: Well, gee, you know, I really appreciate you, um, taking the time to talk to me and, uh, I think maybe I can go along with this, 'cause I want to get out of here.

Person 2: Well, in two or three days I'll get back to you and ... and we'll talk about the scheduling of therapy.

Person 1: So, I'm not going to be on any regular schedule right away?

Person 2: Not right away.

Skill 5. Expressing a Compliment

Learning points
  1. Decide what it is about the other person you want to compliment.

2. Decide whether the other person would like to hear the compliment.
3. Choose the right time and place to express the compliment.
4. Express the compliment in a sincere and friendly manner.

Modeling vignette example
Person 1: *There's John sitting over there. This morning in the group he was really nice to ... uh ... what's her name? ... Mary. He said some nice things to her that made her feel good. Wonder whether he'd like to know that I think that was a good thing for him to do. I think he probably would like to know that I noticed that. Why ... why don't I go over to him right now because he's just ... he's sitting by himself and I'll tell him it was nice.*
John.
Person 2: Yeah?
Person 1: You know, in the group this morning? I think you were very helpful to Mary; I think she really appreciated that and I'd like to let you know that I noticed that you were helpful to her.
Person 2: Well, thanks for telling me that. I was kinda wonderin' whether ... whether that would be helpful to Mary, and ... and it's nice to know that ... that ... probably it was.

Skill 6. Expressing Appreciation

Learning points
1. Clearly describe to the other person *what* he did for you which deserves appreciation.
2. Tell the other person *why* you appreciate what he did.
3. Ask the other person if there is anything you can do for him.

Modeling vignette example
Person 1: Peggy, I would really like to thank you for helping me find my car keys. I don't know what I would have done if you hadn't helped me. I would have missed a very important meeting for one thing and to get them duplicated I would have had to go out of town. So thanks a lot. Is there ....
Person 2: I'm glad I could help.
Person 1: Is there anything I can do? Do you need a lift anywhere?

Skill 7. Expressing Encouragement

Learning points
1. Ask the other person how *he* feels about the way he is handling

the situation.
2. Decide if it might be helpful to encourage the other person.
3. Decide what type of encouragement might be most helpful to the other person.
4. Express encouragement in a sincere and friendly manner.

Modeling vignette example
Person 1: Gee, Barbara, I've noticed that you haven't been talking as much as you used to in group and, um, I wonder, um, is there something different going on?
Person 2: Yeah, It seems that, uh, I've been thinking quite a bit and sometimes I have some pretty valuable thoughts that I'd like to contribute but lately, uh, I just don't seem to be able to get the floor and let people know what I'm thinking and, you know, it's frustrating because I'd really like to share my reactions with the group.
Person 1: *I bet it would be helpful to Barbara if she did speak up more in the group and, . . . and maybe she just does need that extra little bit of encouragement to, uh, give her a little extra confidence to contribute a little bit more. I think I'll tell her that. I think I'll tell her how much the rest of us in the group, uh, respond and appreciate what she has to say.*
You know, Barb, I know that for myself that I . . . I really feel that the things you say in group are very interesting and helpful to me and I think the rest of the folks do also; and I think you really ought to speak up more, and . . . and let us know . . . and . . . that would be helpful to me and I think it would be helpful to the rest of us and maybe helpful to you.
Person 2: Well, you know, thanks very much because that gives me confidence that what I have to say is worth the effort.

Skill 8. Asking for Help

Learning points
1. Define the problem that troubles you.
2. Decide if you want to seek help for the problem.
3. Identify the people who might help you.
4. Make a choice of helper.
5. Tell the helper about your problem.

Modeling vignette example
Person 1: *Oh, I've got a terrible toothache, and I've ignored it for so long, I just can't ignore it any longer. I thought maybe it would go*

*away, like it always did. I think this one, I'm gonna . . . have to
. . . do something about it. I'm gonna have to get some help. Oh
. . . let me see . . . I'm new in town, so I don't have a dentist.
Maybe the lady next door . . . my next door neighbor . . . I don't
know her very well. She doesn't seem too friendly. Uh, . . . I have
an appointment this afternoon for the baby at the pediatrician's.
He'd probably know of a good . . . of a good one. Or maybe the
nurse would. Maybe his nurse would.*
Miss Jones, before I go in to see the doctor, could you recommend
a good dentist? I've got a terrible, terrible toothache.

Person 2: Well, I think I can help you. I've been seeing a dentist for
a long time here in town and I can give you his phone number and
I'm sure, especially if you tell him about how bad your mouth is,
that he'll see you right away. He's like that. He's very nice.

Person 1: Thank you.

Skill 9. Giving Instructions

Learning points
1. Define what needs to be done and who should do it.
2. Tell the other person what you want him to do, and why.
3. Tell the other person exactly how he is to do what you want
   him to do.
4. Ask for his reactions.
5. Consider his reactions and change your directions to him, if
   appropriate.

Modeling vignette example
Person 1: *This light bulb's been burned out for two days now. I
guess I'd better get somebody to do something about it. When I
moved in here they told me the custodian was always supposed to
change the bulbs and that type of thing.*
Mmh . . . Mr. Jones?

Person 2: Yes?

Person 1: My light bulb has been burned out in the livingroom for
two days now and I'd like to see . . . I'd like to have you change it
sometime this afternoon if you would. I'm having a lot of trouble
seeing my way around at night and I'm kind of afraid I'm going to
fall down. If you'd try and get it done this afternoon I could leave
my key under the mat there − and − it's the bulb in the living
room − the one that I want changed. Do you think you could do
it this afternoon?

Person 2: Uh, yeah, I think I'll take care of that. It's O.K.

Person 1: O.K. Well, then, like I said, I'll leave the key there and, uh, thank you very much.

Skill 10. Expressing Affection

Learning points
1. Decide if you have warm, caring feelings about the other person.
2. Decide whether the other person would like to know about your feelings.
3. Decide how you might best express your feelings.
4. Choose the right time and place to express your feelings.
5. Express affection in a warm and caring manner.

Modeling vignette example

Person 1: *There's Dr. Sullivan. I really like him. I think that he's the only person around here that really seems to care a lot about me and I think he's really hip. Like he really knows what's going on, and . . . uh . . . seems to listen. You know, a lot of people around here don't seem to listen when I'm talking to them. Um, I'd like to tell him. I know he probably thinks I'm weird anyway, so, like I could just go ahead and tell him that I like him. I think he'd like to know, too, how I feel about him. Maybe he thinks I don't like him because I don't say very much. Um, I think I'll just tell him . . . just outright . . . that I like him, that I think he's a good doctor. Here he comes now. I might as well tell him. He's not busy and there doesn't seem to be anybody demanding his attention.*
Dr. Sullivan.

Person 2: Hi, Jane. How are you?

Person 1: Really well. . . . I'd . . . you know I'd, uh, like to tell you something. Um, I think you're a really good doctor and I do like you and I think you're really with it and really hip and understand people like me.

Skill 11. Expressing a Complaint

Learning points
1. Define what the problem is, and who is responsible.
2. Decide how the problem might be solved.
3. Tell that person what the problem is and how it might be solved.

4. Ask for his response.
5. Show that you understand his feelings.
6. Come to agreement on the steps to be taken by each of you.

Modeling vignette example

Person 1: *I bought this toaster last month I think it was . . . it must be about four weeks now. And this morning it's not working right. It only toasts on one side. Wonder if maybe I broke it? I . . . I don't know; I thought I was following the instructions . . . I . . . I don't know whether I broke it or whether there's something wrong with it . . . or . . . No, I'm pretty sure I didn't do anything to it. I've been just toasting bread and, uh, it's broken and . . . and I'm sure there's something wrong with the toaster. If I take it back to the store I can tell them that there was something wrong with the toaster and that they should fix it.*

Excuse me. I bought this toaster here four weeks ago . . . Remember when I came into the store?

Person 2: Yeah,. . . . that's one of ours.

Person 1: Um, it seems to be broken, and . . . I think there's something wrong with the toaster and I'd like you to . . . it's on warranty . . . I'd like you to take it back and fix it for me.

Persons 2: Well, these are good toasters . . . they seldom break down. Um . . . you been using it correctly?

Person 1: Yes, I've been using it correctly. I . . . I'd like you to take it in and check it out and make sure that . . . uh, you know . . . and fix it for me. Or if you have some other way that you can check on it?

Person 2: Well . . . uh . . . we never get complaints about these . . . these toasters. And, uh, I don't know . . . I think that maybe . . . uh . . . you been plugging it in the right outlet? You don't hold the button down, you just let it down by itself?

Person 1: Yeah, I've been following all the instructions and I know that you usually sell good merchandise. I've been happy with everything I bought here. And . . . uh, I can understand that you would think that maybe I did something wrong, but . . . I do believe that there's something wrong with this toaster because I've been very careful with it and I . . . I . . . I would hope that you could take it and repair it. Or give me another toaster maybe?

Person 2: Well . . . uh . . . let me do this, ma'am. Let me send it off to the shop and have them check it and, uh, see what the problem is. And, uh, we'll send you a card when it comes back.

Person 1: O.K. Thank you.

Skill 12. Persuading Others

Learning points
1. Decide on your position and what the other person's is likely to be.
2. State your position clearly, completely, and in a way which is acceptable to the other person.
3. State what you think is the other person's position.
4. Restate your position, emphasizing why it is the better of the two.
5. Suggest that the other person consider your position for a while before making a decision.

Modeling vignette example
Person 1: *You know, I really want to get out of the hospital, but only the doctor can give you a pass. I . . . and I know that he's not really willing to do that yet, but I think I'm going to try to convince him that I should have a pass.*
Doctor, I want a pass to go home this weekend, and I feel that I'm ready. If you check with the nurse on the ward, you . . . you'll find that I've been doing very well here. I've been going to all my assignments . . . uh . . . I've been keeping myself clean. I've already contacted my folks and they're more than willing to have me. And I really think that I'm ready to go home. I know that you probably think that I haven't been here long enough because a lot of patients have told me that you like to have us . . . to have people stay here at least a month before going on pass.
Person 2: Yes...
Person 1: Uh ... I think that I ... I ... I'm really ready to go home, and I think that it would be helpful to me. Um, you know, I really think that I'm doing everything here that I should be doing and I feel that going home this weekend would be very helpful to me, and I'd . . . I'd really like a pass. Maybe . . . Maybe . . . Could I check back with you a little later today? If you want to think about it, or maybe you want to check with the nurse?
Person 2: Yeah . . . mmh . . . why don't you do that?

Skill 13. Expressing Anger

Learning points
1. Pay attention to those body signals which help you know what you are feeling.

2. Decide which outside events may have caused you to have these feelings.
3. Decide if you are feeling angry about these events.
4. Decide how you can best express these angry feelings.
5. Express your angry feelings in a direct and honest manner.

Modeling vignette example
Person 1: *Boy, there it is; I've got that throbbing right in my forehead again. Gee, I ... I wonder what it is. Boy, that's uncomfortable. It's really upsetting. Wonder ... what could be causing that. I don't know ... uh, there was a lot of noise this morning, that bothers me, and then in the meeting I wanted to say something, and ... and ... Jane was leading the meeting, and she didn't call on me. I really wanted to say it and she wouldn't call on me. I ... that ... that must be it. 'Cause I know it bothered me right after that ... I've been getting this throbbing ever since then. Boy, that makes me angry, now that I think about it. You know ... I ... I'm just not going to sit on this anymore. I better tell her about that ... tell her that I'm angry about it ... and ... and ... that I don't think she was treating me fairly in the meeting. I'll do it when ... when we're together and there's time to talk about it ... I really have to tell her about it.*

Jane, there's something I've got to tell you. I really am angry about the way you ignored me in that meeting. I had something to say, I had my hand up, I ... I ... wanted to contribute there and ... and ... you know ... you wouldn't even call on me. And I don't think that's fair.
Person 2: Gee, I'm sorry, Bob. I didn't do it intentionally.

Skill 14. Responding to Praise

Learning points
1. Listen openly to the other person's statement of praise.
2. Tell the other person how his statement makes you feel.
3. Thank the other person in a warm and sincere manner.

Modeling vignette example
Person 1: Cliff, I really want to tell you how nice you look. I like that vest — I haven't really seen one around that I like. That really makes you look good.
Person 2: That makes me feel good. Nobody's said anything about it really. Thanks a lot.

Skill 15. Responding to the Feelings of Others

Learning points
1. Observe the other person's words and action.
2. Decide what the other person might be feeling, and how strong the feelings are.
3. Decide whether it would be helpful to let the other person know you understand his feelings.
4. Tell the other person, in a warm and sincere manner, how you think he is feeling.

Modeling vignette example
Person 1: Hi, Bob, I haven't seen you for a while. How've you been doing?
Person 2: God damn it, will you just mind your own business! I had enough today.
Person 1: *Gee, he's really yelling. I don't know what's getting to him. All I asked him was how's he doing and he yelled at me and told me to leave him alone. He must be awfully angry. I just . . . hardly said anything and he yelled, so he must be terribly angry. Wonder if I told him about it . . . that I saw how he's feeling . . . whether that would help? I wonder whether he could tell me about what's bothering him? I'll try it. I'll let him know that I can see how he's feeling.*
Bob, you must be awfully angry about something. What's been happening with you?
Person 2: Well, I'll tell you. I had one hell of a day at work.

Skill 16. Apologizing

Learning points
1. Decide whether there is something for which you want to apologize.
2. Decide how you might best apologize.
3. State your apology in a warm and sincere manner.
4. If appropriate, offer to make up for what happened.

Modeling vignette example
Person 1: *I've really got to say I'm sorry to Dr. Marin for butting in on him when he was talking to the supervisor. I think the best way would be to knock on his door and ask him for a minute of his time. I know he's free now, that he's got no one in his office.*

Person 2: Come in.
Person 1: Dr. Marin, I'm really sorry for butting in on your conversation before with the supervisor. I'll try real hard not to do it again.
Person 2: O.K. All right. That's all right.

Skill 17. Following Instructions

Learning points
   1. Listen carefully while the instructions are being given.
   2. Give your reactions to the instructions.
   3. Repeat the instructions to yourself.
   4. Imagine yourself following the instructions and then do it.

Modeling vignette example
Person 1: Well, Mrs. Allen, now that you're in this class . . . and, by the way, we have this every week at the same time, and this is to sort of help you to . . . uh . . . re-learn things that maybe you've possibly forgotten about cooking, or maybe learn new things. Um, there's going to be eight people altogether in this class and usually when someone new comes into the class, um, we try and give them a fairly simple thing to do until they get used to where things are kept, and that sort of stuff. So, um, today I'd like to have you maybe set the table and not actually do any of the cooking. Um . . . so what you need is, you have to get out the eight plates, cups and saucers, and find out how many people want a beverage, and get glasses out and all the things that you'll need to set the table.
Person 2: O.K. Let's see, there's eight people?
Person 1: That's right.
Person 2: . . . and, where do I get the, like silverware?
Person 1: There's silverware in that drawer over there, and, uh, the plates are right above that.
Person 2: Oh, yeah. O.K. *Um, let's see. I've gotta get eight plates, eight cups. I have to find out how many glasses I need to get, and, uh . . . silverware for eight people. O.K. Right over here. O.K. Let's see. I guess I'll put the plates out first and then the silverware and then I'll ask everybody what they're drinking so I'll know how many glasses and cups to put out. Now. . . .*

Skill 18. Responding to Persuasion

Learning Points
   1. Consider the other person's position.

2. Consider the other person's possible reasons for his position.
3. Ask the other person to explain anything you don't understand about what he has said.
4. Compare the other person's position with your own, identifying the pros and cons of each.
5. Decide on what to do based on what will benefit you most in the long run.

Modeling vignette example
Person 1: C'mon, Bob, ask the Doctor for a pass so we can go out shopping tomorrow afternoon. You can ... if you just ask him, he'll give you the pass.
Person 2: Well. ... *Jane really wants me to ask for that town pass. I know that one of the reasons she's asking me is ... is that she doesn't want to go to town herself, and, uh, I don't know. ... I think maybe she wants to borrow some money from me. That's one of the reasons too. I don't know.*
Jane, do you think that, uh ... uh ... that he'd really give me a pass just by asking him?
Person 1: I know he would. And then you can go shopping tomorrow. Ask him for the pass.
Person 2: Ah ... uh ... I don't know. *She'd like to go and ... but I have some things to do around here. I bet I can do the things here ... and finish them up today. Maybe I will ask him for a ... a, uh, pass.*
Yeah, I think I will ask the Doctor, Jane. I think you're right.
Person 1: We'll have a good time tomorrow.

Skill 19. Responding to Failure

Learning points
1. Decide if you have failed.
2. Think about both the personal reasons and the circumstances which have caused you to fail.
3. Decide how you might do things differently if you tried again.
4. Decide if you want to try again.
5. If appropriate, try again, using your revised approach.

Modeling vignette example
Person 1: *Well, I know I'm not going to get that job. I know the interview didn't go well. Boy, I ... I ... just struck out again. Let's see, I wonder what it was? I know that in some ways I'm not*

really qualified, and that if I had a little more training, I'd be in a better position and, as he said, the job market's tight, so maybe that's another thing. I don't know . . . maybe . . . maybe next time I oughta . . . at least be better prepared for the interview. I can . . . get all the things ready before I go to the interview and tell them exactly what I know how to do and what my skills are and maybe . . . maybe try to interview for jobs that are more appropriate. I'm gonna do it again. Um . . . it's worth it. I . . . I really want a job. In fact, maybe even before I leave here today I'm gonna set up another appointment with the interviewer. That's what I'll do.

Skill 20. Responding to Contradictory Messages

Learning points
1. Pay attention to those body signals which help you know you are feeling trapped or confused.
2. Observe the other person's words and actions which may have caused you to have these feelings.
3. Decide whether his words and actions are contradictory.
4. Decide whether it would be useful to point out the contradiction.
5. Ask the other person to explain the contradiction.

Modeling vignette example
Person 1: Bob, whatta ya want for dinner?
Person 2: Gee, I don't know. Do you have some . . . some chops or . . . maybe a casserole, or something like that?
Person 1: Mmh . . . Are you sure you want chops or a casserole?
Person 2: Yeah . . . I love chops. Casserole is good.
Person 1: You always like meat loaf. How about . . . how about a meat loaf?
Person 2: *There it is again! Boy, I get that tight feeling. I . . . I don't understand that. I just don't understand. There's something about . . . when she says that . . . it just makes me feel uptight and confused. Something's not right there. It . . . it . . . it doesn't make sense. On the one hand she asks me what I want for dinner and then I tell her what I want for dinner and then she tells me that I can't have that, that she wants to make meat loaf. That . . . that . . . that just doesn't make sense to me. You know . . . I have to . . . I've gotta do something about that. I'm gonna have to tell Jane that that's just very confusing to me. And . . . that it's gotta stop. This situation just can't go on. It just gets me uptight every time she does this.*

Jane, there's something that's been going on and I . . . I've gotta talk to you about it, 'cause I just don't understand it. When I come home at night and you ask me what I want for dinner and I tell you what I want for dinner and then you say "no, you can't have that." Why do you ask me? It doesn't make any sense to me.
Person 1: I guess I'm really doing that, huh?
Person 2: You sure are.

Skill 21. Responding to a Complaint

Learning points
1. Listen openly to the complaint.
2. Ask the person to explain anything you don't understand.
3. Show that you understand the other person's thoughts and feelings.
4. Tell the other person your thoughts and feelings, accepting responsibility if appropriate.
5. Summarize the steps to be taken by each of you.

Modeling vignette examples
Person 1: (knock at door) Yeah?
Person 2: Ms. Johnson?
Person 1: Mmh . . . mmh.
Person 2: Uh, there's something I gotta talk to you about. A number of the other tenants in the building have been complaining about all the noise coming from your apartment every evening; and they've been coming to me and they finally forced me to come up and talk to you about it. Uh . . . radio? TV? I don't know what it is, but they . . . they're really up in arms!
Person 1: Gee, I wonder . . . I wonder what it is that is bothering them? I wasn't . . . uh . . . aware I was making so much noise. They didn't tell you that . . . uh . . . it was the TV or? . . .
Person 2: Well, they thought it was the TV or maybe a radio, or . . . I don't know . . . music and stuff . . . um . . . they say it's to all hours of the night.
Person 1: Mmh . . . Mmh. It must be rough when you have to come around, you know . . . come around and tell people about these complaints. I'm really sorry you had to come and tell me about this. Though I wasn't under the impression I was playing my TV that loud and that late. You know, no one's said anything to me. Umh . . . why don't I try turning my TV down a little bit and maybe turning it off a little earlier.

Person 2: That would be good, and I'll tell the other tenants that we're working on the problem.

Skill 22. Responding to Anger

Learning points
1. Listen openly to the other person's angry statement.
2. Show that you understand what the other person is feeling.
3. Ask the other person to explain anything you don't understand about what he has said.
4. Show that you understand why he is feeling angry.
5. If appropriate, express your thoughts and feelings about the situation.

Modeling vignette example
Person 1: Laurie, I wish you'd stop bugging me! You're always hanging around here and you know I have a lot to do. I have to be alone some of the time. You've been here every single day this week.
Person 2: Boy, you're really yelling. I've never seen you so mad. Your face is red. Why don't . . . why don't you sit down. Um, I didn't realize that . . . you know . . . that you had so much to do, and that I'm really bothering you. Um, is it all the time that I bother you, or just . . . just because you're really busy today?
Person 1: Well, it's just that you've been here so much. Uh . . . I . . . like I said — every single day, and I just . . . I don't mind seeing you now and then, but every single day is just too much.
Person 2: Well, no wonder why you're mad. I've been . . . you know . . . I've been kinda lonely lately. That's why I've been doing this but I'll really try to stop.

Skill 23. Setting a Goal

Learning points
1. Decide what you would like to accomplish.
2. Decide what you would need to do to reach this hoped for goal.
3. Decide on the order in which you would do these things.
4. Judge whether your planning is realistic.
5. Set a realistic goal.

Modeling vignette example
Person 1: *Gee, I'd really like to get out of this damn place.*

Everybody tells me I'm doing so well. The doctor says you really ought to start to plan to leave here. I need money. I need a place to stay. I haven't a job. I never worked. And what about my medicine? Boy, I don't think they realize that I've got to get all these things. I don't even know where to start. Well, to get the money, I guess I need a job. Nobody's gonna give you money for nothing. And then, a place to stay. I can't go back with my family. Well, I really should get out of here. I've been here long enough. I . . . I'm not gonna receive any more help than I've already got. I feel good. Maybe I'll ask the doctor for a town pass and I'll look for a job and once I get one I'll start looking for an apartment. That's what I'll do. I'll ask for a town pass first.

Skill 24. Gathering Information

Learning points
1. Decide what specific information you need.
2. Decide who can give you the most accurate information.
3. Ask questions, in a direct manner, to get the information.

Modeling vignette example
Person 1: *Well, it looked like a nice enough apartment, but . . . uh, they warned me to really check on a couple of things . . . to see if the landlord is any good . . . and see if the neighborhood is any good . . . and things like that. Uh, I'd better do that . . . I'm going to find out what kind of landlord this guy is and how he keeps the building up and . . . if he takes the garbage out and all those kinds of things they told me about. Maybe what I ought to do . . . and while I'm here, is just ask one of the other tenants in the building. They probably know better than anyone else.*

Excuse me, sir, do you live in this building?
Person 2: Yes, sir. I do.
Person 1: I've been looking at that apartment that's vacant — 3B, and I wonder if you could tell me a couple of things about the building?
Person 2: Oh, sure. Well, first of all, I'm really happy living here. Uh, the landlord is really nice; he doesn't really press you for the rent . . . on . . . you know . . . every day and, uh, he does keep the place really clean.

Skill 25. Concentrating on a Task

Learning points
1. Set a realistic goal.
2. Decide on a reasonable time schedule.
3. Gather the materials you need.
4. Arrange your surroundings to minimize distraction.
5. Judge whether your preparation is complete and begin the task.

Modeling vignette example
Person 1: *They told me that if I really want to get the job, I'm gonna have to fill out the job application so it makes me look good. I ... I ... I've got the time now. They said I could take as much time as I wanted. I don't think it would take me much more than an hour. I brought that list of jobs with me like the doctor told me, so ... so that I know what to put down ... where I worked and who they can contact for my references. I've got all the names. I've got all the addresses and phone numbers. Umh ... I shouldn't have any problem with that. He said to just sit in this room and ... it should be O.K. He's not going to interrupt me. I'll close the door anyway. That'll help. Let's see, do I have everything? I've got the list of the jobs; I've got the phone numbers, the addresses, the names. I've got a pen. I've got the application. O.K. I'll just start now.*

Skill 26. Evaluating Your Abilities

Learning points
1. Decide what ability you need to evaluate.
2. Think about how you have done in the past when you have tried to use this ability.
3. Get any outside information you can about your ability (ask others, take tests, check records).
4. Use all of this evidence and realistically evaluate your ability.

Modeling vignette example
Person 1: *The doctor told me I could go home for a weekend as soon as I thought I was ready to. I think that what he meant was whether I could control myself ... whether I could control my temper. That's really the problem that there's been at home. I wonder how I've been doing this week controlling my temper. Well, let me think about it. It seems to me I haven't really blown*

*my top at anybody in ... in some time now. And when my
family's come down, I've managed to control it pretty well. Had a
little fight with my sister there, but, well ... I really didn't blow
my stack the way I used to. Let me check with one of the aides
and find out whether I'm seeing that accurately.*
Mr. Smith?

Person 2: Mmh?

Person 1: I was told I could go home for a weekend once I could
control myself ... uh, have I been doing O.K. on the ward lately?

Person 2: Well, let's see. ... Yeah, I think you've been doing pretty
good. I haven't heard any bad reports ... and, one time I saw you
... looked like you just kinda walked away rather than get into
the fight that seemed to be brewing. Sounds O.K. to me.

Person 1: O.K. Thanks a lot for the information. I think when I go
in for my therapy hour, I'm going to tell the doctor that I am
ready to go home for a weekend because I can control myself.

Skill 27. Preparing for a Stressful Conversation

Learning points
1. Imagine yourself in the stressful situation.
2. Think about how you will feel and why you will feel that way.
3. Imagine yourself in the other person's position and think about
   how he will feel and why he will feel that way.
4. Imagine yourself telling the other person what you want to say.
5. Imagine his response.
6. Repeat the above steps, using as many approaches as you can
   think of.
7. Choose the best approach.

Modeling vignette example
Person 1: *Alright, today's the day I've got to do it ... I ... I've
gotta ask for a raise ... gotta do it today. Let's see ... what I'll do
is I'll ... I don't know ... I guess I'll just go in there and knock
on his door. I can just imagine that! Boy! He'll be sitting behind
his desk ... working on his papers there ... and I'll be nervous as
hell, 'cause I'm nervous as hell right now! I'm scared! I know why
I'm scared. I'm scared because I'm scared of him ... and what
he'll say. Gee, I can just see ... I can just see him there now. If I
was in his place, I'd say "What the hell do you want? Always being
bothered by these employees asking for raises." If I were him,
that's what I'd say. Then what would I say? I'd tell him, "Look*

you gotta give me a raise." And he'd say, "No, I don't." Let's see. . . . Maybe . . . maybe he'd . . . you know, instead of being mean, he'd uh, just be feeling a little rushed. Yeah, . . . "What is it now," maybe, and, uh . . . I'd say. . . . "Gee, I need the money . . . I need some more money, boss." What would he say then? Wonder what. . . . "Work harder; work overtime" . . . that's what he'd say to that. Well, maybe I just . . . maybe instead of saying I need the money . . . uh . . . I'll give him some reasons. I'll say, "Look, I've been working here for six months . . . and, uh . . . I've never been late; I've worked overtime every time you asked me to . . . I think I'm doing a good job. . . . My supervisor says I'm doing a good job and everyone else has gotten a raise after three months . . . at least that's what they tell me. What about it, boss?" Well, I don't know . . . maybe he'd say . . . "I'll think about it." I don't know . . . can't be sure about what he'd say. But I think that's the best approach for me. . . . I'll just . . . I'll tell him what I've done and why I think I want the raise. Yeah, that makes some sense to me. That what I'll do.

Skill 28. Setting Problem Priorities

Learning points
1. List all the problems which are currently pressuring you.
2. Arrange this list in order, from most to least urgent problems.
3. Take steps to decrease temporarily the urgency of all but the most pressing problem (delegate, postpone, avoid).
4. Concentrate on the most pressing problem.

Modeling vignette example
Person 1: *What a time for everything to go wrong. My God! Fight with my wife. Here it is the first day of the job and I've . . . I . . . I've gotta make a good impression . . . I gotta . . . Jesus, everything has to . . . has to . . . to be done at once, it seems like. I . . . I've got to go down to the Post Office, change my address down there 'cause I haven't been getting my mail . . . my check . . . where's my medicine? And, uh, geez, the kid has to get set up at school. My God! How am I going to handle all of this? I guess I . . . I'm just going to take a minute and figure out what has to be done. O.K. The most important thing is I've gotta get myself together and get to work and make a good impression — be there on time — that's . . . if I don't do that then it . . . nothing else really matters. I'm sure that I . . . during lunch hour I'll call my wife and try to*

*cool things down with her . . . maybe deal with that a little later
. . . see if maybe she can handle the thing at school. Well, the
medication . . . I've got enough for a couple more days; I'll take
care of that later. Ah, what the hell, I can wait another day for the
Post Office. O.K. First things first; let me get myself together, get
dressed, and get to the job.*

Skill 29. Decision Making

Learning points
   1. Gather accurate information about the topic.
   2. Evaluate the information in light of your goal.
   3. Make a decision which is in your best interest.

Modeling vignette example
Person 1: *Well, I finally made up my mind about buying that new
car and . . . let's see . . . I called the bank today . . . about the loan
. . . and I called the Credit Union and I already talked to Aunt
Mary about borrowing the money from her. Now the bank . . . the
interest isn't too bad there . . . but it's lower at the Credit Union
where I work . . . and they take it out of my pay. And . . . Aunt
Mary'd give me the money at practically no interest. Uh, . . . I
think I'll go with the Credit Union. The interest would be low and
then I wouldn't be obligated to Aunt Mary.*

Skill 30. Identifying and Labeling Your Emotions

Learning points
   1. Pay attention to those body signals which help you know what
      you are feeling.
   2. Decide which outside events may have caused you to have these
      feelings.
   3. Consider all of this information and decide what you are
      feeling.

Modeling vignette example
Person 1: *There's that hot, flushed feeling that I sometimes get,
again. Wonder what that is? I was told that I'm going to see the
doctor this morning. The nurse suggested that I get cleaned up
and, uh, really acted as if this is a really big deal. Maybe I'm mad
at her. She was fussing over me a lot. No . . . I really like her. She's
only trying to help me. God, now that I think about it, I'm really
scared about that meeting. I really want to act right.*

Skill 31. Determining Responsibility

Learning points
1. Decide what the problem is.
2. Consider possible causes of the problem.
3. Decide which are the most likely causes of the problem.
4. Take actions to test out which are the actual causes of the problem.

Modeling vignette example

Person 1: *Boy, I've been wanting a town pass ever since I got to this hospital, and I've ... I've been waiting around for weeks and I haven't gotten a town pass. Must be that doctor. He's really ... he's been giving everybody a hard time, nobody's been getting passes from him. I don't know ... maybe the nurses have been telling him something ... maybe that's why he's not giving me a pass. Boy, I don't know ... I don't know.... Maybe I'm doing something that ... uh ... that says to him I'm not ready for a pass. Can't imagine that. Well, I guess I'm gonna have to find out why it is that I'm not getting that pass. It might be that I'm doing something. I'm gonna ask one of the aides down the hall ... and ask him ... and find out if the doctor told him anything.*
Mr. Smith?

Person 2: Yeah?

Person 1: Do you have any idea why I'm not getting a town pass? I ... I'm.... Has the doctor really been clamping down and not giving anybody town passes?

Person 2: Well, have you asked the doctor yet?

Person 1: Well, no ... but I'm supposed to get a pass if I'm ... if I'm ... but he's just not giving me one.

Person 2: Well, I think you ought to let him know that you'd like one. He's just not going to give you one unless he knows you want one.

Person 1: You mean, that's the reason I haven't gotten one? 'Cause I haven't asked for one?

Person 2: Yeah.

Skill 32. Making Requests

Learning points
1. Decide what you need or want.
2. Decide who can best help you meet your needs or wants.
3. Ask that person in a direct and friendly manner.

Modeling vignette example
Person 1: *Boy, I'd really like to go see that new movie tonight. I don't know whether Bob wants to go to the movies or not. Ah, he probably doesn't want to go. Well . . . uh, actually, I don't know whether he wants to go or not. Maybe I'll just ask him if he wants to go see the movie with me. Ahh . . . I . . . I don't know. I'll just wait and see if he . . . see if he wants to go. No. I'll ask.*
    •Bob, do you want to go to the movies?
Person 2: What's playing?
Person 1: There's that new movie over at the Cinema.
Person 2: A Western?
Person 1: Yeah.
Person 2: Sure.

Skill 33. Relaxation

Learning points
　1. Pay attention to those body signals which help you know you are tense.
　2. Decide whether you would like to relax.
　3. Tell yourself to calm down and relax.
　4. Imagine the scene that you find most calm and peaceful.
　5. Pay attention to those body signals which help you know you are relaxed.

Modeling vignette example
Person 1: *Gee, I got that knot in my stomach . . . I'm sweating. Boy, that . . . that interview is coming up and . . . and . . . I've gotta get that job. I know that's why . . . I . . . I . . . I've really gotta calm down. I've gotta relax, 'cause I can never go to the interview the way I'm feeling now. I'm just too tense. I've got an hour or so until the interview, so I . . . I'm just gonna sit down here in the lounge and try to relax. Yeah, this is a good chair . . . really gotta . . . gotta calm down and relax. That's what I gotta do. Just kinda think about . . . about . . . oh, if I was relaxed like I was when we were at the seashore, sitting on the beach there; it was nice and calm, peaceful. Yeah, that helps. Gotta slow down just like it was then. Gee, that's a little better . . . the knot's kinda easing up in my stomach. I'll just sit here for a little and just try to calm down some more. Yeah, I'm feeling better . . . feeling a little better already.*

Skill 34. Self-control

Learning points
1. Pay attention to those body signals which help you know you are about to lose control of yourself.
2. Decide which outside events may have caused you to feel frustrated.
3. Consider ways in which you might control yourself.
4. Choose the most effective way of controlling yourself and do it.

Modeling vignette example
Person 1: *I can feel myself getting tense . . . teeth are clenched. I'm really getting angry and tense. Been in this restaurant for a half hour now. They haven't . . . the waitress hasn't come over and I'm getting angry. I'm really getting angry. I'm gonna do something. I know that I'm gonna do something. Yeah . . . but . . . it's important to me . . . I told myself that I would be able to go to a restaurant and order a meal and enjoy it and I . . . I'm gonna do that. I really got to . . . really gotta take hold. I really gotta control myself. Maybe I oughta just leave? No . . . no, I wanta stay. Maybe the best thing to do is just try and calm down an' just motion to the waitress to come over . . . 'n' try to deal with it that way. Maybe that's the best way to do it.*
Miss!
Person 2: Yes, sir, can I take your order?
Person 1: Yes, you can.

Skill 35. Negotiation

Learning points
1. State your position.
2. State your understanding of the other person's position.
3. Ask if the other person agrees with your statement of his position.
4. Listen openly to his response.
5. Propose a compromise.

Modeling vignette example
Person 1: You know, Sam, there's a very good movie on television tonight that was just at the theater about a year ago . . . and . . . and I'd . . . very much want to see it. Um . . . I know that the football game's on tonight and you usually wanna watch football.

Is that . . . is that what you probably want to do?

Person 2: Yeah, that's right.

Person 1: I wonder . . . is there a way that we could work something out so that maybe this week we watch the movie since it's the only time it'll be on and, well, football games come on at least three times a week. Could we do something like that?

Person 2: That sounds reasonable.

Skill 36. Helping Others

Learning points
1. Observe whether someone needs help.
2. Decide whether you want to be helpful.
3. Decide how you can be helpful and do it.

Modeling vignette example

Person 1: (crying)

Person 2: *Ann is really in trouble. She looks like she needs some help. Gee, she looks so upset I don't know whether I'm even . . . if I want to get into this or not. It might be . . . might be pretty painful. But . . . uh . . . I can't stand it. I gotta see what I can do for her. I'm just gonna ask her what's wrong and try to say somethin' to make her feel better.*

Ann, what's the matter?

Person 1: Oh . . . uh . . . oh, a lot of things. (crying)

Person 2: Well, come on and sit down and tell me about it.

Skill 37. Assertiveness

Learning points
1. Pay attention to those body signals which help you know you are dissatisfied and would like to stand up for yourself.
2. Decide which outside events may have caused you to feel dissatisfied.
3. Consider ways in which you might stand up for yourself.
4. Take your stand in a direct and reasonable manner.

Modeling vignette example

Person 1: Here's your order, sir.

Person 2: *Did . . . did I order that? Boy . . . right away I get a little tension right in the back of my neck. No, that's not what I ordered. I had the special. I didn't have this hamburger. That*

makes me angry. When you order something in a restaurant, you pay good money and you don't get what you want. I . . . it doesn't look like a bad hamburger. I . . . I could just eat that instead of insisting on the special. I could . . . just . . . throw it back at her . . . what the hell. No, I think I'll just tell her that's not what I ordered and I'd like the special. I think that's what I should do.
Excuse me, Miss.

Person 1: Yes?

Person 2: I think you made a mistake. I ordered the special, not the hamburger.

Person 1: Oh, yes. You're right. That goes to the other table. Thank you.

APPLICATION TAPES

The Application Modeling Tapes, it will be recalled, consist of portrayals of sequences of Basic Skills. In using these tapes in actual Structured Learning Therapy groups it should be kept in mind that the role playing which follows each tape should consist of enactments of that combination and sequence of Basic Skills which will be most likely to deal effectively with the given problem *for that trainee.* This skill selection will often not be identical to that portrayed on the Application Modeling Tapes. How trainers assist trainees in determining which Basic Skills ought to be role played, and in which sequence, in order to deal effectively with a given problem in community living is illustrated in detail in Supplement B.

Skill 38. Finding a Place to Live

1. Setting a Goal
2. Asking for Help
3. Following Instructions
4. Gathering Information
5. Responding to Persuasion
6. Persuading Others
7. Decision Making
8. Negotiation

Skill 39. Moving In (typical)

1. Setting Problem Priorities
2. Concentrating on a Task
3. Making a Request
4. Giving Instructions
5. Expressing Appreciation

Skill 40. Moving In (difficult)

1. Setting Problem Priorities
2. Self-control
3. Preparing for a Stressful Conversation
4. Expressing a Complaint

Skill 41. Managing Money

1. Setting a Goal
2. Gathering Information
3. Persuading Others
4. Decision Making
5. Expressing Appreciation

Skill 42. Neighboring (apartment house)

1. Setting a Goal
2. Starting a Conversation
3. Listening
4. Helping Others
5. Ending a Conversation

Skill 43. Job Seeking (typical)

1. Evaluating Your Abilities
2. Gathering Information
3. Decision Making
4. Preparing for a Stressful Conversation
5. Persuading Others

Skill 44. Job Seeking (difficult)

1. Evaluating Your Abilities
2. Gathering Information
3. Decision Making
4. Preparing for a Stressful Conversation
5. Responding to Failure
6. Relaxation
7. Preparing for a Stressful Conversation
8. Assertiveness

Skill 45. Job Keeping (average day's work)

1. Concentrating on a Task
2. Asking for Help
3. Following Instructions
4. Responding to Failure
5. Gathering Information
6. Responding to Praise

Skill 46. Job Keeping (strict boss)

1. Following Instructions
2. Evaluating your Abilities
3. Preparing for a Stressful Conversation
4. Responding to a Complaint
5. Concentrating on a Task

Skill 47. Receiving Telephone Calls (difficult)

1. Listening
2. Responding to the Feelings of Others
3. Responding to a Complaint
4. Giving Instructions
5. Responding to Anger

Skill 48. Restaurant Eating (typical)

1. Making Requests

2. Listening
3. Decision Making
4. Making Requests
5. Expressing Appreciation

Skill 49. Organizing Time (typical)

1. Setting a Goal
2. Concentrating on a Task
3. Evaluating Your Abilities

Skill 50. Using Leisure Time (learning something new)

1. Setting a Goal
2. Gathering Information
3. Decision Making
4. Concentrating on a Task
5. Expressing Encouragement

Skill 51. Using Leisure Time (interpersonal activity)

1. Relaxation
2. Evaluating Your Abilities
3. Asking for Help
4. Gathering Information
5. Helping Others

Skill 52. Social (party)

1. Preparing for a Stressful Conversation
2. Starting a Conversation
3. Determining Responsibility
4. Identifying and Labeling Emotions
5. Asking for Help
6. Expressing Appreciation
7. Decision Making

Skill 53. Social (church supper)

1. Concentrating on a Task
2. Relaxation
3. Making Requests
4. Expressing Appreciation
5. Responding to the Feelings of Others
6. Making Requests

Skill 54. Marital (positive interaction)

1. Responding to the Feelings of Others
2. Expressing Appreciation
3. Expressing Encouragement
4. Helping Others
5. Expressing Affection

Skill 55. Marital (negative interaction)

1. Responding to Contradictory Messages
2. Apologizing
3. Giving Instructions
4. Setting Problem Priorities
5. Expressing a Compliment

Skill 56. Using Community Resources (seeking money)

1. Setting Problem Priorities
2. Gathering Information
3. Making Requests
4. Responding to Failure
5. Assertiveness

Skill 57. Using Community Resources (avoiding red tape)

1. Asking for Help
2. Self-control
3. Asking for Help

4. Responding to Contradictory Messages
5. Assertiveness

Skill 58. Dealing with Crises (inpatient to nonpatient transition)

1. Identifying and Labeling your Emotions
2. Relaxation
3. Setting Problem Priorities
4. Evaluating your Abilities
5. Setting a Goal

Skill 59. Dealing with Crises (loss)

1. Identifying and Labeling Your Emotions
2. Asking for Help
3. Determing Responsibility
4. Evaluating Your Ability

JOB SEEKING (difficult)*

Narrator: I'm Dr. Harris, Director of the Regional Psychiatric Center. A problem commonly facing many people, some of whom have been hospitalized, is that of Job Seeking. When a person deals with this problem effectively, he is able to handle himself well in interviews and able to find the kind of work for which he is best suited. If he does not do an effective job in seeking employment, he will frequently become discouraged and will be less likely to persevere and to find the job he wants. The tape you will hear is one good example of the steps a particular person followed in Job Seeking. As you will hear Cliff, the actor on the tape, begin to look for employment, you will notice that he uses a number of skills. These skills are: first, Evaluating Your Abilities; second, Gathering Information; Third, Decision Making; fourth, Preparing for a Stressful Conversation; fifth, Responding to Failure; sixth, Relaxation; seventh, Preparing for a Stressful Conversation; and eighth, Assertiveness. Listen carefully as Cliff begins to work on the task of Job Seeking. As you will hear, he is about to leave the

*Tape #44

hospital and needs to look for work. He has to evaluate his ability to succeed at different kinds of work, particularly sales. The learning points for Evaluating Your Abilities are: first, decide what ability you need to evaluate; second, think about how you have done in the past when you have tried to use this ability; third, get any outside information you can about your ability; and fourth, use all of this evidence and realistically evaluate your ability.

Person 1: *Now that I'm out of the hospital, I need to get some kind of a job. But I really don't know what I'm good at. I don't really have any special training or anything . . . no real skills, I guess. I . . . I think what I'd like to do is maybe some kind of sales work. That seems like something I could do and I might be able to get a job that way. I . . . I really don't know how good I'd be at it. I . . . I really haven't sold things before except when I worked for a few months when I got out of school . . . and I sold encyclopedias. That was kind of . . . kind of a hassle, but I did manage to sell some. Even in the hospital I used to be pretty good at selling raffle tickets. That's not much experience, but . . . it was selling. I . . . I don't know . . . I don't really know who I could ask about my ability to sell things. But . . . I did sell those encyclopedias and I think . . . I think I could really sell clothes. My friends tell me that I've got good taste, and I . . . I like clothes and things like that. And . . . and just . . . just before I left the hospital I took some of those aptitude tests at the employment office and the counselor there told me that they indicate that I might be good in that area. I don't know . . . I'd like to do it. I think maybe I should go to an employment office. There . . . maybe there I could pursue it a little bit more.*

Narrator: Having decided that he probably has the ability to succeed in sales work, Cliff now has to find out what jobs are available in sales. He has to gather information on job openings. The learning points for Gathering Information are: first, decide what specific information you need; second, decide who can give you the most accurate information; third, ask questions, in a direct manner, to get the information.

Person 1: *I guess what I really need to know is what jobs there are in the area, for maybe sales, especially in selling clothes. Um, I checked the newspapers already. There doesn't seem to be much there. I talked to some of my friends, but they don't seem to*

*know of any jobs in the area. I think maybe what I should do . . .
is . . . I could go back to the State Employment Office where I
took those tests and there might be someone there that I could
talk to. Maybe that Mr. Stacey that I talked to before.*
Mr. Stacey?

Person 2: Yes, sir.

Person 1: I don't know if you remember me or not, but I was in
here a few months ago and I took some of those tests . . . those
aptitude tests?

Person 2: Mmh, mmh.

Person 1: Well, since then, I got out of the hospital and I've been
trying to figure out what kind of a job I'd like to apply for. Um,
I've been thinking it over and I think what I'd really like is some
kind of sales work, especially maybe clothes. Um, huh . . . you
know . . . especially selling men's clothes, or something along,
maybe, those lines. Is there any kind of information you have that
. . . of any jobs available that I could look into?

Person 2: It seems to me I saw somewhere there was an opening in a
discount store and one in a men's shop. Here's the listing we have
here of the available employment. Why don't you check through
that and I'm . . . I think it's listed here.

Person 1: O.K. Thanks.

Narrator: He has gotten two leads on different job openings in sales.
He has to decide which job to apply for. The learning points for
Decision Making are: first, gather accurate information about the
topic; second, evaluate the information in light of your goal; and
third, make a decision which is in your best interest.

Person 1: *Mr. Stacey gave me those job descriptions, and those two
openings — there's the one at the discount store and the one at the
men's shop downtown. Well, the men's shop pays more — the
discount store might be easier to get into — they hire more people.
It might be a little bit easier to start out there too. But, it doesn't
say anything on either job description about needing experience.
It says they're both willing to train . . . and, uh . . . I don't know.
The men's store pays more too. I think even though the job at the
discount store might be easier, I really need the money, and I
think I might like working at that men's shop a little bit more. I
think I'll make an appointment with this Mr. Allen at the men's
store.*

Narrator: Cliff has scheduled an interview with Mr. Allen at the men's store. The interview may be difficult and stressful. So Cliff will have to prepare for a stressful conversation. The learning points for Preparing for a Stressful Conversation are: first, imagine yourself in the stressful situation; second, think about how you will feel and why you will feel that way; third, imagine yourself in the other person's position and think about how he will feel and why he will feel that way; fourth, imagine yourself telling the other person what you want to say; fifth, imagine his response; sixth, repeat the above steps, using as many approaches as you can think of; and seventh, choose the best approach.

Person 1: *I can just see myself at that appointment this afternoon. I've been in that store before and it's a really fancy place. It really looks good. It's kinda frightening actually. I'll probably feel very uncomfortable, 'cause I know I'm gonna be worried about whether I'm dressed well or not. And I'll have to look pretty good if I'm applying for a job to sell clothes. I know I'm going to be nervous too about ... about my hospitalization, whether that's going to come up. I'm sure he's very concerned about the person looking good, because the person he hires will be selling in his store. I wanta tell him how interested I am in the job, tell him that my only experience is selling encyclopedias. I don't know ... that's probably kinda silly. It's probably just ... he'll probably say that doesn't have much to do with selling clothes. Um ... I could tell him that I really like clothes and all that kind of stuff and I think I could ... I think I could be good at it, but that I don't have any real experience. I could just not even mention that business with the encyclopedias — but that I'm willing to learn and I ... I think that I want to bring it up myself — about the hospitalization. I might as well just tell him. Oh, he'll probably say that that's all fine but he can't afford to hire someone who's not stable. I don't know, though — he might be interested in giving me a chance if I just tell him the truth. I think that's what I'll do. I'm just gonna say that I'm interested, that I don't have any experience, and that I just got out of the hospital.*

[Interview occurs]

Cliff: Uh, well, Mr. Allen, is there anything else that you'd like to ask?

Mr. Allen: Uh, no ... I think you've told me pretty much everything we need to know. Uh, I guess I should mention to you there have been a number of other applicants. Uh . . . though we haven't made up our minds yet, and I do have your phone number. Um, we'll make a decision and if we decide to hire you, I'll give you a call within the next few days.

Cliff: Uh . . . oh . . . O.K.

Mr. Allen: See ya.

Narrator: Cliff feels as if the interview at the men's store did not go too well and that he's failed. He now has to respond to failure. The learning points for Responding to Failure are: first, decide if you have failed; second, think about both the personal reasons and the circumstances which have caused you to fail; third, decide how you might do things differently if you tried again; fourth, decide if you want to try again; and fifth, if appropriate, try again, using your revised approach.

Cliff: *Well, I think I really blew it. He sure didn't seem very interested in hiring me. I . . . I . . . noticed right away when I got in there that, uh . . . he didn't seem to be paying too much attention. I probably didn't sell myself very well. I don't know if I even should have mentioned about the hospital. He didn't ask. Plus, maybe . . . maybe it's just the place too. It'd kinda . . . kind of a classy store and I really don't have much experience — and maybe I emphasized that too much. Well, if I try again, uh, I'd probably pick someplace that isn't quite as tough a challenge. Yeah, like that discount store. That's probably where I should have gone in the first place. I think I'd like to try again. I . . . I . . . um, I'm pretty sure I still like that kind of work, and I sure need a job. It's just that, next time when I try, I'll just . . . I'm gonna be a little more positive about what I've done and what I haven't done and . . . try and sell myself a little bit better.*

Narrator: Cliff is still tense even after the job interview and he has to relax in order to relieve the tension. The learning points for Relaxation are: first, pay attention to those body signals which help you know you are tense; second, decide whether you would like to relax; third, tell yourself to calm down and relax; fourth, imagine the scene that you find most calm and peaceful; and fifth, pay attention to those body signals which help you know you are relaxed.

Cliff: *Jeez, my hands are sweating. I'm getting a headache, too. I must be getting upset about the whole thing. I . . . I wish I could relax and just calm down a bit. Jeez, Cliff, now just cool it. Relax a little bit. Uh, I'd like to . . . I'd like to just get comfortable somehow. Sort of just like sitting in a hot tub for a while, just sitting there soaking — with my eyes closed and just cooling off and relaxing. Uh, I'm feeling a little bit better already, just thinking about it. Feels like my headache's starting to go away. I know I'm less tense. Uh, I almost feel like taking a nap.*

Narrator: Cliff has scheduled another employment interview and wants to do a better job, but he's still nervous. He needs to prepare for the interview which again may be stressful. The learning points for Preparing for a Stressful Conversation are: first, imagine yourself in the stressful situation; second, think about how you will feel and why you will feel that way; third, imagine yourself in the other person's position and think about how he will feel and why he will feel that way; fourth, imagine yourself telling the other person what you want to say; fifth, imagine his response; sixth, repeat the above steps, using as many approaches as you can think of; and seventh, choose the best approach.

Cliff: (Sigh) *Well, I called up that discount store and they gave me an appointment with a Miss Anderson down at the store this afternoon at 2 o'clock. (Sigh) I don't know — I can't imagine what it's gonna be like at that place. It probably won't be anything like the men's store. Those places are always so crowded and everything that . . . it'll probably be just some kind of a little office off to the side . . . be a lot of people running in and out . . . no real privacy. I know I'm gonna be nervous when I get there after being at the last interview — screwing it up the way I did. I don't know . . . this lady probably feels just like Mr. Allen did — doesn't want to take any chances. Well, this time I could just try again like I did before. Maybe she's a lot different than the other guy — uh, I could just tell her that I don't have any real experience — that I just got out of the hospital. I don't know — after the last time — she'll probably just say what he said — don't call us, we'll call you. I think maybe what would be better — if I just went in there a little more positive, and uh, if the hospital thing doesn't come up, I'm not going to mention it. And if it does, I'm certainly not going to apologize. I feel like it helped me, and I'm capable, and I . . . I know I can hold a job and I think I can do a good job. I . . . I don't know. She may say that she'll give me a try. It's worth it. I think I'm gonna try that when I go in this afternoon.*

Narrator: Cliff is at the second job interview and the interviewer has asked him some difficult questions. He wants to stand up for himself and assert himself in the interview. The learning points for Assertiveness are: first, pay attention to those body signals which help you know you are dissatisfied and would like to stand up for yourself; second, decide which outside events may have caused you to feel dissatisfied; third, consider ways in which you might stand up for yourself; and fourth, take your stand in a direct and reasonable manner.

Miss Anderson: Now, Mr. Wilson, we have your application here and there are two things I'm just not clear on. As far as your qualifications uh, I don't understand this − this is . . . a few things you've done, but you've never really worked in a store. Is that so? And mental illness in your family or within you, I don't see . . . maybe you just overlooked it? Is that the case?

Cliff: *I'm starting to feel angry, feel my blood pressure going up − I just don't wanna lose out on this job too − not again. I don't know what to do − I'm out of the hospital now. I'm well and I feel capable of getting this job and I want her to know that. And, those questions are . . . they're getting me. She's just trying to get me on the defensive or something. I don't know. I'm gonna tell her about that encyclopedia job and also that I've held down other jobs for a long time. I did . . . they weren't sales but I was able to hold a job and follow directions and do everything I could. Uh, I'm gonna tell her about those aptitude tests at the employment office, and also the fact that . . . they wouldn't just discharge me from the hospital unless I was able to cope with things − I know I'm better now. I feel good and I know I can handle this job and I'm going to tell her so!*

Miss Anderson, excuse me, but I . . . I really . . . have the feeling that you're not listening . . . on those questions you asked, I didn't check off anything about mental illness. Frankly, I . . . recently was released from a psychiatric center. Um, there's nothing too serious involved. I got counseling before I went in and the doctor felt that I should go in for awhile to, you know . . . learn how to handle pressure a little bit. I think maybe before I was a little too involved with my job, and, uh, I really feel like the hospital helped me. I feel much better now. Pressure doesn't upset me a lot. I feel like I can handle this job or a lot of other jobs and also, just before I left the hospital, I took several tests at the employment office — aptitude tests and things like that and they seem to feel that I did have interests in this area and, you know, that this would be something I could handle. I just feel ready for this kind of job and I feel, uh, capable and I hope you'll take that into consideration. Even though I really haven't had a lot of experience in sales except the, uh . . . in selling encyclopedias — I think I put that down — I know it doesn't have much to do with selling clothes, but it was a selling experience and I've had two other jobs before going into the hospital that I held for a long time. Again, not directly involved with sales, but I was able to come to work on time and do what I was supposed to do and, uh . . . I think I . . . I've done this in the past and I know I can do it again. I just . . . I really hope that you will seriously consider me for this job.

Miss Anderson: Well, I can see where you might have been under pressure selling encyclopedias. That's a very hard job and I think if you did that, uh, I think we have a place for you.

Cliff: Good.

Narrator: You have just heard a good example of steps involved in Job Seeking. In order to help you solve this kind of problem, the persons leading your group will help you decide on and practice the skills necessary for you to succeed in Job Seeking.

USING COMMUNITY RESOURCES (avoiding red tape)*

Narrator: I'm Dr. Harris, Director of the Regional Psychiatric Center. A problem commonly facing many people, some of whom have been hospitalized, is that of Using Community Resources. When a person deals with this problem effectively, he's able to use community agencies, facilities, and services without being overwhelmed by red tape, regulations, and needless bureaucratic delays. He is able to get what he needs and deserves. If a person does not demonstrate this skill, he is likely to become frustrated, overwhelmed, and not get what he is entitled to. The tape you will hear is one good example of the steps a particular person follows in using community resources. As you hear Mr. Williams, the actor, using community resources, you will notice that he uses a

*Tape #57

number of skills. These skills include Asking for Help, Self-control, Asking for Help, Responding to Contradictory Messages, and Assertiveness. Listen carefully as Mr. Williams begins to attempt to use community resources. The first skill he'll need to use is that of Asking for Help. He wants to find out about getting money in order to go to school. He has to ask for help to find out about available funds. The learning points for Asking for Help are: first, define the problem that troubles you; second, decide if you want to seek help for the problem; third, identify the people who might help you; fourth, make a choice of helper; fifth, tell the helper about your problem.

Person 1: *I . . . I've been out of the hospital now quite a while and I've got a job. It's not really a very good job. I . . . I . . . really would like to go back and take some night courses. I got . . . I've got almost a year of college. Maybe just one more year. At least I could get my associate degree or something. Um . . . the problem is, though, I really need money if I was gonna take some courses. The job I've got really doesn't pay enough for that. I guess I'll probably have to ask somebody for some help, to get some information about getting some money or . . . 'cause I know I want to take the courses, but I've gotta get money if I want to do it. I could ask my case worker about it, or . . . I was over to the Community College to look at their catalog. I could probably go to the financial aid office over there. Or I could go to the V.A. office too. I'm a veteran. Well, I don't know . . . this is sort of out of my case worker's territory I think, and besides I'd kinda like to do the whole thing on my own if I could. Mmh . . . if I go to the financial aid office that'll probably mean a loan. I don't really want to take out a loan right now. I think maybe my best bet is probably the V.A. office. I'm a veteran and I . . . I must be eligible for education benefits. I think that's where I'll go.*
Excuse me. Could you help me? . . . Uh, I'm planning to take some night courses and I'd just like to know what . . . uh . . . what funds are available and . . . uh . . . what kinds of . . . uh . . . how much money I could get if I was gonna take some courses.
Person 2: Were you next in line?
Person 1: Yeah, . . . I . . . I'm next in line.
Person 2: Have you registered here before?
Person 1: No. . . . No, I haven't.
Person 2: Well, you have to give your discharge papers to me. I have to fill out a form, you know. I also want your Social Security

card. It has to be photostated. I don't want the card itself. Now, I want you to file for an eligibility card also. I want both cards and, really, we can't do anything for you until I have all of these in front of me. It's really a waste of time.

Narrator: In his first attempt to gain the information he needs, he finds that the bureaucratic clerk is evasive and impolite. He becomes angry and needs to control himself. The learning points for Self-control are: first, pay attention to those body signals which help you know you are about to lose control of yourself; second, decide which outside events may have caused you to feel frustrated; third, consider ways in which you might control yourself; and fourth, choose the most effective way of controlling yourself and do it.

Person 1: *Boy, I'm burning up . . . so tense and angry. I'm a little shaky. Feel like punching her. I know what's making me feel this way. It's that woman. All I asked was a simple question and she's giving me a big runaround. I . . . I've got to control myself somehow . . . I feel like telling her off. I probably should just walk out of here and give up. Or . . . I could stick with it and try to get some answers. I guess I'd better do that . . . if I tell her off I won't get anyplace and if I leave that won't solve the problem. I'm just gonna have to ask her another question I guess.*

Narrator: He decides that the best approach would be to ask for help again. The learning points for Asking for Help are: first, define the problem that troubles you; second, decide if you want to seek help for the problem; third, identify the people who might help you; fourth, make a choice of helper, and fifth, tell the helper about your problem.

Person 1: *The problem is I . . . I just haven't been able to get any information from this woman. But I wanta get some answers. Maybe I could ask her another question . . . or . . . or . . . I could ask to see somebody else. I guess . . . I . . . I'll just stick with her and try one more time.*
Um . . . excuse me.
Person 2: Oh, you're here again.
Person 1: Yes. Um . . . maybe you misunderstood my question. See, I'm not actually trying to apply now for anything. All I want to know is if I could be eligible for educational benefits, and, if so,

you know, about how much money they'd allocate for courses.

Person 2: Well, you know that we're here to help you. I mean, we set up this booth here for you people . . . look at the lines. I gave you information but you know there is red tape. You must fill out these forms.

Narrator: Mr. Williams is again frustrated in his dealings with the clerk. What she is saying is very confusing to him because she seems to be giving him contradictory messages. He needs to respond to these contradictory messages. The learning points for Responding to Contradictory Messages are: first, pay attention to those body signals which help you know you are feeling trapped or confused; second, observe the other person's words and actions which may have caused you to have these feelings; third, decide whether his words and actions are contradictory; fourth, decide whether it would be useful to point out the contradiction; and fifth, ask the other person to explain the contradiction.

Person 1: *I . . . I'm clenching my teeth. I feel so bottled up. This woman makes me feel like I'm backed into a corner! She . . . she's got such a vacant look on her face and . . . and she's saying she wants to help but she's also saying that I've got to do a hundred things. This . . . this just isn't making sense to me. She's telling me here that . . . you know . . . that she wants to help me but at the same time she's saying that she won't help me. I . . . I don't know if it's gonna do any good to tell her, but I've got to. I've got to say something.*

Person 2: Next!

Person 1: I . . . I'm sorry, but I feel like you're telling me a couple of different things. I only wanted some information when I came in here. I . . . I've . . . I've been here 20 minutes already, and I just wanted a simple answer, about . . . about, you know, educational benefits.

Person 2: Well, did you bring your forms with you?

Person 1: No, I didn't bring any forms with me. 'Cause I only came in here for some general information. I only wanted to know, uh . . . approximately how much, you know, money I could get if I took courses. I don't want to have to fill out forms now . . . or anything. And . . . you know . . . like on the one hand you're telling me that you're willing to help. And on the other hand you . . . you're not answering a very simple question.

Person 2: Well apparently you don't understand that you have to fill out the forms. We go by the forms on how much money you will get. You have to follow our procedure, too, young man.

Narrator: Mr. Williams still has gotten nowhere in his attempt to gain information from the clerk. He decides that he must assert himself. The learning points for Assertiveness are: first, pay attention to those body signals which help you know you are dissatisfied and would like to stand up for yourself; second, decide which outside events may have caused you to feel dissatisfied; third, consider ways in which you might stand up for yourself; and fourth, take your stand in a direct and reasonable manner.

Person 1: *I'm getting tense again. I'm starting to perspire. I feel just like punching that woman. I . . . I know she's the cause. I came in here just . . . just for . . . information and she's not helping me at all. She's giving me all this crap about paper work and . . . and . . . I feel just as though she's trying to get rid of me. Well, I'm not going to leave here without some kind of answer. I am a veteran, so I must be entitled to some money for school. I want a know what! I want to know how much before I sign up for classes. I don't feel like I have to . . . I don't feel like I have to put up with this, and I'm not asking her for a favor. This is a right! I'm not leaving here . . . I'm not leaving here without an answer. The secretary told me that . . . that man over by the file cabinet is the supervisor here, I think that I'm just gonna talk to him.*

Excuse me, sir. Are you . . . are you the boss here . . . the supervisor?
Person 3: Yes, sir, I am. Can I help you?
Person 1: Well, uh . . . I hope so. My name is Williams and I've been in this office almost a half hour already and I only came in to ask for some general information and I've been talking to that woman over there and I feel like I've been talking to a wall. She's telling me all this stuff about procedure and paper work and I don't really want to do that now. I just want some answers about educational benefits with the V.A. Do you think you could help me with that?
Person 3: I . . . I think we have the information. Why don't you come on right into my office and I'll give it to you.
Person 1: Thank you very much.

Narrator: You have just heard a good example of steps involved in Using Community Resources. In order to help you solve this kind of problem, the persons leading your group will help you decide on, and practice, the skills necessary for you to use community resources.

5
Structured Learning Therapy Research:
An Annotated Bibliography and
Research Directions

Treatment approaches which aspire to assist people lead more effective and more satisfying lives must not be permitted to endure indefinitely simply on the basis of the faith and enthusiasm of their proponents. Therapies must be subjected to careful, objective, and continuing evaluation. Those approaches, and only those approaches, which such research demonstrates to be effective are deserving of society's continued use and development. Those that fail such outcome evaluations justly must pass out of current usage.

The present chapter reports, in annotated bibliographic form, a number of completed and ongoing evaluative studies examining the effectiveness of Structured Learning Therapy, as well as a small number of other reports dealing with particular aspects or implications of this approach. In general terms, the several evaluative studies combine to support the effectiveness of SLT with diverse trainee groups and diverse skill-training targets. Much remains to be learned about this therapy approach, and continuing tests of its efficacy are necessary. But, on the basis of evidence described below, we are confident in recommending its continued and expanded use with inpatient, outpatient, and ex-patient trainees.

Several of the studies summarized below, as well as a wealth of related studies by other investigators examining the impact of SLT components, are examined in much greater detail in *Structured Learning Therapy: Toward a Psychotherapy for the Poor* (see Goldstein, 1973).

Berlin, R.J. Training of hospital staff in accurate affective perception of fear-anxiety from vocal cues in the context of varying facial cues. Unpublished masters thesis, Syracuse University, 1974.
Trainees: Attendants and nurses (N=52)
Skill: Recognition of vocal cues of anxiety
Experimental design: (1) SLT for vocal and facial cues, (2) SLT for vocal cues with exposure to but no training for facial cues, (3) SLT for vocal cues, (4) No-training control.
Results: No significant between-group differences. For group receiving SLT for both vocal and facial cues, a significant pre-post recognition gain on both training and test cues of anxiety.

Berlin, R.J. Teaching acting-out adolescents prosocial conflict resolution with Structured Learning Therapy. Unpublished doctoral dissertation, Syracuse University, in progress.
Trainees: Adolescent boys with history of acting-out behaviors (N=42)
Skill: Empathy, Compromise
Experimental design: (1) SLT for empathy in conflict situations, (2) SLT for empathy in nonconflict situations, versus (3) No-treatment control by (1) High Interpersonal Maturity Level versus (2) Low Interpersonal Maturity Level.
Results: In progress.

Cobb, F.M. Acquisition and retention of cooperative behavior in young boys through instructions, modeling, and structured learning. Unpublished doctoral dissertation, Syracuse University, 1973.
Trainees: First-grade boys (N=80)
Skill: Cooperation
Experimental design: (1) SLT for cooperation, (2) Instructions plus modeling of cooperation, (3) Instructions for cooperation, (4) Attention control, (5) No-treatment control.
Results: SLT significantly > all other conditions on both immediate and delayed tests of cooperative behavior.

Cross, W. An investigation of the effects of therapist motivational predispositions in Structured Learning Therapy under task versus relationship stress conditions. Unpublished doctoral dissertation, Syracuse University, in progress.
Trainees: College undergraduates (N=120)
Skill: Structured Learning Therapy group leadership skills
Experimental design: Task-motivated versus relationship-motivated

trainers by task-relevant versus relationship-relevant trainee-originated trainer stress plus no-treatment control.
Results: In progress.

Davis, C. Training police in crisis intervention skills. Unpublished manuscript, Syracuse University, September 1974.
Description of a training program utilizing SLT to develop skills among a 225-person urban police force for the competent handling of family fights, rapes, accidents, suicides, and a variety of other crises common in everyday police work. Skills taught included: (1) Preparing to deal with threats to your safety, (2) Calming the emotional aspects of the crisis, (3) Gathering relevant information, and (4) Taking appropriate action.

Edelman, E. Behavior of high versus low hostility — guilt structured learning trainers under standardized client conditions of expressed hostility. Unpublished masters thesis, Syracuse University, in progress.
Trainers: Nurses and attendants at state mental hospital (N=60)
Skill: Structured learning trainer group leadership behaviors
Experimental design: SLT trainers high versus low in hostility — guilt by (1) High, (2) Low or (3) No expressed client hostility.
Results: In progress.

Fleming, D. Teaching negotiation skills to preadolescents. Unpublished doctoral dissertation, Syracuse University, in progress.
Trainees: Adolescents (N=96)
Skill: Negotiation
Experimental design: High self-esteem versus Low self-esteem adolescents by Adult SLT trainer versus Peer SLT trainer by Presence versus Absence of pre-SLT enhancement of expectancy for success.
Results: In progress.

Fleming, L.R. Training aggressive and unassertive educable mentally retarded children for assertive behaviors, using three types of Structured Learning Therapy. Unpublished doctoral dissertation, Syracuse University, in progress.
Trainees: Mentally retarded children (N=96)
Skill: Assertiveness
Experimental design: (1) SLT for assertiveness plus fear-coping training, (2) SLT for assertiveness · plus anger-coping training,

(3) SLT for assertiveness, (4) Attention control by Aggressive versus Unassertive children.
Results: In progress.

Friedenberg, W.P. Verbal and nonverbal attraction modeling in an initial therapy interview analogue. Unpublished masters thesis, Syracuse University, 1971.
Trainees: Psychiatric inpatients (N=60, all male, mostly schizophrenic)
Skill: Attraction
Experimental design: High versus low attraction to interviewer displayed via nonverbal cues by high versus low attraction to interviewer displayed via verbal cues.
Results: Significant modeling effect for attraction for the High-High group (High modeled attraction using both the verbal and nonverbal cues) as compared to the other three conditions.

Gilstad, R. Acquisition and transfer of empathic responses by teachers through self-administered and leader-directed Structured Learning Training and the interaction between training method and conceptual level. Unpublished doctoral dissertation, Syracuse University, in progress.
Trainees: Elementary school teachers (N=60)
Skill: Empathy
Experimental design: SLT for empathy, training conducted by a trainer in "standard" SLT groups versus SLT for empathy, self-instructional training format by High versus Low conceptual level trainees, plus attention control.
Results: In progress.

Gold, G., and Goldstein, A.P. Training self-control in behavior problem children.
Trainees: Behavior problem children (N=33, age 8-14)
Skill: Self-control
Experimental design: (1) SLT for self-control, (2) Play therapy, (3) No-treatment control.
Results: In progress.

Golden, R. Teaching resistance-reducing behavior to high school students. Unpublished doctoral dissertation, Syracuse University, 1975.
Trainees: High school students (N=43)

Skill: Resistance-reducing behavior (reflection of the other's feeling plus appropriate assertiveness regarding one's own view in an interpersonal conflict situation with authority figures)
Experimental design: (1) Discrimination training ("good" modeled skill behavior versus "bad" modeled skill behavior) for resistance-reducing behavior, (2) SLT for resistance-reducing behavior, (3) No-treatment control by Internal versus External locus of control.
Results: In progress.

Goldstein, A.P. A prescriptive psychotherapy for the alcoholic patient based on social class. *Proceedings of the second annual alcoholism conference of NIAAA,* Washington, D.C. U.S. Department of Health, Education and Welfare, 1973, pp. 234-241.

An overview of the development of Structured Learning Therapy and relevant evaluative research, with special emphasis upon its implications for alcoholic patients.

Goldstein, A.P. *Structured learning therapy: Toward a psychotherapy for the poor.* New York: Academic Press, 1974.

A comprehensive statement of the origin and rationale for Structured Learning Therapy, and a full presentation of relevant evaluative research. Modeling scripts from both inpatient and outpatient studies are presented.
Contents:
1. Psychotherapy: Income and outcome
2. Personality development and preparation for patienthood
3. Language and malcommunication
4. Psychopathology and sociopathology
5. Structured Learning and the middle-class patient
6. Structured Learning and the lower-class inpatient
7. Structured Learning and the lower-class outpatient
8. Structured Learning and the working-class paraprofessional
9. Future directions
   Appendix: Modeling scripts

Goldstein, A.P., Cohen, R., Blake, G., and Walsh, W. The effects of modeling and social class structuring in paraprofessional psychotherapist training. *Journal of Nervous and Mental Disease,* 1971, 153, 47-56.
Trainees: Nurses and attendants (N=135)
Skill: Attraction, empathy, warmth

Experimental design: High, low, and no attraction modeling by middle, low, and no social class structuring.
Results: Significant modeling by social class structuring interaction effects for attraction, empathy, and warmth.

Goldstein, A.P., Gershaw, N.J., and Sprafkin, R.P. Structured Learning Therapy: Training for community living. *Psychotherapy: Theory, Research and Practice,* in press.

An overview of the development and current status of Structured Learning Therapy. This article places special emphasis on the failure of other approaches to skill deficit reduction in schizophrenic patients to adequately foster transfer of newly learned skills to community functioning. The relative success of Structured Learning Therapy in this regard is described.

Goldstein, A.P., and Goedhart, A.W. The use of Structured Learning for empathy enhancement in paraprofessional psychotherapist training. *Journal of Community Psychology,* 1973, 1, 168-173.
Experiment I.
Trainees: Student nurses (n=74)
Skill: Empathy
Experimental design: (1) SLT for empathy (professional trainers), (2) SLT for empathy (paraprofessional trainers), (3) No-training control.
Results: Both SLT conditions significantly > No-training control on both immediate and generalization measures of empathy.
Experiment II.
Trainees: Hospital staff (N=90); nurses, attendants, OT, RT
Skill: Empathy
Experimental design: (1) SLT plus transfer training for empathy, (2) SLT for empathy, (3) No-training control.
Results: Significant SLT effect for immediate empathy measurement (Groups 1 and 2 >3); significant transfer effect for generalization empathy measure (Group 1 > 2 and 3).

Goldstein, A.P., Goedhart, A.W., and Wijngaarden, H.R. Modeling in de psychotherapie bij patienten uit de lagere sociale klasse. In A.P. Cassee, P.E. Boeke, and J.T. Barendregt (Eds.), *Klinische Psychologie in Nederland.* Deventer: Van Loghum Slaterus, 1973, pp. 279-288.

A presentation (in Dutch) of the origin, rationale, and current status of Structured Learning Therapy. The particular usefulness of this approach with low-income Dutch and American patient populations is stressed.

Goldstein, A.P., Martens, J., Hubben, J., Van Belle, H., Schaaf, W., Wiersema, H., and Goedhart, A. The use of modeling to increase independent behavior. *Behavior Research and Therapy,* 1973, 11, 31-42.

Experiment I.
   Trainees: Psychiatric outpatients (N=90, all psychoneurotic or character disorders)
   Skill: Independence (assertiveness)
   Experimental design: (1) Independence modeling, (2) Dependence modeling, (3) No-modeling control.
   Results: Significant modeling effect for Independence, and a significant modeling effect for Dependence − both as compared to each other and to the No-modeling control condition.

Experiment II.
   Trainees: Psychiatric outpatients (N=60, all psychoneurotic or character disorders)
   Skill: Independence (assertiveness)
   Experimental design: Independence modeling plus (1) Structuring model as warm, (2) Structuring model as cold, (3) No structuring of model by Male versus Female plus a No-structuring/No-modeling control.
   Results: Warm and No-structuring modeling conditions significantly > Cold structuring and Control on independence for males and females.

Experiment III.
   Trainees: Psychiatric inpatients (N=54, all schizophrenic)
   Skill: Independence (assertiveness)
   Experimental design: Presence versus Absence of independence modeling by Presence versus Absence of instructions to behave independently.
   Results: Significant main and interaction effects for Modeling and Instructions on independence as compared to No-modeling/No-instructions conditions.

Goldstein, A.P., and Sorcher, M. Changing managerial behavior by applied learning techniques. *Training and Development Journal,* 1973, 36-39.

   An examination of inadequacies characterizing most managerial training approaches, including (1) the singular focus on attitude change rather than behavior change, (2) unresponsiveness to changing characteristics of the American work force, and (3) insufficient attention to the implication of research on human learning for managerial training. The manner in which Structured Learning seeks to correct these inadequacies and provide an effective approach to training managers is presented.

Goldstein, A.P., and Sorcher, M. *Changing supervisor behavior.* New York: Pergamon Press, 1974.

A presentation of theory and research on the components of Structured Learning — modeling, role playing, social reinforcement, and transfer training. Emphasis throughout is upon the teaching of supervisory skills, especially in industry. Relevant evaluative research in an industrial context is reported.

Contents:
1. Supervisor training: Perspectives and problems
2. A focus on behavior
3. Modeling
4. Role playing
5. Social reinforcement
6. Transfer training
7. Applied learning: Applications and evidence

Goldstein, A.P., Sprafkin, R.P., and Gershaw, N.J. Structured Learning Therapy: Skill training for schizophrenics. *Schizophrenia Bulletin,* 1975, 14, 83-88.

A description of the procedures which constitute Structured Learning Therapy and their evaluation. Relevant modeling tapes and related materials are also described. This article places special emphasis on the community-relevant needs of a variety of types of schizophrenic patients, and the manner in which daily living skill deficits may be systematically reduced by the use of this approach.

Goldstein, A.P., Sprafkin, R.P., Gershaw, N.J., and Sherman, M. Training in the teaching of coping and mastery skills.
Trainees: Hospital staff (N=64)
Skill: Structured Learning Therapy group leadership skills
Experimental design: Hospital staff "master trainers" (N=6) trained hospital staff "staff trainers" (N=64) in SLT leadership skills. Staff trainers led patient groups in (1) SLT for Giving Instructions,

(2) Discussion groups for Giving Instructions, or (3) No-treatment control. In addition to between-condition comparisons, trainee skill development will be examined as a function of trainer leadership skills, trainer task vs. relationship orientation, and relevant trainer attitudes.
Results: In progress.

Goldstein, A.P., Stein, N., Driscol, S., and Sheets, J. The use of Structured Learning for teaching role taking to psychiatric inpatients. In A.P. Goldstein, *Structured Learning Therapy: Toward a psychotherapy for the poor.* New York Academic Press, 1973, pp. 137-143.
Trainees: Schizophrenic inpatients (N=30, all female)
Skill: Role taking in a marital context
Experimental design: (1) SLT for role taking, (2) Attention control, (3) No-treatment control.
Results: Trend only for SLT > Attention or No-treatment control on immediate post-test for gain in role-taking skill. No significant generalization effect.

Gutride, M.E., Goldstein, A.P., and Hunter, G.F. The use of modeling and role playing to increase social interaction among schizophrenic patients. *Journal of Consulting and Clinical Psychology,* 1973, 40, 408-415.
Trainees: Psychiatric inpatients (N=133, all "asocial, withdrawn")
Skill: Social interaction (an array of conversational and physical approach skill behaviors)
Experimental design: SLT versus No SLT by Psychotherapy versus No Psychotherapy by Acute versus Chronic.
Results: A substantial number of significant interaction and main effects for SLT across several social interaction behavioral criteria.

Gutride, M.E., Goldstein, A.P., and Hunter, G.F. Structured Learning Therapy with transfer training for chronic inpatients. *Journal of Clinical Psychology,* July 1974, 277-280.
Trainees: Psychiatric inpatients (N=106, all "asocial, withdrawn")
Skill: Social interaction in a mealtime context
Experimental design: (1) SLT plus transfer training, (2) SLT plus additional SLT, (3) SLT, (4) Companionship control, (5) No-treatment control.
Results: A substantial number of significant effects for SLT across several social interaction behavioral criteria. Significant effects are

mainly for groups 1, 2, and 3 compared to the control conditions, rather than between the SLT conditions.

Guzzetta, R.A. Acquisition and transfer of empathy by the parents of early adolescents through Structured Learning Training. Unpublished doctoral dissertation, Syracuse University, 1974.
Trainees: Mothers of early adolescents (N=37)
Skill: Empathy
Experimental design: (1) SLT for empathy taught to mothers and their children together (to maximize transfer), (2) SLT for empathy taught to mothers and their children separately, (3) SLT for empathy taught to mothers only, (4) No-training control.
Results: All three SLT conditions showed significantly greater acquisition and transfer of empathy than did No-training control mothers. No significant differences between SLT conditions.

Healy, J.A. Training of hospital staff in accurate effective perception of anger from vocal cues in the context of varying facial cues. Unpublished masters thesis, Syracuse University, 1975.
Trainees: Nurses and attendants (N=44)
Skill: Recognition of vocal cues of anger
Experimental design: (1) SLT for vocal and facial cues, (2) SLT for vocal cues with exposure to but no training for facial cues, (3) SLT for vocal cues, (4) No-training control.
Results: All SLT groups significantly $>$ controls on vocal training and test cues; no significant generalization to new (untrained) vocal cues.

Hollander, T.G. The effects of role playing on attraction, disclosure, and attitude change in a psychotherapy analogue. Unpublished doctoral dissertation, Syracuse University, 1970.
Trainees: V.A. Hospital psychiatric inpatients (N=45, all males)
Skill: Attraction to the psychotherapist
Experimental design: Role play versus Exposure versus No-treatment control.
Results: No significant role-playing effects for attraction or disclosure.

Jennings, R.L. The use of Structured Learning techniques to teach attraction enchancing interviewee skills to residentially hospitalized, lower socioeconomic emotionally disturbed children and adolescents: A psychotherapy analogue investigation. Unpublished

doctoral dissertation, University of Iowa, 1975.
Trainees: Emotionally disturbed, lower socioeconomic children and adolescents (N=40)
Skill: Interviewee behaviors: Initiation, Terminating silences, Elaboration, and Expression of affect
Experimental design: (1) SLT for interviewee behaviors versus (2) Minimal treatment control in a 2 x 2 x 4 factorial design reflecting (a) repeated measures, (b) treatments, and (c) interviewers.
Results: SLT > significantly Minimal treatment control on Interview initiation and Terminating silences. No significant effects on Interview elaboration or Expression of affect. SLT significantly > Minimal treatment control on attractiveness to interviewer on portion of study measures.

Lack, D.Z. The effect of a model and instructions on psychotherapist self-disclosure. Unpublished masters thesis, Syracuse University, 1971.
Trainees: Attendants (N=60)
Skill: Self-disclosure
Experimental design: Presence versus Absence of modeled self-disclosure by Presence versus Absence of instructions to self-disclose.
Results: Significant modeling and instruction effects for self-disclosure.

Lack, D.Z. Problem-solving training, structured learning training, and didactic instruction in the preparation of paraprofessional mental health personnel for the utilization of contingency management techniques. Unpublished doctoral dissertation, Syracuse University, 1975.
Trainees: Nurses and attendants (N=50)
Skill: Contingency management
Experimental design: SLT for problem solving and contingency management versus SLT for contingency management by Instruction for problem solving and contingency management versus Instruction for contingency management plus No-training control.
Results: Significant SLT effects for problem solving.

Liberman, B. The effect of modeling procedures on attraction and disclosure in a psychotherapy analogue. Unpublished doctoral dissertation, Syracuse University, 1970.

Trainees: Alcoholic inpatients (N=84, all males)

Skill: Self-disclosure; attraction to the psychotherapist

Experimental design: High versus Low modeled self-disclosure by High versus Low modeled attraction plus Neutral-tape and No-tape controls.

Results: Significant modeling effect for self-disclosure; no modeling effect for attraction.

Litwak, S.E. The use of the helper therapy principle to increase therapeutic effectiveness and reduce therapeutic resistance: Structured Learning Therapy with resistant adolescents. Unpublished doctoral dissertation, Syracuse University, in progress.

Trainees: Junior high school students (N=48)

Skill: Following instructions

Experimental design: (1) SLT for following instructions, trainees anticipate serving as SLT trainers, (2) SLT for following instructions, no trainee anticipation of serving as trainers, versus (3) No-treatment control by three parallel conditions involving Expressing a compliment, i.e., a skill target not concerned with resistance reduction.

Results: Group 1 significantly > Group 2 significantly > Group 3 on both skills on immediate and transfer measures.

Lopez, M.A. The influence of vocal and facial cue training on the identification of affect communicated via paralinguistic cues. Unpublished masters thesis, Syracuse University, 1974.

Trainees: Nurses and attendants (N=52)

Skill: Recognition of vocal cues of depression

Experimental design: (1) SLT for vocal and facial cues, (2) SLT for vocal cues with exposure to but no training for facial cues, (3) SLT for vocal cues, (4) No-training control.

Results: SLT for vocal cues plus either facial cue training (Group 1) or facial cue exposure (Group 2) significantly > SLT for vocal cues (Group 3) or Control (Group 4) on both post-test and generalization criteria.

McManus, S. Conceptual level and structured learning for parental empathy enhancement. Unpublished doctoral dissertation, Syracuse University, in progress.

Trainees: Parents of emotionally disturbed children (N=40)

Skill: Empathy

Experimental design: (1) SLT for empathy, (2) Lecture presenta-

tions of empathy, (3) Brief instructions for empathy, (4) No treatment.
Results: In progress.

Moses, J. *Supervisory relationship training: A new approach to supervisory training, Results of evaluation research.* New York: Human Resources Development Department, AT&T, May 1974.
Trainees: Supervisor trainees (N=183)
Skill: Effective management of any array of supervisor-supervisee relationship problems involving discrimination, absenteeism, and theft
Experimental design: SLT for supervisory relationship skills versus No training.
Results: Trained supervisors significantly > untrained supervisors on all behavioral and questionnaire criteria.

O'Brien, D. Trainer-trainee FIRO-B compatability as a determinant of certain process events in Structured Learning Therapy.
Trainers: Nurses and attendants at state mental hospital (N=60)
Skill: Structured learning trainer group leadership behaviors vis á vis low affection (actor) trainees
Experimental design: Trainers with High versus Low Originator Compatability for FIRO-B Control by Compatible or Incompatible trainees. Also, Trainers with High versus Low Originator Compatability for FIRO-B Affection by Compatible or Incompatible trainees.
Results: In progress.

Orenstein, R. The influence of self-esteem on modeling behavior in a psychotherapy analogue. Unpublished masters thesis, Syracuse University, 1969.
Trainees: University undergraduates (N=80, all females)
Skill: Attraction to the psychotherapist
Experimental design: High versus Low modeled attraction by High versus Low subject self-esteem.
Results: Significant modeling effect for attraction; no modeling effect for self-esteem. Subjects viewing a high attraction model were also significantly more willing to disclose, as were high self-esteem subjects. Low self-esteem subjects were significantly more persuasible.

Orenstein, R. Effect of teaching patients to focus on their feelings on level of experiencing in a subsequent interview. Unpublished doctoral dissertation, Syracuse University, 1973.

Trainees: Psychiatric inpatients (N=75, all female)
Skill: Focusing (ability to be aware of one's own affective experiencing)
Experimental design: (1) SLT for focusing, (2) Focusing manual, (3) Brief instructions for focusing, (4) Attention control, (5) No-treatment control.
Results: No significant between-group differences in focusing ability.

Perry, M.A. Didactic instructions for and modeling of empathy. Unpublished doctoral dissertation, Syracuse University, 1970.
Trainees: Clergymen (N=66)
Skill: Empathy
Experimental design: High empathy modeling versus Low empathy modeling versus No modeling by Presence versus Absence of instructions to be empathic.
Results: Significant modeling effect for empathy. No significant instructions or interaction effects for empathy.

Perry, M.A. Structured Learning Therapy for skill training of mentally retarded children.
Trainees: Mildly and moderately retarded halfway house residents (N=36)
Skill: Social interaction skills
Experimental design: SLT for social interaction skills versus Attention control versus No-treatment control.
Results: In progress.

Raleigh, R. Individual versus group Structured Learning Therapy for assertiveness training with senior and junior high school students. Unpublished doctoral dissertation, Syracuse University, in progress.
Trainees: Senior and junior high school students (N=80)
Skill: Assertiveness
Experimental design: Individual versus group SLT by senior versus junior high school student trainees plus attention control and no-treatment control.
Results: In progress.

Robertson, B. The effects of structured learning trainer's need to control on their group leadership behavior with aggressive and withdrawn trainees. Unpublished masters thesis, Syracuse University, in progress.

Trainers: Nurses and attendants at state mental hospital (N=60)
Skill: Structured learning trainer group leadership behaviors.
Experimental design: Trainers High or Low on need to control in interpersonal contexts versus controlling or cooperative actor trainees.
Results: In progress.

Robinson, R. Evaluation of a Structured Learning empathy training program for lower socioeconomic status home-aide trainees. Unpublished masters thesis, Syracuse University, 1973.
Trainees: Home-aide trainees (N=29)
Skill: Empathy
Experimental design: (1) SLT for empathy, (2) Didactic training of empathy, (3) No-treatment control.
Results: SLT > Didactic training or No-treatment control on immediate and generalization measures of empathy.

Rosenthal, N. Matching counselor trainees' conceptual level and training approaches: A study in the acquisition and enhancement of confrontation skills. Unpublished doctoral dissertation, Syracuse University, 1975.
Trainees: Counselor trainees (N=60)
Skill: Confrontation (ability to point out to clients discrepancies in the verbal and/or nonverbal contents of their statements)
Experimental design: (1) SLT for confrontation, training conducted by a trainer in "standard" SLT groups versus SLT for confrontation, self-instructional training format, by High versus Low conceptual level trainees, plus Attention Control.
Results: Significant interaction effects on confrontation skill for type of SLT (leader-led versus self-instructional) by conceptual level (high versus low). Also, SLT (both types) > Attention Control on confrontation skill.

Schneiman, R. An evaluation of Structured Learning and didactic learning as methods of training behavior modification skills to lower and middle socioeconomic level teacher-aides. Unpublished doctoral dissertation, Syracuse University, 1972.
Trainees: Teacher aides (N=60, 30 middle-class and 30 lower-class)
Skill: Disciplining (appropriate use of rules, disapproval and praise)
Experimental design: (1) SLT for disciplining, (2) Didactic training for disciplining, (3) No-training control by Middle-class versus Lower-class aides.

Results: Across social-class levels, SLT > Didactic or No-training on immediate and generalization behavioral measures of disciplining.

Sorcher, M., and Goldstein, A.P. A behavior modeling approach in training. *Personnel Administration,* 1973, 35, 35-41.
An overview of the nature and potential impact of Structured Learning in an industrial context. Topics examined include the need for a concrete, behavioral training focus; the basis for the choice of modeling, role playing, social reinforcement, and transfer training as the desirable components of this behavioral approach; and a brief example of how these procedures are utilized.

Sutton, K. Effects of modeled empathy and structured social class upon level of therapist displayed empathy. Unpublished masters thesis, Syracuse University, 1970.
Trainees: Attendants (N=60)
Skill: Empathy
Experimental design: High versus Low modeled empathy by Middle-class versus Lower-class structuring of the model's patient interviewee.
Results: Significant modeling effect for empathy on immediate but not generalization measurement. No significant social class structuring or interaction effects.

Sutton-Simon, K. The effects of two types of modeling and rehearsal procedures upon schizophrenics' social skill behavior. Unpublished doctoral dissertation, Syracuse University, 1974.
Trainees: Psychiatric inpatients (N=83, all male, all schizophrenic)
Skill: Social interaction behaviors
Experimental design: (1) SLT with behavioral and cognitive models, (2) SLT with behavioral models, (3) SLT with cognitive models, (4) Attention control, (5) No-treatment control.
Results: No significant between-condition differences.

Trief, P. The reduction of egocentrism in acting-out adolescents by Structured Learning Therapy. Unpublished doctoral dissertation, Syracuse University, in progress.
Trainees: Adolescent boys with history of acting-out behaviors (N=50)
Skill: Perspective-taking; Cooperation

Experimental design: Presence versus Absence of SLT for affective perspective taking by Presence versus Absence of SLT for cognitive perspective taking plus No-treatment control.
Results: In progress.

Walsh, W.G. The effects of conformity pressure and modeling on the attraction of hospitalized patients toward an interviewer. Unpublished doctoral dissertation, Syracuse University, 1971.
Trainees: Psychiatric inpatients (N=60, all female, mostly schizophrenic)
Skill: Attraction
Experimental design: Presence versus Absence of high attraction modeling by Presence versus Absence of high attraction conformity pressure plus No-treatment control.
Results: Significant main and interaction effects for modeling and conformity pressure on attraction. No significant generalization effect.

FUTURE RESEARCH: A CONCLUDING NOTE

As we observed earlier in this chapter, and as has now been annotated, evaluative studies of Structured Learning Therapy have yielded largely supportive findings. More such investigation is an obvious necessity, with particular emphasis on transfer and generalization effects. The transfer training principles examined in considerable detail in Chapter 1 should be viewed as guideposts, from which specific techniques for transfer enhancement may be drawn, tested, and, if found successful, incorporated into the practice of Structured Learning Therapy.

Beyond the crucial matter of transfer of training, there are several other potential effectiveness-enhancing procedures, suggested by experimental findings, which may prove to be valuable additions or modifications to Structured Learning Therapy as it is currently constituted. We wish to briefly consider below a number of these possible directions for future research and application.

Trainee motivation

From at least the time of Clark Hull (Hull, 1943), it has been appropriate to view an individual's behavior to be, at minimum, a function of both his ability or skill and his motivation to utilize that skill at any given time. While Structured Learning Therapy reflects some concern with motivation via its social reinforcement component and its attention to coaching trainees' real-life reinforcement dispensers, it is accurate to note an important reservation. Structured Learning Therapy remains essentially a skill-training approach which, in common with most therapies and training efforts, is relatively weak in its ability to arouse adequate levels of trainee motivation to learn or use given skill behaviors when such motivation is low. Research on "impression management" (Braginsky, Braginsky, and Ring, 1969), which shows that a substantial percentage of hospitalized psychiatric patients are actually motivated to appear "sick" or "incompetent," serves to underline the value of both research and clinical efforts concerned with increasing patient motivation for competent skill performance. These efforts might take several forms. While the trainee is still an inpatient, staff must serve as reinforcers of those skill behaviors (learned through Structured Learning Therapy or otherwise) that are necessary for successful living in the community, rather than as rewarders of those behaviors constituting the Social Breakdown Syndrome or a "colonization effect." Once discharged, perhaps greater motivational use can be made of both the patient's friends and relatives, as well as the patient himself. Tharp and Wetzel (1969) have begun to show us how real-life contingency managers (friends, relatives, and others unrelated to the ex-patient) can be trained and used effectively in delivering the social reinforcement necessary to motivate the development or maintenance of prosocial skill behaviors. Watson and Tharp (1972) go one step further and have trainees develop and apply their own incentives. By a self-modification use of contracts "written" by the trainee with himself, certain types of behavior change may be enhanced — though the usefulness of such contracting with ex-inpatients from public mental hospitals has not yet been tested.

But, it is not enough to look for means for enhancing trainee motivation by turning to staff, relatives, friends, or the patient himself. Motivation for prosocial behavior, for social, vocational, financial, and marital competence and satisfaction, is also a matter of societal incentive. Acting perhaps more as concerned citizen than expert therapist or trainer, it is incumbent on all of us to urge upon societal and community leaders the provision of adequate facilities, funding, and opportunities so that rewarding use of coping and mastery skills is in fact a possible reality and, thus, a potential incentive.

Modification of Structured Learning Therapy

It is almost true in the helping professions that a therapeutic or training approach more than 24 hours old has achieved "traditional" or "classical" status. Whatever its bases, such instant rigidification serves the helping effort poorly. Both research findings and clinical experience yield new information, new directions, and new leads to which we must remain continuously open. The four components of Structured Learning Therapy combine to yield an approach of at least moderate effectiveness. Can we do better? We think so, and would urge continuing concern and investigation of both current and potential Structured Learning Therapy components. For example, would it be productive for skill-learning purposes to also engage trainees in a discrimination-training procedure whereby both good and bad or competent and incompetent examples of a skill's learning points are modeled, labeled, contrasted, and discussed? Certainly, in laboratory contexts, such training has proven valuable on perceptual tasks. Its psychoeducational efficacy as a possible addition to Structured Learning Therapy deserves careful trial. Other features of the modeling component ought to be examined. We have utilized film, videotape, and audiotape modeling displays, and settled mostly on the last as our approach of choice. But what of the relative efficacy of (more elaborate) multi-media modeling displays and (less elaborate) live displays? We have typically employed anonymous, adult actor-models. Would prominent persons in such roles be worthwhile, as has apparently proven to be the case both in commercial advertising and our own modeling tape narrations?

Earlier in this book, we emphasized the importance of *realistic* role playing, of "setting the stage" so that role playing is, as much as possible, behavioral rehearsal for real-life skill usage in a real-life setting. To what extent, therefore, can Structured Learning Therapy be moved out of a formal training setting and actually conducted in real-life application settings? Such "park bench therapy" (Goldstein, Heller, and Sechrest, 1966) might be conducted in homes, offices, factories, or leisure-time settings, and might involve as co-actors, not anonymous strangers, but one's spouse, parents, children, or actual friends.

In addition to new or modified technique components, and use of new and transfer-enhancing training settings, there remains a wide array of procedures and materials of demonstrated value in aiding people develop new skills and change old behaviors (see Bergin and Garfield, 1971; Kanfer and Goldstein, 1975; Rimm and Masters,

1974). We urge the reader to contemplate and examine such procedures and materials, and do so in a spirit which considers not only Structured Learning Therapy, but all approaches to therapy and training as perpetually incomplete and unfinished.

Prescriptive utilization.

In the early 1950s, when evaluative research on psychotherapy was but a few years old, outcome studies usually sought to answer some variation of the question: "Is treatment A better than treatment B?" But even if A did appear to "work better" than B, answers to such global questions never told us why, never shed light on which were the active ingredients in the treatment A package that helped people change, and which ingredients were inactive and thus dispensible. In 1976, a different and more prescription-seeking outcome question is being asked: "Which treatment(s) used by which treaters on which patients yields which outcomes?" Here research concern is simultaneously focused upon *all* outcome-relevant aspects of the given treatment context. In the case of Structured Learning Therapy, such prescriptive concern for identifying active and inactive ingredients should lead to factorial studies of trainers X trainees X procedures. A number of such investigations were outlined earlier in this chapter, but many, many prescriptive questions remain (Goldstein and Stein, 1976). There are, for example, a number of potential trainee populations which might derive considerable benefit from participation in a skill-training approach such as Structured Learning Therapy, but with whom such a training effort has either barely begun or has not yet been attempted at all. These populations include parents, the elderly, mentally retarded adults and children, emotionally disturbed children, prison populations, and diverse types of mildly disturbed outpatient neurotics. For maximally effective skill training with such populations, much research remains to be done to identify relevant trainer, trainee, and technique characteristics, and optimally prescriptive combinations of these characteristics. We urge such research efforts upon the reader, as but one example of an investigative and creative spirit we hope will characterize formal and informal efforts to aid trainees to develop the skills necessary for them to lead effective and satisfying lives in the community.

References

Action for mental health. Final report of the Joint Commission on Mental Illness and Health. New York: Basic Books, 1961.

Ayllon, T., and Azrin, N.H. *The token economy: A motivational system for therapy and rehabilitation.* New York: Appleton-Century-Crofts, 1968.

Bandura, A. *Principles of behavior modification.* New York: Holt, Rinehart & Winston, 1969.

Bandura, A., Blanchard, E.B., and Ritter, B. The relative efficacy of desenitization and modeling approaches for inducing behavioral, affective and attitudinal changes. *Journal of Personality and Social Psychology,* 1969, **13**, 173-199.

Bergin, A.E. and Garfield, S.L. (Eds.) *Handbook of psychotherapy and behavior change.* New York: Wiley, 1971.

Bernstein, B. Social structure, language and learning. *Educational Research,* 1961, 3, 163-176.

Binder, A., McConnell, D., and Sjoholm, N.A. Verbal conditioning as a function of experimenter characteristics. *Journal of Abnormal and Social Psychology,* 1957, **55**, 309-314.

Braginsky, B.M., Braginsky, D.D., and Ring, K. *Methods of madness.* New York: Holt, Rinehart & Winston, 1969.

Brehm, J.W., and Cohen, A.R. *Explorations in cognitive dissonance.* New York: Wiley, 1962.

Brock, T.C., and Blackwood, J.E. Dissonance reduction, social comparison, and modification of others' opinion. *Journal of Abnormal and Social Psychology,* 1962, **65**, 319-324.

Bryan, J.H., and Test, M.A. Models and helping: Naturalistic studies in aiding behavior. *Journal of Personality and Social Psychology,* 1967, **6**, 400-407.

Burrs, V., and Kapche, R. Modeling of social behavior in chronic hospital patients. Unpublished manuscript, California State College at Long Beach, 1969.

Callantine, M.F., and Warren, L.M. Learning sets in human concept formation. *Psychological Reports,* 1955, **1** 363-367.

Carlsmith, J.M., Collins, B.E., and Helmreich, R.K. Studies in forced compliance: I. The effect of pressure for compliance on attitude change produced by face-to-face role playing and anonymous essay writing. *Journal of Personality and Social Psychology,* 1966, **4**, 1-13.

Chittenden, G.E. An experimental study in measuring and modifying assertive behavior in young children. *Monographs of the Society for Research in Child Development,* 1942, **7**, Number 31.

Cohen, A.R., and Latane, B. An experiment on choice in commitment to counter-attitudinal behavior. In J.W. Brehm and A.R. Cohen, *Explorations in cognitive dissonance.* New York: Wiley, 1962, Pp. 88-91.

Cohen, B.D., Kalish, H.I., Thurston, J.R., and Cohen, E. Experimental manipulation of verbal behavior. *Journal of Experimental Psychology,* 1954, **47**, 106-110.

Crafts, L.W. Transfer as related to number of common elements. *Journal of General Psychology,* 1935, **13**, 147-158.

Culbertson, F.M. Modification of an emotionally held attitude through role playing. *Journal of Abnormal and Social Psychology,* 1957, **54**, 230-233.

Davis, K., and Jones, E.E. Changes in interpersonal perception as a means of reducing cognitive dissonance. *Journal of Abnormal and Social Psychology,* 1960, **61**, 402-410.

Davison, G.C. Appraisal of behavior modification techniques with adults in institutional settings. In C.M. Franks (Ed.), *Behavior therapy: Appraisal and status.* New York: McGraw-Hill, 1969.

Dolger, L., and Ginandes, J. Children's attitudes toward discipline as related to socioeconomic status. *Journal of Experimental Education,* 1946, **15**, 161-165.

Duncan, C.P. Transfer after training with single versus multiple tasks. *Journal of Experimental Psychology,* 1958, **55**, 63-73.

Duvall, E.M. Conceptions of parenthood. *American Journal of Sociology,* 1946, **52**, 193-203.

Ekman, P. A comparison of verbal and non-verbal behavior as reinforcing stimuli of opinion responses. Unpublished doctoral dissertation, Adelphi College, 1958.

Fahmy, S.A. Conditioning and extinction of a referential verbal response class in a situation resembling a clinical diagnostic interview. *Dissertation Abstracts,* 1953, **13**, 873-874.

Feshback, S. The function of aggression and the regulation of aggressive drive. *Psychological Review,* 1964, **71**, 247-272.

Freeman, H.E., and Simmons, O.G. *The mental patient comes home.* New York: Wiley, 1963.

Friedenberg, W.P. Verbal and non-verbal attraction modeling in an initial therapy interview analogue. Unpublished masters thesis, Syracuse University, 1971.

Gelfand, D.M., and Singer, R.D. Generalization of reinforced personality evaluations: A further investigation. *Journal of Clinical Psychology,* 1968, **24**, 24-26.

Goffman, E. *Asylums.* New York: Doubleday-Anchor, 1961.

Goldstein, A.P. *Structured Learning Therapy: Toward a psychotherapy for the poor.* New York: Academic Press, 1973.

Goldstein, A.P., Cohen, R., Blake, G., and Walsh, W. The effects of modeling and social class structuring in paraprofessional psychotherapist training. *Journal of Nervous and Mental Disease,* 1971, **153**, 47-56.

Goldstein, A.P., and Goodhart, A. The use of structured learning for empathy enhancement in paraprofessional psychotherapist training. *Journal of Community Psychology,* 1973, **1**, 168-173.

Goldstein, A.P., Heller, K., and Sechrest, L.B. *Psychotherapy and the psychology of behavior change.* New York: Wiley, 1966.

Goldstein, A.P., Martens, J., Hubben, J., VonBelle, H.A., Schaaf, W., Wiersema, H., and Goodhart, A. The use of modeling to increase independent behavior. *Behavior Research and Therapy,* 1973, **11**, 31-42.

Goldstein, A.P., and Stein, N. *Prescriptive psychotherapies.* New York: Pergamon Press, 1976.

Greenspoon, J. The effect of two non-verbal stimuli on the frequency of members of two verbal response classes. *American Psychologist,* 1954, **9**, 384.

Grotjahn, M. The qualities of the group therapist. In H.I. Kavlan and B.J. Sadock (Eds.), *Comprehensive Group Psychotherapy.* Baltimore: Williams & Wilkens, 1971. Pp. 757-773.

Harvey, O.J., and Beverly, G.D. Some personality correlates of concept change through role playing. *Journal of Abnormal and Social Psychology,* 1961, **63**, 125-130.

Harvey, O.J., Hunt, D.E., and Schroder, H.M. *Conceptual systems and personality organization.* New York: Wiley, 1961.

Herzberg, F., Mausner, B., and Snyderman, B. *The motivation to work.* New York: Wiley, 1959.

Hildum, D.C., and Brown, R.W. Verbal reinforcement and interviewer bias. *Journal of Abnormal and Social Psychology,* 1956, **53**, 108-111.

Hollander, T.G. The effects of role playing on attraction, disclosure and attitude change in a psychotherapy analogue. Unpublished doctoral dissertation, Syracuse University, 1970.

Hovland, C.I., Janis, I., and Kelley, H.H. *Communication and persuasion: Psychological studies of opinion change.* New Haven: Yale University Press, 1953.

Hull, C.H. *Principles of Behavior.* New York: Appleton-Century-Crofts, 1943.

Hunt, D.A., and Dopyera, J. Personality variation in lower-class children. *The Journal of Psychology,* 1966, **62**, 47-54.

Janis, I.L., and Hovland, C.I. An overview of persuasibility research. In Hovland and Janis (Eds.) *Personality and Persuasibility.* New Haven, Conn.: 1959, Yale University Press. Pp. 1-26.

Janis, I.L., and Mann. L. Effectiveness of emotional role playing in modifying smoking habits and attitudes. *Journal of Experimental Research in Personality,* 1965, **1**, 84-90.

Kanfer, F.H., and Goldstein, A.P. *Helping People Change.* New York: Pergamon Press, 1975.

Kleinsasser, L.D. The reduction of performance anxiety as a function of desensitization, pre-therapy vicarious learning, and vicarious learning alone. Unpublished doctoral dissertation, Pennsylvania State University, 1968.

Klinger, B.I. Effect of peer model responsiveness and length of induction procedure on hypnotic responsiveness. *Journal of Abnormal Psychology,* 1970, **75**, 15-18.

Kohn, M.L. Social class and schizophrenia: A critical review. In H. Wechsler, L. Soloman, and B.M. Kramer (Eds.), *Social psychology and mental health.* New York: Holt, 1970. Pp. 113-127.

Krumboltz, J.D., and Thoresen, C.E. The effect of behavioral counseling in group and individual settings on information seeking behavior. *Journal of Counseling Psychology,* 1964, **11**, 324-333.

Krumboltz, J.D., Varenhorst, B.B., and Thoresen, C.E. Non-verbal factors in the effectiveness of models in counseling. *Journal of Counseling Psychology,* 1967, **14**, 412-418.

Lack, D.Z. The effects of a model and instructions on psychotherapist self-disclosure. Unpublished masters thesis, Syracuse University, 1971.

Theodore Lownik Library
Illinois Benedictine College
Lisle, Illinois 60532

Lefkowitz, M., Blake, R.R., and Mouton, J.S. Status factors in pedestrian violation of traffic signals. *Journal of Abnormal and Social Psychology,* 1954, **51**, 704-706.

Liberman, B. The effect of modeling procedures on attraction and disclosure in a psychotherapy analogue. Unpublished doctoral dissertation, Syracuse University, 1970.

Lichtenstein, E., Keutzer, C.S., and Himes, K.H. Emotional role playing and changes in smoking attitudes and behavior. *Psychological Reports,* 1969, **25**, 379-387.

Mann, J.H. Experimental evaluations of role playing. *Psychological Bulletin,* 1956, **53**, 227-234.

Marlatt, G.A., Jacobson, E.A., Johnson, D.L., and Morrice, D.J. Effect of exposure to a model receiving evaluative feedback upon subsequent behavior in an interview. *Journal of Consulting and Clinical Psychology,* 1970, **34**, 194-212.

Matarazzo, J.D., Wiens, A.N., and Saslow, G. Studies in interview speech behavior. In L. Krasner and L.P. Ullman (Eds.), *Research in behavior modification.* New York: Holt, Rinehart & Winston, 1965. Pp. 179-210.

McFall, R.M., and Marston, A.R. An experimental investigation of behavior rehearsal in assertive training. *Journal of Abnormal Psychology,* 1970, **76**, 295-303.

McGehee, N., and Thayer, P.W. *Training in business and industry.* New York: Wiley, 1961.

McNair, D.M. Reinforcement of verbal behavior. *Journal of Experimental Psychology,* 1957, **53**, 40-46.

Milby, J.B. Modification of extreme social isolation by contingent social reinforcement. *Journal of Applied Behavior Analysis,* 1970, **3**, 149-152.

Miller, D. Retrospective analysis of posthospital mental patients' worlds. *Journal of Health and Social Behavior,* 1967, **8**, 136-140.

Murray, E.J., and Cohen, M. Mental illness, milieu therapy, and social organization in ward groups. *Journal of Abnormal and Social Psychology,* 1959, **58**, 48-54.

Nuthman, A.M. Conditioning of a response class on a personality test. *Journal of Abnormal and Social Psychology,* 1957, **54**, 19-23.

Oakes, W.F., Droge, A.E., and August, B. Reinforcement effects on conclusions reached in group discussion. *Psychological Reports,* 1961, **9**, 27-34.

Paul, G.L. Chronic mental patient: Current status — future directions. *Psychological Bulletin,* 1969, **71**, 81-94.

Pearlin, L.I., and Kohn, M.L. Social class, occupation, and parental values: A cross-national study. In A.L. Grey (Ed.), *Class and personality in society.* New York: Atherton Press, 1969. Pp. 161-184.

Perry, M.A. Didactic instructions for and modeling of empathy. Unpublished doctoral dissertation, Syracuse University, 1970.

Phillips, E.L. Achievement place: Token reinforcement procedures in a home-style rehabilitation setting for "pre-delinquent" boys. *Journal of Applied Behavior Analysis,* 1968, 1, 213-223.

Poser, E.G. The effect of therapists' training on group therapeutic outcome. *Journal of Consulting Psychology,* 1966, 30, 4, 283-289.

Quay, H. The effect of verbal reinforcement on the recall of early memories. *Journal of Abnormal and Social Psychology,* 1959, 59, 254-257.

Riessman, F. *The culturally deprived child.* New York: Harper, 1962.

Rimm, D.C., and Masters J.C. *Behavior Therapy.* New York: Academic Press, 1974.

Ritter, B. Treatment of acrophobia with contact desensitization. *Behavior Research and Therapy,* 1969, 7, 41-45.

Rosenbaum, M.E., and Tucker, I.F. The competence of the model and the learning of imitation and non-imitation. *Journal of Experimental Psychology,* 1962, 63, 183-190.

Salzinger, K., and Pisoni, S. Reinforcement of verbal affect responses of schizophrenics during the clinical interview. Presented at American Psychological Assocation, New York, 1957.

Schaefer, H.H., and Martin, P.L. *Behavioral therapy.* New York, McGraw-Hill, 1969.

Schatzman, L., and Strauss, A. Social class and modes of communication. *American Journal of Sociology,* 1955, 60, 329-338.

Schofield, W. *Psychotherapy, the purchase of friendship.* Englewood Cliffs, N.J.: Prentice-Hall, 1964.

Shore, E., and Sechrest, L.B. Concept attainment as a function of number of positive instances presented. *Journal of Educational Psychology,* 1961, 52, 303-307.

Sidowski, J.B. Influence of awareness of reinforcement on verbal conditioning. *Journal of Experimental Psychology,* 1954, 48, 355-360.

Sobey, F. *The nonprofessional revolution in mental health.* New York: Columbia University Press, 1970.

Sutton, K. Effects of modeled empathy and structured social class upon level of therapist displayed empathy. Unpublished masters thesis, Syracuse University, 1970.

Taffel, C. Anxiety and the conditioning of verbal behavior. *Journal of Abnormal and Social Psychology,* 1955, 51, 496-501.

Tharp, R., and Wetzel, R. *Behavior Modification in the Natural Environment.* New York: Academic Press, 1969.

Truax, C.B., and Carkhuff, R.R. *Toward effective counseling and psychotherapy.* Chicago: Aldine, 1967.

Truax, C.B., and Wargo, D.G. Effects of vicarious therapy pretraining and alternate sessions on outcome in group psychotherapy with outpatients. *Journal of Counseling and Clinical Psychology,* 1969, 33, 440-447.

Tuma, E., and Livson, N. Family socioeconomic status and adolescent attitudes to authority. *Child Development,* 1960, 31, 387-399.

Verplanck, W.S. The control of the content of conversation: Reinforcement of statements of opinion. *Journal of Abnormal and Social Psychology,* 1955, 51, 668-676.

Walsh, W. The effects of conformity pressure and modeling on the attraction of hospitalized patients toward an interviewer. Unpublished doctoral dissertation, Syracuse University, 1971.

Wasik, B.H., Senn, K., Welch, R.H., and Cooper, B.R. Behavior modification with culturally deprived school children: Two case studies. *Journal of Applied Behavior Analysis,* 1969, 2, 181-194.

Watson, D.L., and Tharp, R.G. *Self-Directed Behavior: Self-Modification for Personal Adjustment.* Belmont, California: Brooks Cole, 1972.

Whalen, C. Effects of a model and instructions on group verbal behavior. *Journal of Consulting and Clinical Psychology,* 1969, 3, 409-521.

Yalom, I.D. *The theory and practice of group psychotherapy.* New York: Basic Brooks, 1970.

Zimbardo, P.G. The effect of effort and improvisation on self-persuasion produced by role playing. *Journal of Experimental Social Psychology,* 1965, 1, 103-120.

Zusman, J. Some explanations of the changing appearance of psychiatric patients: Antecedents of the Social Breakdwon Syndrome Concept. *International Journal of Psychiatry,* 1967, 3, 216-237.

Author Index

Subject Index

by homework, 53-56
by identical elements, 24
by performance feedback, 25

by response availability, 23-24
by stimulus variability, 24-25

Supplement A

Trainer's Manual
for
Structured Learning Therapy

SKILL TRAINING FOR COMMUNITY LIVING: APPLYING STRUCTURED LEARNING THERAPY is a complete text for use of the multimedia Skill Training Program. It provides the reader with the basic background of Structured Learning Therapy, and fully describes its techniques, procedures and materials. How to apply this approach effectively is discussed and illustrated, as are procedures for training professional and paraprofessional staff in its use.

The Skill Training Program was developed to provide hospitals, clinics, halfway houses, and other institutions and agencies with an effective tool for teaching patients basic skills for getting along well with other people and functioning effectively in the community. Patients are taught such basic social and personal skills as starting a conversation, responding to anger, setting a goal, making requests, etc. These basic skills are then combined to teach competent functioning in such realistic situations as job seeking, dealing with crisis, using leisure time, etc.

THE SKILL TRAINING FOR COMMUNITY LIVING PROGRAM

BASIC SKILLS PROGRAM, including Basic Skill Tapes in an attractive binder with 10 sets of SKILL CARDS and 10 TRAINEES' NOTEBOOKS.

APPLICATION SKILLS PROGRAM, including the Application Skill Tapes in an attractive binder.

TRAINER INSTRUCTION PROGRAM, including the test, trainer preparation tapes, and the brief guide, TRAINER'S MANUAL FOR STRUCTURED LEARNING THERAPY in an attractive binder.

For further information, contact Pergamon Press, Fairview Park, Elmsford, N.Y. 10523.

Supplement A

TRAINER'S MANUAL
for
STRUCTURED
LEARNING
THERAPY

ARNOLD P. GOLDSTEIN
Psychology Department
Syracuse University
Syracuse, New York

N. JANE GERSHAW and ROBERT P. SPRAFKIN
Syracuse Veterans Administration Hospital
Syracuse, New York
and
SUNY Upstate Medical Center

PERGAMON PRESS/STRUCTURED LEARNING ASSOCIATES
New York • Toronto • Oxford • Sydney • Frankfurt • Paris

162

Pergamon Press Offices:

U.S.A.	Pergamon Press Inc., Maxwell House, Fairview Park, Elmsford, New York 10523, U.S.A.
U.K.	Pergamon Press Ltd., Headington Hill Hall, Oxford OX3, OBW, England
CANADA	Pergamon of Canada, Ltd., 207 Queen's Quay West, Toronto 1, Canada
AUSTRALIA	Pergamon Press (Aust) Pty. Ltd., 19a Boundary Street, Rushcutters Bay, N.S.W. 2011, Australia
FRANCE	Pergamon Press SARL, 24 rue des Ecoles, 75240 Paris, Cedex 05, France
WEST GERMANY	Pergamon Press GmbH, 6242 Kronberg/Taunus, Frankfurt-am-Main, West Germany

Copyright © 1976 Pergamon Press Inc. and Structured Learning Associates

The preparation of this Manual was supported in part by PHS Research Grant MH 13669 from the National Institute of Mental Health. Their assistance is gratefully acknowledged.

All Rights Reserved. No part of this publication may be reproduced, stored in a retrieval system or transmitted in any form or by any means: electronic, electrostatic, magnetic tape, mechanical, photocopying, recording or otherwise, without permission in writing from the publishers.

ISBN 0-08-021110-0
Printed in the United States of America

Contents

Introduction

The primary purpose of this Trainer's Manual is to provide detailed guidelines for effectively conducting Structured Learning Therapy groups. Structured Learning is a therapy approach which has been demonstrated to be successful in teaching psychiatric outpatients, inpatients, and a variety of other trainees, skills helpful to them in leading satisfying and effective lives. It is an approach which focuses on the teaching of personal and interpersonal coping and mastery skills, including such skills as initiating, carrying out, and ending a conversation; listening; initiating and responding to a complaint; negotiation; role taking; asking for help; self-control; stress rehearsal; problem solving; affective perception; aggression reduction, and a host of other skills relevant to the interpersonal and planning components of the work, social, financial, and personal aspects of daily living.

Structured Learning consists of four components, each of which is a well-established behavior change procedure. These procedures are modeling, role playing, social reinforcement, and transfer training.

In each training session, a group of six to 12 patients: (1) listen to a brief audiotape (or watch live persons) depicting specific skill behaviors shown to be helpful in dealing with common problems of daily living (MODELING)*, (2) are given extensive opportunity, encouragement, and training to behaviorally rehearse or practice or practice the effective behaviors which have been modeled (ROLE PLAYING), (3) are provided corrective feedback and approval or praise as their role playing of the behaviors becomes more and more similar to the tape model's behavior (SOCIAL REINFORCEMENT), and (4) discuss Homework Reports completed between sessions as but one of a variety of procedures used to encourage the transfer of the newly learned behaviors from the training setting to their real-life setting (TRANSFER TRAINING).

Before describing in further detail the procedures involved in organizing and actually running Structured Learning sessions, we wish to mention briefly what Structured Learning is *not*. First, it is important to stress that the behavioral steps which make up each skill (learning points) portrayed on each audiotape should not be viewed as the one and only way to enact the skill effectively. The goal of Structured Learning Therapy is to help build a flexible repertoire of socially effective and satisfying behaviors which can be

---

*See Appendix A, Tables 3 and 4 for a complete listing of the Structured Learning Therapy modeling tapes.

1

adjusted to the demands of the patients' life situations. Thus, we urge the reader to consider the taped behaviors as good examples, as they indeed have been shown to be, but not as the only way to effectively perform the skill involved.

A second caution may be stated by noting that the Structured Learning modeling tapes are not instructional tapes in the usual sense. An instructional tape is most typically played to an audience which passively listens to it and then, at some later date, is supposed to do what was played. Such passive learning is not likely to be enduring learning. Thus, the Structured Learning modeling tapes should not be played alone — i.e., without role playing and feedback following them. We have demonstrated experimentally that all four components of our training approach are necessary and sufficient for enduring behavior change, and these results should be reflected in the use of these materials and procedures. Finally, Structured Learning is not an approach that can be used effectively by all possible trainers. Later in this Manual we shall describe in detail the knowledge, skills, and sensitivities which a trainer must possess to be effective with this approach.

ORGANIZING THE STRUCTURED LEARNING GROUP

Selection of Patients

Each Structured Learning group should consist of trainees who are clearly deficient in whatever skill is going to be taught. If possible, trainees should also be grouped according to the *degree* of their deficiency in the given skill. The optimal size group for effective Structured Learning sessions consists of six to 12 trainees plus two trainers. For both learning and transfer to occur, each trainee must have ample opportunity to practice what he has heard or seen modeled, receive feedback from other group members and the trainers, and discuss his attempts to apply at home, on the job, or on the ward what he has learned in the therapy sessions. Yet, each session should typically not exceed two hours in length, since Structured Learning is intensive and trainees' efficiency of learning diminishes beyond this span. A group size of six to 12, therefore, is optimal in that it permits the specific therapy tasks to be accomplished within the allotted time period. If most trainees in a given group show a particularly brief span of attention, the session can be shortened to as little as one-half hour, although in this instance it is advisable to meet more often than the usual two or three times per week.

The trainees selected need not be from the same ward (if inpatients) nor from the same community area (if outpatients). However, again to maximize transfer, trainees are asked to "set the stage" when role playing by enacting the modeling tape's specific behaviors, or "learning points," as they fit their real situation on the ward, at home, or at work. Each role play involves at least two participants, the trainee himself (main actor) and another trainee (co-actor) chosen by him to play the role of wife, boss, nurse, or whatever role is appropriate for the given skill problem. We ask the main actor playing himself to describe in detail an actual situation of his in which he is having or could be having difficulty performing the skill behaviors which have been modeled. The co-actor plays the part of the other person in the main actor's life who is involved in the skill problem area. In this way, the role playing becomes real — i.e., rehearsal for solving real-life problems. Thus, while participants need not come from the same ward or community, they should be familiar enough with one another's real-life situations so that they can role play these situations realistically.

Number, Length, and Spacing of Sessions

The Structured Learning modeling tapes and associated procedures typically constitute a training program from three to 15 sessions long, depending on the level of the group and the number and complexity of skills being taught. For each interpersonal or personal skill we have sought to teach, we have developed a different modeling tape. The specific behaviors comprising the skill are concretely demonstrated on each tape. The order in which the modeling tapes are utilized should (1) give trainees a sense of making progress in skill mastery (thus, the easier skills should come first), and (2) provide them (in each session) with useful knowledge that can be applied in real-life settings between sessions.

It is most desirable that treatment occur at a rate of two or, at the most, three times per week. *Spacing is crucial.* Most trainees in all therapy or skill-training programs learn well in the training setting. Most, however, fail to transfer this learning to where it counts . . . on the ward, at home, at work, in the community. As will be seen below, Structured Learning includes special procedures which maximize the likelihood of transfer of training, including between-sessions

3

"homework." For there to be ample opportunity for trainees to try out in real-life what was learned in the training setting, sessions must be well spaced. One sequence of modeling, several role plays, feedback, and assignment of homework is ideally covered in each training session of one to two hours in length. The following session should open with a review of the previous session's homework.

TRAINERS

The role playing and feedback activities which constitute most of each Structured Learning session are a series of "action-reaction" sequences in which effective skill behaviors are first rehearsed (role playing) and then critiqued (feedback). As such, the trainer must both lead and observe. We have found that one trainer is very hard pressed to do both of these tasks well at the same time, and thus, we recommend strongly that each session be led by a team of two trainers. Their professional credentials are largely irrelevant; on the other hand, their group leadership skills, interpersonal sensitivity, enthusiasm, and the favorableness of the relationship between them are the qualities that appear crucial to the success of treatment. Furthermore, proficiency in two types of skills are required of Structured Learning trainers.

The first might best be described as *General Trainer Skills* — i.e., those skills requisite for success in almost any training or therapy effort. These include:

    a) oral communication and group discussion leadership,

    b) flexibility and capacity for resourcefulness,

    c) enthusiasm,

    d) ability to work under pressure,

    e) empathic ability,

    f) listening skill,

    g) broad knowledge of human behavior, demands of community living, etc.,

    h) group management skills.

The second type of requisite skills are *Specific Trainer Skills* — i.e., those germane to Structured Learning in particular. These include:

    a) knowledge, in depth, of Structured Learning — its background, procedures, and goals,

    b) ability to orient both patients and supporting staff to Structured Learning,

    c) ability to initiate and sustain role playing,

4

d) ability to present material in concrete, behavioral form,

e) ability to reduce trainees' resistance,

f) sensitivity in providing corrective feedback.

For both trainer selection and development purposes, we have found it most desirable to have potential trainers participate, as if they were actual trainees, in a series of Structured Learning sessions. After this experience, we have had them co-lead a series of sessions with an experienced trainer. In doing so, we have shown them how to conduct such sessions, given them several opportunities to practice what they have seen, and provided them with feedback regarding their performance. In effect, we have used Structured Learning to teach Structured Learning. To aid in this regard, we have developed and utilized a series of Trainer Preparation tapes portraying Initial, Advanced, and Resistive Structured Learning Therapy sessions.

THE STRUCTURED LEARNING SESSIONS

The Setting

One major principle for encouraging transfer from the therapy to the real-life setting is the rule of identical elements. This rule states that the more similar the two settings — i.e., the greater number of identical physical and social qualities shared by them — the greater the transfer. Therapy in a fancy office or at a mountaintop work-play retreat may be great fun, but it results in minimal transfer of training. We urge that Structured Learning be conducted in the same general setting as the real-life environment of most participating trainees and that the treatment setting be furnished to resemble or simulate as much as possible the likely application settings.

The horeshoe seating arrangement, illustrated in Fig. 1, is one good example of how furniture might be arranged in the therapy room. Participating trainees sit at desk or tables so that some writing space is provided. Two chairs are placed up front for the role players. Behind and to the side of one of the role players is a chalkboard on which is written the learning points (specific skill behaviors) for the skill being worked with at that time. If possible, other parts of this same room should be furnished with props which resemble (at least in rudimentary form) a kitchen, a store counter, an office, a bedroom, or other relevant application setting. When no appropriate furniture or materials are available to "set the scene," substitute or even imaginary props can readily be used.

5

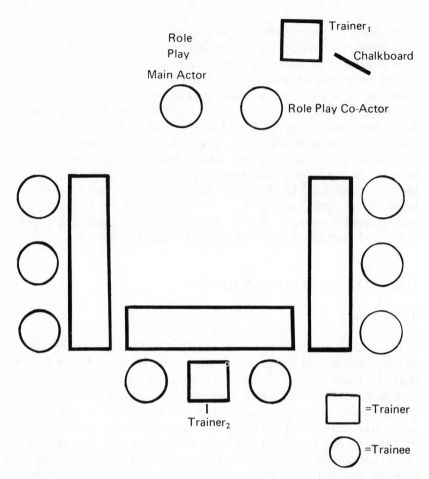

Fig. 1. A Functional Room Arrangement for Structured Learning Therapy

We have found it useful in the majority of Structured Learning Therapy groups to provide each trainee with a simplified and structured guide which explains group procedures and which is useful for taking notes during and between training sessions. This guide, the *Trainee's Notebook for Structured Learning Therapy** outlines the procedural details for Structured Learning Therapy and provides note pages for the trainee to write learning points, role play notes, and homework assignments. The *Notebook* also serves as a convenient reference for trainees as they build a repertoire of skills.

*See Supplement B for Table of Contents of the *Trainee's Notebook for Structured Learning Therapy.*

6

The Introduction

The initial session is opened by the trainers first introducing themselves and having each trainee do likewise, being sure that every trainee has the opportunity to tell the group something about his background and training goals. After such an initial warm-up or familiarization period, the trainers introduce the program by providing trainees with a brief description of its rationale, training procedures, targets, and so forth. Typically, the introduction also covers such topics as the centrality of interpersonal skill for effective and satisfying community living, the value of skill knowledge and skill flexibility on the part of the trainee, the variety of skills needed in relation to the complex demands made in contemporary society, and the manner in which training focuses on altering specific behaviors and not attitude change. The specific training procedures (modeling, role playing, etc.) are then described, as is the implementation (dates, time, place, etc.) of these procedures. A period of time is spent discussing these introductory points, and then the actual training begins.

Modeling

Trainers describe the first skill to be taught and hand out cards (SKILL CARDS) to all trainees on which the name of the skill and learning points are printed. The first modeling tape is then played. Trainees are told to listen closely to the way the actors in each vignette on the tape follow the learning points.

To ease trainees into Structured Learning, it is recommended that the first skill taught be one that trainees can master with relative ease. It is particularly important that a trainee's first experience with Structured Learning be a successful one.

All modeling audiotapes begin with a narrator setting the scene and stating the name of the skill and the learning points that make up that skill. Sets of actors portray a series of vignettes in which each learning point is clearly enacted in sequence. The narrator then returns on the tape, makes a summary statement, restates the learning points, and urges their continued use. In our view, this sequence of narrator's introduction, modeling scenes, and narrator's summary constitutes the minimum requirement for a satisfactory modeling audiotape. We have described in detail elsewhere (see Goldstein, 1973) those tape, model, and patient characteristics that

7

usually enhance or diminish the degree of learning that occurs. We refer the reader interested in developing modeling displays to this source (and see Appendix C). We have found that live modeling by trainers can also often provide those elements that promote satisfactory learning by trainees.

Role Playing

A brief spontaneous discussion almost invariably follows the playing of a modeling tape. Trainees comment on the learning points, the actors, and, very often, on how the situation or skill problem portrayed occurs in their own lives. Since our primary goal in role playing is to encourage realistic behavioral rehearsal, a trainee's statements about his individual difficulties using the skill being taught can often develop into material for the first role play. To enhance the realism of the portrayal, have him (now the main actor) choose a second trainee (co-actor) to play the role of the significant other person in his life who is relevant to the skill problem. One trainer should be responsible for keeping a record of who has role played, which role, and for which skill — to be sure that all participate about equally.

It is of crucial importance that the main actor seek to enact the learning points he has just heard modeled. He is told to refer to his skill card on which the learning points are printed. As noted, the learning points should also be written on a chalkboard for him to see while role playing. Before role playing begins, the following instructions should be delivered:

1. *To the main actor:* Follow and enact the learning points. Do so with the real skill problem you have chosen in mind.
2. *To the co-actor:* Respond as realistically as possible, doing what you think the actual other person in the main actor's real-life situation would do.
3. *To the other trainees in the group:* Observe how well the main actor follows the learning points and take notes on this for later discussion.

The main actor is asked to briefly describe the real skill problem situation and the real person(s) involved in it, with whom he could try these learning point behaviors in real life. The co-actor should be called by the name of the main actor's significant other during the role play. The trainer then instructs the role players to begin. It is the trainers' main responsibility, at this point, to be sure that the main actor keeps role playing and that he attempts to follow the learning points while doing so. If he "breaks role" and begins making comments, explaining background events, etc., the trainers should firmly instruct him to resume his role. One trainer should position himself near the chalkboard and point to each learning point, in turn, as the role play unfolds, being sure none are either missed or enacted out of order. If the trainers or actors feel the role play is not progressing well and wish to start it over, this is appropriate. Trainers should make an effort to have the actors complete the skill enactment before stepping down. Observers should be instructed to hold their comments until the role play is completed.

The role playing should be continued until all trainees have had an opportunity to participate (in either role) and preferably until all have had a chance to be the main actor — even if all of the same learning points must be carried over to a second or third session. Note that while the framework (learning points) of each role play in the series remains the same, the actual content can and should change from role play to role play. It is the problem as it actually occurs, or could occur, in each trainee's real-life environment that should be the content of the given role play. When completed, each trainee should be better armed to act appropriately in the given reality situation.

A few further procedural matters relevant to role playing should be noted, as each will serve to increase its effectiveness. Role reversal is often a useful role play procedure. A trainee role playing a skill problem may have a difficult time perceiving his co-actor's viewpoint, and vice versa. Having them exchange roles and resume the role playing can be most helpful in this regard.

At times, it has been worthwhile for the trainer to assume the co-actor role, in an effort to expose trainees to the handling of types of reactions not otherwise role played during the session. It is here that the trainer's flexibility and creativity will certainly be called upon. We might add in this context that while we sometimes suggest that trainers play the co-actor role, we urge them to be especially cautious when taking on the main actor role. Errors in the enactment of this live modeling role can be most serious, destroy trainer credibility, and severely decrease his value as a trainer for that group of trainees.

Real-life problems very often require effective use of a combination of Basic Skills for their satisfactory solution. To reflect this fact in our training procedures, we have developed a series of modeling Application Tapes which portray sequences and combinations of

9

Basic Skills necessary to deal with such daily living matters as finding a place to live, job seeking, marital interactions, and dealing with crises.* The procedures utilized with the Application Skill tapes are essentially the same as those used for the Basic Skill tapes, though individualized skill combinations will have to be constructed prior to role playing. Application groups, using Basic Skills in combination, should only be started once trainees have a firm grasp of Basic Skills used separately.

Feedback

Upon completion of each role play, a brief feedback period should ensue. The goals of this activity are to let the main actor know how well he followed the learning points or in what ways he departed from them, to explore the psychological impact of his enactment on his co-actor, and to provide him encouragement to try out his role play behaviors in real-life. To implement this process, the recommended feedback sequence is:

A. The co-actor is asked, "How did your (friend, husband, wife, boss, etc.) make you feel?" "What were your reactions to him?" "What would you be likely to do if you really were _____ ?"
B. The observing trainees are asked: "How well were the learning points followed?" "What *specific* behaviors did you like or dislike?" "How was the co-actor helpful?"
C. The trainers should comment in particular on the following of the learning points, and provide social reinforcement (praise, approval, encouragement) for close following. To be most effective, reinforcement provided by the trainers should be offered in accordance with the following rules:
  1. Provide reinforcement at the earliest appropriate opportunity after role plays which follow the learning points.
  2. Provide reinforcement only after role plays which follow the learning points.
  3. Vary the specific content of the reinforcements offered.
  4. Provide enough role-playing activity for each group member to have sufficient opportunity to be reinforced.
  5. Provide reinforcement in an amount consistent with the quality of the given role play.
  6. Provide no reinforcement when the role play departs signifi-

*See Appendix A (Table 4) for a complete list of Application Tapes.

cantly from the learning points (except for "trying" in the first session or two).

7. In later sessions, space out the reinforcement you provide so that not every good role play is reinforced.

D. The main actor is asked to comment on his own enactment, on the comments of others, and on his specific expectations regarding how, when, and with whom he might attempt the learning points in his real-life environment.

In all these critiques, it is crucial that the behavioral focus of Structured Learning be maintained. Comments must point to the presence or absence of specific, concrete behaviors, and not take the form of general evaluative comments or broad generalities. Feedback, of course, may be positive or negative in content. At minimum, a "poor" performance (major departures from the learning points) can be praised as "a good try" at the same time as it is being criticized for its real faults. If at all possible, trainees failing to follow the relevant learning points in their role play should be given the opportunity to re-role play these same learning points after receiving corrective feedback. At times, as a further feedback procedure, we have audiotaped or videotaped entire role plays. Giving them later opportunities to observe themselves on tape can be an effective aid to learning, by enabling them to reflect on their own behavior.

Since a primary goal of Structured Learning is skill flexibility, a role play enactment which departs markedly from the learning points may not be "wrong." That is, it may in fact "work" in some situations. Trainers should stress that they are trying to teach effective alternatives and that the trainees would do well to have the learning points in their repertoire of skill behaviors — available to use when appropriate.

As the final feedback step, after all role playing and discussion are completed, the modeling tape can be replayed. This step, in a sense, summarizes the session and leaves trainees with a final review of the learning points.

Transfer Training

Several aspects of the training sessions described above had, as their primary purpose, augmentation of the likelihood that learning in the therapy setting will transfer to the trainee's actual real-life environment. We would suggest, however, that even more forthright steps need to be taken to maximize transfer. When possible, we would urge a homework technique which we have used successfully with most groups. In this procedure, trainees are openly instructed to try in their own real-life settings the learning point behaviors they have practiced during the session. The name of the person(s) with whom they will try it, the day, the place, etc., are all discussed. The trainee is urged to take notes on his first transfer attempt on Homework Report 1 (see Appendix D) provided by the trainers. This form requests detailed information about what happened when the homework assignment was attempted, how well the relevant learning points were followed, the trainee's evaluation of his performance, and his thoughts about what his next assignment might appropriately be.

As is true of our use of the modeling tapes, it has often proven useful (to insure success experiences) to start with relatively simple homework behaviors and, as mastery is achieved, work up to more complex and demanding assignments. The first part of each session is devoted to a presentation and discussion of these homework reports. Trainers should meet patient failure to "do their homework" with some chagrin and expressed disappointment. However, when trainees do attempt to complete their homework assignments, social reinforcement (praise, approval, encouragement) should be provided by the trainers. It cannot be stressed too strongly that without these, or similar attempts to maximize transfer, the value of the entire therapy effort is in severe jeopardy.

Of the several principles of transfer training for which research evidence exists, the principle of performance feedback is clearly most consequential. A trainee can learn very well in the therapy setting, do all his transfer homework, and yet the training program can be a performance failure. "Learning" concerns the question: *Can* he do it? "Performance" is a matter of: *Will* he do it? Trainees will perform as trained if and only if there is some "payoff" for doing so. Stated simply, new behaviors persist if they are rewarded, diminish if they are ignored or actively challenged.

We have found it useful to implement several supplemental programs outside of the Structured Learning Therapy setting which can help to provide the rewards or reinforcements trainees need so that their new behaviors are maintained. These programs include provision for both external social reward (provided by people in the trainee's real-life environment) and self-reward (provided by the trainee himself).

In several hospitals and agencies, we have actively sought to identify and develop environmental or external support by holding orientation meetings for hospital staff and for relatives and friends of trainee's — i.e., the real-life reward and punishment givers. The purpose of these meetings was to acquaint significant others in the trainee's life with Structured Learning Therapy theory and procedures. Most important in these sessions is the presentation of procedures whereby staff, relatives, and friends can encourage and reward trainees as they practice their new skills. We consider these orientation sessions for such persons to be of major value for transfer of training.

Frequently, environmental support is insufficient to maintain newly learned skills. It is also the case that many real-life environments in which trainees work and live will actively resist a trainee's efforts at behavior change. For this reason, we have found it useful to include in our transfer efforts a method through which trainees can learn to be their own rewarders. Once a new skill has been practiced through role playing, and once the trainee has made his first homework effort and gotten group feedback, we recommend that trainees continue to practice their new skill as frequently as possible. It is at this time that a program of self-reinforcement can and should be initiated. Trainees can be instructed in the nature of self-reinforcement and encouraged to "say something and do something nice for yourself" if they practice their new skill well. Homework Report 2 (see Appendix D) will aid both trainers and trainees in this effort. On this form, trainees can specify potential rewards and indicate how they rewarded themselves for a job well done. Trainees' notes can be collected by the trainer in order to keep abreast of independent progress being made by trainees without consuming group time.

Resistance and Resistance Reduction

As happens in all treatment and training approaches, trainees participating in Structured Learning Therapy will sometimes behave in a resistive manner. In one or more of a variety of ways, they may seek to block or avoid trainer efforts to conduct the session as we have defined it throughout this Manual. We have identified 18 different ways in which such resistance may occur. These types of resistance are listed in Table 1, along with brief mention of the general approaches to reducing such resistance which we have found useful. These several means for dealing effectively with trainee resistance are identified more fully in Table 2.

13

Table 1. Types of Trainee Resistance

I. *Active resistance to participation*
   1. participation, but not as instructed
   2. refusal to role play
   3. lateness
   4. walking out
   5. cutting

Reduce this resistance by: (a) empathic encouragement, (b) threat reduction, (c) instruction.

II. *Inappropriate behavior due to pathology*
   1. inability to remember
   2. inattention
   3. excessive restlessness
   4. bizarre behavior

Reduce this resistance by: (a) simplification, (b) termination of responses, (c) instruction.

III. *Hyperactivity*
   1. interruption
   2. monopolizing
   3. trainer's helper
   4. jumping out of role
   5. digression

Reduce this resistance by: (a) empathic encouragement, (b) termination of responses, (c) threat reduction.

Table 2. Method for Reducing Trainee Resistance

I. *Simplification Methods*
   1. Reinforce minimal trainee accomplishment.
   2. Shorten the role play.
   3. Have the trainee read a script portraying the learning points.
   4. Have the trainee play a passive role (responder or even nonspeaking) in role playing.
   5. Have trainee follow one learning point.
   6. Have trainer "feed" sentences to the trainee.

II. *Threat Reduction Methods*
1. Have live modeling by the trainer.
2. Reassure the trainee.
3. Clarify any aspects of the trainee's task which are still unclear.

III. *Elicitation of Responses Methods*
1. Call for volunteers.
2. Introduce topics for discussion.
3. Ask specific trainee to participate, preferably choosing someone who has made eye contact with leader.

IV. *Termination of Responses Methods*
1. Interrupt ongoing behavior.
2. Cause extinction through inattention to trainee behavior.
3. Discontinue contact and get others to participate.
4. Urge trainee to get back on correct track.

V. *Instruction Methods*
1. Coach and prompt.
2. Instruct in specific procedures and applications.

VI. *Empathic Encouragement Method*
Step 1. Offer the resistant trainee the opportunity to explain in greater detail his reluctance to role play, and listen non-defensively.
Step 2. Clearly express your understanding of the resistant trainee's feelings.
Step 3. If appropriate, respond that the trainee's view is a viable alternative.
Step 4. Present your own view in greater detail, with both supporting reasons and probable outcomes.
Step 5. Express the appropriateness of delaying a resolution of the trainer-trainee difference.
Step 6. Urge the trainee to tentatively try to role play the given learning points.

Prescriptive Utilization

While Structured Learning Therapy has been shown to be effective with many different types of psychiatric populations

varying greatly in their initial levels of skill deficit, its effectiveness
may be enhanced even further by responsiveness on the part of
trainers to special characteristics of the trainees with whom they are
working. For example, with long-term hospitalized patients – whose
attention span is short and whose motivation for skill enhancement is
low – we have adapted the procedures set forth earlier in this manual
by (1) having the trainers be more active and participate more
actively in role playing, (2) having the trainers offer social (token and
material) reinforcement more frequently and for lesser skill incre-
ments, (3) having the trainers begin thinking of reinforcements later,
(4) having shorter and more repetitiive group sessions, (5) having
fewer trainees per group, (6) paying more relative attention to
simpler levels of a given skill, (7) allowing more total time per skill,
and (8) requiring less demanding homework assignments. We urge
those using Structured Learning Therapy to consider implementing
analogous alterations in any and all aspects of this approach as a
function of the special needs, potentialities, or limitations of the
trainees they are trying to assist.

FURTHER READINGS

1. Goldstein, A.P. *Structured Learning Therapy: Toward a psychotherapy for the poor.* New York: Academic Press, 1973.
2. Goldstein, A.P. A prescriptive psychotherapy for the alcoholic
patient based on social class. *Proceedings of the second annual
alcoholism conference of NIAAA,* Washington, D.C., U.S. Department of Health, Education and Welfare, 1973. Pp. 234-241.
3. Goldstein, A.P., Gershaw, N.J., and Sprafkin, R.P. Structured
Learning Therapy: Skill training for schizophrenics. *Schizophrenia
Bulletin,* 1975, 14, 83-86.
4. Goldstein, A.P., and Goedhart, A. The use of Structured Learning
for empathy enhancement in paraprofessional psychotherapist
training. *Journal of Community Psychology,* 1973, 1, 168-173.
5. Goldstein, A.P., and Sorcher, M. *Changing supervisor behavior.*
New York: Pergamon Press, 1973.
6. Goldstein, A.P., Sprafkin, R.P., and Gershaw, N.J. *Skill training
for community living: Applying Structured Learning Therapy.*
New York: Pergamon Press, 1976.
7. Goldstein, A.P., Sprafkin, R.P., and Gershaw, N.J. Structured
Learning Therapy: Training for community living. *Psychotherapy:
Theory, research and practice,* in press.

8. Gutride, M.E., Goldstein, A.P., and Hunter, G.F. The use of modeling and role playing to increase social interaction among schizophrenic patients. *Journal of Consulting and Clinical Psychology,* 1973, 40, 408-415.
9. Gutride, M.E., Goldstein, A.P., and Hunter, G.F. The use of Structured Learning Therapy with transfer training for chronic inpatients. *Journal of Clinical Psychology,* 194, 32, 277-280.

APPENDIX A

Table 3. Structured Learning Therapy Modeling Tapes: Basic Skills

Series I.   Conversations: Beginning Skills
        Skill   1.   Starting a Conversation
        Skill   2.   Carrying on a Conversation
        Skill   3.   Ending a Conversation
        Skill   4.   Listening

Series II.   Conversations: Expressing Oneself
        Skill   5.   Expressing a Compliment
        Skill   6.   Expressing Appreciation
        Skill   7.   Expressing Encouragement
        Skill   8.   Asking for Help
        Skill   9.   Giving Instructions
        Skill 10.   Expressing Affection
        Skill 11.   Expressing a Complaint
        Skill 12.   Persuading Others
        Skill 13.   Expressing Anger

Series III. Conversations: Responding to Others
        Skill 14.   Responding to Praise
        Skill 15.   Responding to the Feelings of Others (Empathy)
        Skill 16.   Apologizing
        Skill 17.   Following Instructions
        Skill 18.   Responding to Persuasion
        Skill 19.   Responding to Failure
        Skill 20.   Responding to Contradictory Messages
        Skill 21.   Responding to a Complaint
        Skill 22.   Responding to Anger

Series IV. Planning Skills
        Skill 23.   Setting a Goal
        Skill 24.   Gathering Information
        Skill 25.   Concentrating on a Task
        Skill 26.   Evaluating Your Abilities
        Skill 27.   Preparing for a Stressful Conversation
        Skill 28.   Setting Problem Priorities
        Skill 29.   Decision Making

Series V. Alternatives to Aggression
Skill 30. Identifying and Labeling Your Emotions
Skill 31. Determining Responsibility
Skill 32. Making Requests
Skill 33. Relaxation
Skill 34. Self-control
Skill 35. Negotiation
Skill 36. Helping Others
Skill 37. Assertiveness

Table 4. Structured Learning Therapy Modeling Tapes:
Application Skills*

Skill 38. Finding a Place to Live (through formal channels)
Skill 39. Moving In (typical)
Skill 40. Moving In (difficult)
Skill 41. Managing Money
Skill 42. Neighboring (apartment house)
Skill 43. Job Seeking (typical)
Skill 44. Job Seeking (difficult)
Skill 45. Job Keeping (average day's work)
Skill 46. Job Keeping (strict boss)
Skill 47. Receiving Telephone Calls (difficult)
Skill 48. Restaurant Eating (typical)
Skill 49. Organizing Time (typical)
Skill 50. Using Leisure Time (learning something new)
Skill 51. Using Leisure Time (interpersonal activity)
Skill 52. Social (party)
Skill 53. Social (church supper)
Skill 54. Marital (positive interaction)
Skill 55. Marital (negative interaction)
Skill 56. Using Community Resources (seeking money)
Skill 57. Using Community Resources (avoiding red tape)
Skill 58. Dealing with Crises (inpatient to nonpatient transition)
Skill 59. Dealing with crises (loss)

*Each application tape portrays a model enacting three to eight Basic Skills, in a sequence and combination chosen to deal completely with a real-life problem

19

APPENDIX B

Trainee's Notebook for Structured Learning Therapy

Contents

APPENDIX C

Modeling Tape Format*

I.   *Narrator's Introduction*
   1. Introduction of self:
      a)   Name and title
      b)   High status position — e.g., Hospital Director
   2. Introduction of skill:
      a)   Name
      b)   General (descriptive) definition
      c)   Behavioral (learning points) definition
   3. Incentive statement — How and why skill-presence may be rewarding
   4. Discrimination statement — Examples of skill-absence, and how and why skill-absence may be unrewarding
   5. Repeat statement of learning points and request for attention to what follows

II.   *Modeling Displays*
Ten brief vignettes of the learning point behaviors, each vignette portraying the complete set of learning points which constitute the given skill. A variety of actors (models) and situations are used. Model characteristics (age, sex, apparent socioeconomic level, etc.) are similar to typical trainee characteristics; situation characteristics should also reflect common, trainee real-life environments. The displays portray both overt model behaviors as well as ideational and self-instructional learning points. Models are provided social reinforcement for skill enactment.

III.   *Narrator's Summary*
   1. Repeat statement of learning points
   2. Description of rewards to both models and actual trainees for skill usage
   3. Urging of trainees to enact the learning points in the Structured Learning Therapy session which follows and, subsequently, in their real-life environments

*See references cited under Further Readings for a fuller description of model, tape display, and observer characteristics demonstrated to enhance imitative learning.

APPENDIX D

Homework Reports

HOMEWORK REPORT 1

NAME: _____ DATE:_____

GROUP LEADERS:_____

FILL IN DURING THIS CLASS:

1. Homework assignment:

2. Learning points to be followed:

_____

FILL IN BEFORE NEXT CLASS:

3. Describe what happened when you did the homework assignment:

4. Learning points you actually followed:

5. Rate yourself on how well you used the skill (check one):

    a. Excellent _____

    b. Good_____

    c. Fair _____

    d. Poor _____

6. Describe what you feel should be your *next* homework assignment:

HOMEWORK REPORT 2

NAME: _____ DATE:_____

GROUP LEADERS: _____

FILL IN BEFORE DOING YOUR HOMEWORK:

1. Homework assignment:

2. Learning points to be followed:

3. Rewarding yourself:

    a. An excellent job will be rewarded with:

    b. A good job will be rewarded with:

    c. A fair job will be rewarded with:

FILL IN AFTER DOING YOUR HOMEWORK:

4. Describe what happened when you did the homework assignment:

5. Learning points you actually followed:

6. Rate yourself on how well you used the skill (check one):

    a. Excellent_____

    b. Good _____

    c. Fair _____

    d. Poor_____

7. Describe how you rewarded yourself:

8. Describe what you feel should be your next homework assignment:

Supplement B

Trainee's Notebook
for
Structured Learning Therapy

Robert P. Sprafkin
N. Jane Gershaw
Arnold P. Goldstein

Trainee's Name _____

Address _____

_____

TRAINEE'S NOTEBOOK
for
STRUCTURED
LEARNING
THERAPY

ROBERT P. SPRAFKIN
N. JANE GERSHAW
Syracuse Veterans Administration Hospital
Syracuse, New York
and
SUNY Upstate Medical Center

ARNOLD P. GOLDSTEIN
Psychology Department
Syracuse University
Syracuse, New York

PERGAMON PRESS/STRUCTURED LEARNING ASSOCIATES
New York • Toronto • Oxford • Sydney • Frankfurt • Paris

Pergamon Press Offices:

U.S.A.   Pergamon Press Inc., Maxwell House, Fairview Park,
                  Elmsford, New York 10523, U.S.A.

U.K.   Pergamon Press Ltd., Headington Hill Hall, Oxford OX3, OBW,
                  England

CANADA   Pergamon of Canada, Ltd., 207 Queen's Quay West,
                  Toronto 1, Canada

AUSTRALIA   Pergamon Press (Aust) Pty. Ltd., 19a Boundary Street,
                  Rushcutters Bay, N.S.W. 2011, Australia

FRANCE   Pergamon Press SARL, 24 rue des Ecoles,
                  75240 Paris, Cedex 05, France

WEST GERMANY   Pergamon Press GmbH, 6242 Kronberg/Taunus,
                  Frankfurt-am-Main, West Germany

Copyright © 1976 Pergamon Press Inc. and Structured Learning Associates

The preparation of this Manual was supported in
part by PHS Research Grant MH 13669 from the
National Institute of Mental Health. Their
assistance is gratefully acknowledged.

---

*All Rights Reserved. No part of this publication may be
reproduced, stored in a retrieval system or transmitted
in any form or by any means: electronic, electrostatic,
magnetic tape, mechanical, photocopying, recording or
otherwise, without permission in writing from the publishers.*

ISBN 0-08-021111-9
Printed in the United States of America

CONTENTS

*These are noted here because they appear in Notebook (8 pages of Skill Notes, 56 pages of Role Playing Notes, 8 pages of Homework Report 1 and 56 pages of Homework Report 2) but are not reproduced because copies are shown on pages indicated above.

A Note to Trainees

This Trainee's Notebook is yours. It is designed to help you learn as much as you can in your Structured Learning Therapy group. The notebook is divided into two parts. The first part contains information about what Structured Learning Therapy is and what you and your group will be doing. The second part of the notebook is the place for you to do some writing, both during your group meetings and between meetings.

INFORMATION ABOUT YOUR GROUP

1. Your Structured Learning Therapy group will meet on _____ at _____ o'clock. Your group leaders are_____ _____ and _____.
   You are expected to attend all group meetings and to arrive on time for meetings. If you cannot attend a meeting, please notify your group leader before that meeting.
2. At the group meeting, you are invited to say what you like about the topics which are being discussed.
3. All members of the group will be asked to participate in the activities of the group, including discussions, role playing, feedback, and homework.
4. It is important for you to listen and pay close attention when group leaders or other group members are speaking.
5. You are encouraged to write down notes on the pages provided in this notebook.

2

WHAT IS STRUCTURED LEARNING THERAPY

Structured Learning Therapy is a highly effective method for teaching you a number of useful *skills* that can help you to get along more successfully in your daily life. These skills will help you to feel more comfortable with yourself and with other people. Learning the skills well can help you to live a more independent and satisfying life.

The skills that are taught using Structured Learning Therapy are taught to groups or classes. When your group meets, you and your group leaders will follow certain procedures. These procedures are designed to help you learn new skills quickly and well. Listed below are the procedures you will follow:

1. *Discussion of new skill.* Your group leaders will help you to decide which skill should be taught first. They will discuss the skill with you and show you a series of steps which make up each skill. The steps that make up a skill are called *learning points*. You will receive a card or paper which has on it the name of the skill and the learning points for that skill. You can copy the information from the card into this notebook on the pages provided for *Skill Notes*. The next page is an example of a Skill Notes page.

Date: _____

SKILL NOTES

Skill Name: _____

Learning points:

_____

_____

_____

_____

_____

_____

_____

Notes: _____

_____

_____

_____

_____

_____

_____

_____

_____

_____

2. *Modeling.* After you have become familiar with the steps or learning points that make up the skill, you will listen to a tape recording or watch your group leaders demonstrate how a number of people use the skill well. This tape recorded or live demonstration is called *modeling* because it presents several models or examples of people using the skill. As you listen to the tape or watch your leaders, you will see that the models follow the learning points in order to use the skill well. During modeling, it is very important for you to do two things. *First,* listen for the learning points. Your group leaders will help you to do this by pointing out each learning point on the chalkboard. *Second,* think about situations in your daily life in which you could benefit from using the skill more effectively than you have in the past.

3. *Role playing.* The best way to learn a skill is to practice or rehearse it for the times when you will actually want to use the skill in your daily life. This practice is called *role playing.* Role playing is preparation or rehearsal for the real-life situations in which you can use the skill being taught. During role playing, you will be asked to do one of three things.

You may be the *main actor.* As the main actor, your job is to rehearse for a situation in your daily life by using the skill being taught. Your group leaders will help you to pick out a situation which you can role play. The main actor follows the learning points in the same way that the model did.

At other times, you may be the *co-actor* while another group member is the main actor. The co-actor's job is to help the main actor rehearse by responding in a realistic and positive way to what the main actor does and says. Your group leaders will help you to decide what to do and say as the co-actor.

A third thing you may be asked to do during role playing is to be an *observer.* As an observer, it is your job to pay close attention to what the main actor and co-actor are doing and saying during the role playing. Listen carefully to which learning points the main actor follows and which ones he fails to follow. Notice what the main actor does well and what needs improvement. Notice the ways in which the co-actor is helpful in rehearsing the skill. You can write down your observations on the pages provided in this notebook for *Role Playing Notes.* This will help you to remember what you observe. The next page is an example of a Role Playing Notes page.

5

Date: _____

ROLE PLAYING NOTES

Skill Name: _____

Main actor:. _____

Co-actor: _____

Describe role playing situation: _____

_____

_____

Learning points really followed:

_____

_____

_____

_____

What did the main actor do well:

_____

_____

What could the main actor do better?

_____

How was the co-actor helpful?

_____

Notes:

_____

4. *Feedback.* After the role playing has been completed, the co-actor, the observers, and the group leaders will share their reactions to the role playing with the main actor. This is called *feedback.* Feedback helps the main actor to see what he did well and what he may want to improve. Those group members who have been observers during the role playing can read what they have written in their *Role Playing Notes.* In learning how to use a new skill well, it is very important that the main actor get all the help and encouragement that he can. When you are asked to give feedback, you can be helpful by commenting on those things the main actor did well. If you have a negative comment, it will also be helpful if you say it and then offer some suggestion about how the main actor could improve or correct his use of the skill.

5. *Homework.* Since the skills taught through Structured Learning Therapy are useful in solving real-life problems, it is important that you use what you have rehearsed in real-life situations. Therefore, after you have role played a skill successfully in the group, you will be asked to try to use that skill outside of the group. Using the skill outside of the group is your *homework* assignment. The first time you practice a new skill outside of class, you will be asked to keep a record of your homework by filling out *Homework Report 1.* Once you have completed your homework, you will report back to the group on how you used your new skill. The second time, and all other times you use the same skill outside of class, you will be asked to keep a record by filling out *Homework Report 2.* Doing your homework is extremely important in order to learn a skill well and to enjoy the benefits of using that skill.

HOW TO COMPLETE HOMEWORK REPORT 1

In order for you to use the skills you have learned in the group, it is important that you practice those skills outside of the group in a number of real-life settings. This practice in real-life settings is called *homework.*

For your homework assignment, you will be expected to practice each skill after you have role played or rehearsed it in the group. After practicing a skill in the group, you will be asked to complete the first two parts of Homework Report 1. This Report has six parts altogether. *Before* you leave the group, you should complete parts 1 and 2 of this Report. You will be asked to fill in:

1. *Homework assignment.*
   Here you should write the name of the skill you plan to practice, with whom you will practice it, and where and when the practice will occur.
2. *Learning points to be followed.*
   Here you should write the learning points for the skill which you will practice. Do so even if you have written these learning points elsewhere in the notebook or have them on a printed card. Writing them down will help you to learn and remember them.
   After you have done your homework, fill in the rest of Homework Report 1. Do this by completing parts 3, 4, 5, and 6 of the Report.
3. *Describe what happened when you did the homework assignment.*
   Here you should write what you said and did, what the other person said and did, how you felt, and what the result or outcome was of trying the skill.
4. *Learning points you actually followed.*
   Here you should write exactly which of the learning points you really used.
5. *Rate yourself on how well you used the skill* (check one).
   a. Excellent _____
   b. Good   _____
   c. Fair   _____
   d. Poor   _____
   Here you should rate how well you did in completing your homework assignment. If you did your homework exactly as you planned in the group and followed all of the learning points, you should check *Excellent.* If you missed one learning point, you should check *Good.* If you tried to do your homework, but missed more than one learning point, you should check *Fair.* If you did not do any part of your homework, you should check *Poor.*
6. *Describe what you feel should be your next homework assignment.*
   Once you have finished practicing your new skill in a real-life setting, and in order to really learn your new skill well, it will be useful for you to continue to practice it. Perhaps you should practice in exactly the same setting as you did on this first assignment or perhaps you can think of another real-life setting in which you can benefit from using your new skill. In this space, write what homework assignment would be most useful to you in continuing to practice your new skill. Here are some examples of homework assignments completed by trainees in other groups.

HOMEWORK REPORT 1 – EXAMPLE 1

Joe was practicing the skill, "Starting a Conversation" for the first time. He decided in the group that his first homework assignment would be to start a conversation with the new aide on his ward. Therefore, on part 1 of the homework report he wrote down the name of the skill (Starting a Conversation), with whom he was planning to practice it (the new aide), where and when he was planning to practice it (on the ward on Wednesday evening). He also wrote the learning points for Starting a Conversation on part 2.

Joe carried out his assignment on Wednesday evening. Afterwards, he filled out the rest of his homework report. He wrote down exactly what he did (part 3). He remembered that he had missed one learning point (part 4), so he checked that he had done a *Good* job (part 5).

When Joe reported to the group, the other group members also told him that he had done a good job. Joe was pleased with the way he had done his homework assignment and felt good about himself for having started a conversation well. Joe planned to continue practicing his new skill by starting a conversation with his new neighbor at home. He wrote this plan under part 6 on his homework report.

Joe's homework report appears on the next page.

HOMEWORK REPORT 1

NAME: *Joe*   DATE:_____

GROUP LEADERS: *Ann and Robert*_____

FILL IN DURING THIS CLASS:

1. Homework assignment:

    Start a conversation with the new aide on the ward on Wednesday evening.

2. Learning points to be followed:

    1. Choose the right time and place.

    2. Greet the other person.

    3. Make small talk.

    4. Judge if the other person is listening and wants to talk with you.

    5. Open the main topic.

FILL IN BEFORE NEXT CLASS:

3. Describe what happened when you did the homework assignment:

I chose a quiet time on Wednesday night. I went
up to the aide and said "hello." He asked him
where he was from. I started talking about the
main topic (whether he would go downtown with me)
before I judged if he was listening. I felt
pretty comfortable talking, and he agreed to go
downtown with me.

4. Learning points you actually followed:

1, 2, 3, 5 — I missed number 4.

5. Rate yourself on how well you used the skill (check one):

    a. Excellent _____

    b. Good _____✓_____

    c. Fair _____

    d. Poor _____

6. Describe what you feel should be your *next* homework assignment:

Start a conversation with the new neighbor
at home.

11

HOMEWORK REPORT 1 — EXAMPLE 2

Mary was practicing the skill of "Giving Instructions" in the group. In the past she had had difficulty in giving instructions to her teenage daughter, so she decided to work on instructing her daughter on how to clean the kitchen floor properly. She filled in the first part of the homework report on which she wrote the name of the skill (Giving Instructions), with whom she was planning to practice it (her daughter), where and when she was planning to practice it (at home on Saturday morning). On the second part of the report she also listed the learning points for Giving Instructions.

After practicing the skill on Saturday morning, Mary filled out the rest of her Homework Report 1. She wrote down what she said and did, and what her daughter said and did (part 3). When she wrote down the learning points that she actually followed (part 4), she realized that she had missed two learning points. She decided that she had done a *Fair* job at giving instructions to her daughter (part 5).

When Mary reported back to the group, they agreed that she had done a fair job, and several group members made helpful suggestions on how she might do things differently. After discussing her homework in the group, Mary felt encouraged to practice the skill again with her daughter. She wrote that down as her next homework assignment (part 6).

Mary's Homework Report 1 is on the next page.

HOMEWORK REPORT 1

NAME: *Mary*   DATE: _____

GROUP LEADERS: *Robert and Ann*

FILL IN DURING THIS CLASS:

1. Homework assignment:

I plan to give instructions to Sally on how to clean the kitchen floor properly. I will do it on Saturday morning at home.

2. Learning points to be followed:

1. Define what needs to be done and who should do it.

2. Tell the other person what you want her to do, and why.

3. Tell the other person exactly how she is to do what you want her to do.

4. Ask for her reactions.

5. Consider her reactions and change your directions to her, if appropriate.

FILL IN BEFORE NEXT CLASS:

3. Describe what happened when you did the homework assignment:

I told Sally to clean the floor, but I didn't tell her exactly how—and I didn't consider her reactions very well. She didn't do a good job cleaning the floor and I felt a little angry at her and at myself

4. Learning points you actually followed:

I followed learning points 1, 2 and 4 but I missed 3 and I didn't do a good job on 5.

5. Rate yourself on how well you used the skill (check one):

a. Excellent _____

b. Good _____

c. Fair ___✓_____

d. Poor _____

6. Describe what you feel should be your *next* homework assignment:

I will try again to give instructions to Sally. This time I will tell her exactly how to clean the floor, and I will consider her reactions

14

After you have filled out your Homework Report, bring it to your next group meeting where you will have an opportunity to discuss it with the other members of your group. Your group leaders as well as other group members will give you *feedback* on how well you did your homework assignment. Group members will comment on how well you did your homework, and perhaps make comments on how you might have done it differently. Feedback from other group members may also help you to think about different ways to practice your new skill. Based on this feedback, you may want to revise your plan for your next homework assignment.

HOW TO COMPLETE HOMEWORK REPORT 2

Homework Report 2 is provided so that you will be able to continue to practice your new skill and learn it well. After you have role played a new skill in the group for the first time and then practiced it for the first time outside of the group (using Homework Report 1), you will be asked to keep a record of all the other times you use that skill outside of the group. You will use Homework Report 2 to keep track of the times you use this skill. Using a skill often is extremely important in order for you to learn the skill well and enjoy the benefits of using that skill. Homework Report 2 should be discussed with your group leaders, so that you and your group leaders can keep a record of how well you are practicing your new skill outside of the group. You will find that the more often you practice your skill in many different real-life settings, the more comfortable you will become in using your new skill.

The best way to learn your new skill as you practice is to *reward* your efforts when you use the skill well. A reward consists of doing something nice for yourself and saying something nice to yourself when you have done a job well. People tend to do things more frequently and more willingly after they have been rewarded for doing those things. By rewarding yourself for practicing a new skill, you will be more likely to want to practice that skill again in the future.

There are some important things to keep in mind about rewarding your efforts at practicing your new skill. *First,* choose your rewards carefully. A reward should be a special treat, and something special that you tell yourself. For example, if you want to reward yourself by buying something for yourself, be sure to buy a special thing that you would not have bought otherwise. *Second,* always reward yourself right after you do your homework successfully. Arrange your rewards so that you can enjoy them right away, or as soon as possible. *Third,* always try to reward yourself by doing something nice for yourself *and* saying something nice to yourself when you have done your homework well. For instance, when you practice your new skill well, you might want to buy yourself a special treat, like a dessert, *and* saying something nice to yourself, like "I'm proud of myself." *Fourth,* reward yourself frequently when you are beginning to learn a new skill. These frequent rewards help to encourage you to use the skill often. The more often you practice the new skill, the easier it will be for you to use it. After you have used the skill often, it will not be necessary to reward yourself each time you use it. When you first begin to use the skill, however, be sure to reward yourself each time you use it well.

Homework Report 2 helps you to continue to practice skills until you become very comfortable using them. You and your group leaders should discuss which skills you should continue to practice. Each time that you practice your new skill you should complete Homework Report 2. This form has eight parts altogether. Before you begin the continuing practice of your new skill, you should fill in parts 1, 2, and 3 of this form. Fill in:

1. *Homework assignment.*
   Here you write the name of the skill that you will continue to practice, with whom you will practice it, and where and when you will practice.
2. *Learning points to be followed.*
   Here you write the learning points for the skill that you will practice.
3. *Rewarding yourself.*
   Here you describe what you will do for yourself or say to yourself if you do an *Excellent* job, a *Good* job, or a *Fair* job. For example, you may write that an *Excellent* job will be rewarded by treating yourself to a good dinner and telling yourself that you are proud of the way you did your homework, a *Good* job will be rewarded by telling yourself that you did pretty well and by buying yourself a soda, a *Fair* job will be rewarded by telling yourself that you made a good start at working on the skill and that you will keep trying, and by treating yourself to a cup of coffee.

   After you have done your homework assignment, fill in the rest of Homework Report 2.
4. *Describe what happened when you did the homework assignment.*
   Here you write what you said and did, what the other person said

and did, and how you felt.

5. *Learning points you actually followed.*
   Here you write exactly which of the learning points you really used.

6. *Rate yourself on how well you used the skill* (check one).
   a. Excellent _____
   b. Good _____
   c. Fair _____
   d. Poor _____
   Here you rate how well you did in completing your homework assignment. If you did your homework assignment exactly as planned, and followed all of the learning points, you should check *Excellent.* If you missed one learning point, you should check *Good.* If you tried to do your homework, but missed more than one learning point, you should check *Fair.* If you did not do any part of your homework, you should check *Poor.*

7. *Describe how you rewarded yourself.*
   Here you write what you did for yourself and said to yourself as a reward for completing your homework.

8. *Describe what you feel should be your next homework assignment.*
   Here you write what homework assignment would be most useful to you in continuing to practice your new skill. After you have completed your Homework Report 2, hand it in to your group leaders. You may wish to discuss with them how you are doing on your continuing practice of your new skill. They may be able to offer suggestions for additional ways of practicing your new skill.
      Here are some examples of homework assignments completed by trainees in other groups.

HOMEWORK REPORT 2 – EXAMPLE 1

Joe decided that he should continue to practice starting more conversations. The next person he wanted to start a conversation with was his new neighbor at home. Therefore, he wrote down, on Homework Report 2 (part 1) the name of the skill (Starting a Conversation), with whom he planned to practice it (his new neighbor), and where and when he planned to practice it (on the porch at home on Saturday afternoon). He also wrote down the learning points for Starting a Conversation (part 2).

Joe also figured out how he should reward his attempts at starting a conversation with his new neighbor. He decided that he would reward an excellent job by treating himself to a night at the movies and by telling himself that he was proud of the way he did his homework; he decided that a good job would be rewarded by buying a soda for himself and by telling himself that he had done well; a fair job would be rewarded by telling himself that he was off to a good beginning at working on the skill, and by having a cup of coffee (part 3).

Joe was able to start a conversation with his new neighbor as he had planned (part 4). As he noted on his Homework Report, he completed all of the learning points (part 5). Since he had performed the skill exactly as planned, he rated his attempt as an *excellent* job (part 6). He felt proud of himself, and he told himself that he felt proud. Saturday evening he treated himself to the movie that he had wanted to see (part 7).

At his next group meeting, Joe handed his completed Homework Report 2 to his group leaders. Joe decided that he wanted more practice at Starting a Conversation so that he would feel even more comfortable with the skill, so he selected as his next homework assignment to start a conversation with one of the storekeepers downtown (part 8).

HOMEWORK REPORT 2

NAME: _Joe_ _____   DATE: _____

GROUP LEADERS: _Ann and Robert_ _____

FILL IN BEFORE DOING YOUR HOMEWORK:

1. Homework assignment:

Start a conversation with my new neighbor on the porch at home on Saturday afternoon.

2. Learning points to be followed:

1. Choose the right time and place.
2. Greet the other person.
3. Make small talk.
4. Judge if the other person is listening and wants to talk with me.
5. Open the main topic I want to talk about.

3. Rewarding yourself:

   a. An excellent job will be rewarded with:

   Go to a movie and tell myself that I'm proud of how I did the homework.

   b. A good job will be rewarded with:

   Buy a soda and tell myself I did well.

   c. A fair job will be rewarded with:

   Have a cup of coffee and tell myself I'm off to a good start.

19

FILL IN AFTER DOING YOUR HOMEWORK:

4. Describe what happened when you did the homework assignment:

I saw my neighbor on the porch at home on Saturday. I walked up to him, said 'hello', and told him my name. I asked him how he liked living here. He seemed to be paying attention, so I asked him if he would like to go to a ballgame with me. He said 'yes', and thanked me for asking. I felt real good about talking to him.

5. Learning points you actually followed:

1, 2, 3, 4, 5

6. Rate yourself on how well you used the skill (check one):

    a. Excellent_____✓_____

    b. Good _____

    c. Fair _____

    d. Poor_____

7. Describe how you rewarded yourself:

I went to a movie and told myself that I was proud of how I did my homework.

8. Describe what you feel should be your next homework assignment:

Start another conversation — this time with a storekeeper downtown.

HOMEWORK REPORT 2 – EXAMPLE 2

Mary decided that she needed more practice with the skill of "Giving Instruction" since her first attempt at giving instructions to her daughter had not been completely successful. This time she wanted to give better instructions to her daughter on how to clean the kitchen floor. On the first part of Homework Report 2 Mary wrote the name of the skill (Giving Instructions), with whom she planned to practice it (her daughter), where and when she planned to practice it (at home, on Saturday morning). Next she wrote down the learning points for Giving Instructions (part 2).

Giving Instructions was an important skill for Mary to learn and feel comfortable with. She knew that she had to practice it, and that by rewarding herself she would be able to encourage herself to practice it more often. She decided that if she did an *excellent* job at giving instructions to her daughter she would buy herself a new hat and tell herself that she was really proud of her progress. If she did a *good* job she would buy a cake for dessert, and tell herself that she was doing well at learning to give instructions. If she did a *fair* job she would tell herself that the practice was helpful to her and she would watch a special TV program (part 3).

After completing her homework assignment, Mary filled out the rest of Homework Report 2. She was able to give instructions to her daughter on how to clean the kitchen floor properly (part 4). She only missed one learning point (part 5). Since she only missed one learning point, she rated her attempt as *good* (part 6). Right after giving her daughter the instructions she told herself that she had done well and then went out and bought a cake for dessert (part 7). Mary felt that she still needed some more practice at giving instructions. She decided that her next homework assignment should be to give instructions to her daughter on how to prepare a meat loaf for dinner (part 8).

Mary brought her Homework Report 2 to her next group meeting and reported on her progress to her group leaders. They agreed that she was doing well and that continued practice at giving instructions would be helpful.

Mary's Homework Report 2 is on the next page.

21

HOMEWORK REPORT 2

NAME: _Mary_ DATE: _____

GROUP LEADERS: _Robert and Ann_

FILL IN BEFORE DOING YOUR HOMEWORK:

1. Homework assignment:

Give instructions to Sally on how to clean the kitchen floor at home on Saturday morning.

2. Learning points to be followed:

1. Define what needs to be done and who should do it.

2. Tell the other person what you want her to do and why.

3. Tell the other person exactly how you want her to do what you want her to do.

4. Ask for her reaction.

5. Consider her reactions, and change your directions to her if appropriate.

3. Rewarding yourself:

a. An excellent job will be rewarded with:

Buy a new hat for myself and tell myself I'm really proud of my progress.

b. A good job will be rewarded with:

Buy a cake for dessert and tell myself I'm doing well.

c. A fair job will be rewarded with:

Watch the TV special and tell myself that the practice is helpful.

FILL IN AFTER DOING YOUR HOMEWORK:

4. Describe what happened when you did the homework assignment:

I had decided that Sally should learn how to clean the kitchen floor right. On Saturday morning I told her that I wanted her to clean the floor, and I told her how. I checked to make sure she understood but I didn't give her a chance to react. Even though I missed the last learning point I felt that I did a good job in giving instructions to Sally. and the floor finally got cleaned.

5. Learning points you actually followed:

1, 2, 3, 4 — I missed 5.

6. Rate yourself on how well you used the skill (check one):

a. Excellent_____

b. Good _____✓_____

c. Fair _____

d. Poor_____

7. Describe how you rewarded yourself:

I told myself that I did well and I went right out and bought a cake for dessert.

8. Describe what you feel should be your next homework assignment:

I still need more practice Giving Instructions. I want to Give Instructions to Sally on how to make a meat loaf for dinner.

Supplement C
An Advanced
Structured Learning Therapy Session*

My name is Dr. Robert Sprafkin. Dr. Arnold Goldstein, Dr. Jane Gershaw, and I have developed a series of Modeling and Trainer Preparation Tapes for use with Structured Learning Therapy. The tape you will hear is a trainer preparation tape which demonstrates the running of an advanced group of people (many of whom have been hospitalized) who are being seen in an outpatient clinic. The problems that are being covered are the problems that confront people who are living in a community and attempting to deal with problems involved in living productive and satisfying lives. As you will recall, the components of Structured Learning Therapy are modeling, role playing, feedback or social reinforcement, and transfer training. In the tapes that you will hear, the modeling component involves the use of an application tape. An application tape involves the combination of a series of basic skills into a story line or into a process where they fit together and deal directly with a real-life problem situation applicable for the person. The skills that are portrayed on a given modeling tape are good examples of those skills that might be used in solving a particular problem. But the selection of specific skills for solving a particular person's problem is dependent on the nature of his problem. Thus, what you will hear is the group discuss and decide on which skills in which order are the most appropriate for solving a particular person's problem. Following this skill selection discussion, the stage is set and the role playing of the skills is begun. When the role playing is completed, the main actor is provided with feedback, or social reinforcement, and transfer training. It should be recalled that since this is an advanced session, the participants will have practiced the individual skills in previous sessions. However, they have never practiced skills in combination before.

Dr. Gershaw: O.K. Well, we've just finished listening to the Job Seeking tape which is one of the Application Series that we've been working on in recent weeks. And that was in response to your request, Alex, that we do start working on finding a job because I know that's a problem that you've talked about for some time now . . . that it's been continuing . . .

Patient 1: Yeah.

Dr. Gershaw: What we'd like to do now, as we've done in past weeks, is begin to talk about your specific problems in finding a

*Transcript of Trainer Preparation Tape #2

job, Alex, and for the rest of us as we listen to you talk about it, ask questions to find out what . . . the details of the trouble you've had and begin to look down our list of the Basic Skills to find out what skills in Job Seeking that Alex needs to practice. And then we'll put those all together and come up with a series of role playing skits. O.K.? Is that . . . does anybody have any questions about that? We've done it a couple of time before but, uh . . . is there any problem with that?

Patient 2: We've got to come up with what we think he wants?

Dr. Gershaw: Right. So, get your list of Basic Skills in front of you.

Dr. Goldstein: Needs . . . needs.

Patient 3: Or what he's got to be able to do?

Dr. Goldstein: Yeah. Those skills that would best help him actually go out and seek a job. So, it's as you say, uh, what he needs.

Dr. Gershaw: How about if you start at the beginning, Alex. And give us a little bit of background about the trouble you've had finding a job in the past and what the present problem seems to be. O.K.?

Patient 1: Well, uh, that's one of the problems. I have a hard time figuring out what I want to do for a job to begin with. Let's see, uh, it's always been difficult looking for a job. Well, for one thing, my parents usually go away for the summer and they really like me to come along and that . . . that's kind of . . . it's bad. I mean it's very hard to find a full-time job where you can be away for the summer.

Dr. Gershaw: Right. You can't . . .

Patient 1: They really like me to come along with them. And . . .

Dr. Gershaw: Nobody's going to give you two months off.

Patient 1: Also, my parents really feel that I shouldn't, um, just, you know, like take any kind of job. They want me to finish school. I was a Liberal Arts major and I've been taking courses on and off and, um . . . I did work for awhile. I had a couple of jobs through the employment office. Um, one of them was a shoe clerk but that didn't work out very good. I had a real hard time dealing with customers and I didn't really sell very many shoes. I . . . I . . . so I really don't know where to start. I, uh, I don't know whether I want to finish school or whether . . . I think I really want a job because I really would like to maybe move into my own place. My parents are supporting me. . . .

Patient 3: Yeah, but Alex, that's got to stop, sometime, and you really, you want to earn some money of your own. So, you know. . . .

Patient 1: Yeah, but I don't have a job right now. That's why I live with my parents. . . .

Patient 3: But, the idea is to get one — any kind, maybe to begin with.

Patient 4: He's got to learn to assert himself first, with his parents.

Patient 2: First he's . . .

Patient 4: You do whatever they tell you to do. Don't you think it's about time, you know. . . .

Patient 1: Well, they support me. I should really do . . . I mean I try to do the things that they . . .

Patient 4: Well, but if you get a job, you wouldn't have to be dependent on them.

Patient 2: Well, what do you want to do?

Patient 3: Yeah, what are you good at?

Patient 1: What kind of a job do you think I should get?

Patient 2: I think you want us to decide.

Patient 3: We can't do that for you.

Patient 4: Obviously, you're going to have to evaluate your abilities.

Patient 3: Right.

Patient 1: I don't know if I have any abilities.

Dr. Gershaw: So, Mrs. Nelson, you figure that's kind of the first skill that, uh, that Alex needs to work on?

Patient 3: Yeah, I think so.

Dr. Goldstein: That sounds like a pretty good idea. Do some of the rest of you think that would be a good starting place?

Patient 4: Yeah, he's gotta . . .

Patient 2: No, I don't agree with Mrs. Nelson. I think that at first he's got to make a decision.

Dr. Goldstein: Mmh, mmh.

Patient 3: I think he's got to assert himself first. He can't do anything until he stands up to his parents.

Dr. Goldstein: O.K. Now, let's see, we've talked about Evaluating Your Abilities, about Decision Making, and about Assertiveness. I think those are three good ideas and you should get some more. Let me write these on the board. We'll sort of put them all down — all the skills that you think Alex needs more training in, or practice in, and then we'll decide from that list which ones to include, and we'll arrange them in order. Let's go on, Alex, if you will, talking about . . . I'll be writing on the board . . . talking about this problem for you, this area, and let's see what other skills we can come up with.

Dr. Gershaw: I have a feeling that we need a little bit more information from Alex. . .

Dr. Goldstein: Yeah. . .

Dr. Gershaw: Kind of the specifics of how he gets into trouble. And then we can really get into the skills and see who he has to use them with and how he has to use the skills to find a job.

Patient 1: Um, what kind of trouble do you mean? Let me see . . . um . . . well, like I've said, I've only been looking for a couple of jobs and I . . . I got one through the employment office but it really wasn't anything I wanted and I didn't do well at it at all.

Patient 4: What. . . .

Dr. Gershaw: What happened . . . I'm sorry, excuse me, Mrs. Wolf . . .

Patient 4: Well, I just wondered what went wrong with that job. I always thought that would be kind of neat.

Patient 1: To work in a shoe store?

Patient 4: Yeah.

Patient 1: Oh, I don't know. People seemed to . . . you know, just really know what they want and I wasn't really able to sell them the things. . .

Patient 3: What, you didn't know where the things were?

Patient 1: No, I knew where the things were. I just . . . I guess I just wasn't a very good salesman is all.

Patient 4: How about Persuading Others, then you couldn't do that, right?

Dr. Gershaw: That's kind of once he got into the job, he couldn't hold on to it.

Dr. Goldstein: Right.

Dr. Gershaw: Let's . . . let's stay back one step from that and, you know, it sounds like one of the problems was kind of getting talked into a job that really didn't suit you. . . .

Patient 1: Yeah. . .

Dr. Gershaw: When you went to the employment office? You knew that when you went there that you really didn't want it, but you . . . somehow you wound up there anyway.

Patient 1: But I didn't know what I did want. That . . . I think that . . . you know the man at the employment office was really nice about it. He was really helpful and everything.

Dr. Gershaw: Could you tell us what happened when you went there, to the employment office?

Patient 1: Well, uh, he asked me, you know, if I'd had any experience, any kinds of jobs and what kinds of work I would like to do and I didn't have very many answers. I didn't really have any experience in anything and . . . the same problem as now. I didn't really know what I wanted to do either. So, he was just sort of . . . like you said, he was just sort of deciding for me. But I didn't know what else to do. He was. . . .

Dr. Gershaw: That's kind of what the group got into for a couple of minutes right at the beginning of decid . . . trying to help, uh . . . Alex make a decision before really finding out and then somebody, was it you, Mrs. Gill, said that he needs to do it for himself? No, it was you, Mr. Richmond. . .

Patient 2: Yeah, yeah. . .

Dr. Gershaw: You commented that we can't decide for him, that he really needs to make a decision . . .

Patient 2: Yeah, and I still hear him saying that he's . . . well, he's having problems with decision making and looking for other people to decide for him.

Patient 3: Well, he doesn't . . .

Patient 2: He doesn't really know what he wants.

Patient 3: He doesn't . . . he doesn't . . . really have a goal, almost. He says a job, but it's a very general kind of thing.

Patient 4: You know, if you go into the employment office and you know what you want, they never help you very much there.

Patient 1: If you want . . .

Patient 5: You got to know what kind of job you want . . .

Dr. Goldstein: Are you both saying, then, that Setting a Goal might be another skill to include here?

Patient 5: I think so.

Dr. Goldstein: Good, I'll put that down.

Patient 1: I still don't understand how you do that, when you don't know what you want to do? How do you set a goal?

Patient 2: You don't even know if you want to do anything. You know, you just sort of . . .

Patient 3: He sounds as if he's too afraid to make a mistake.

Dr. Goldstein: Let's pursue that a little. Would you go on about that, being too afraid to make a mistake?

Patient 3: Yeah, he's so afraid to make up his mind about anything, because he's so afraid he might not succeed at what he decides and . . . and he doesn't want to do anything wrong, it seems.

Patient 4: Yeah, he already screwed up once. So, he . . .

Patient 3: Well, a lot of times you have to make a mistake in order to, you know, in order to do what you're gonna have to do.

Dr. Goldstein: What kind of mistake do you think is . . .

Patient 3: Well, he might choose . . . well, say maybe that job wasn't you know, for him, so select another field, maybe . . . try something else.

Patient 5: This job that he tried, the shoe salesman?

Patient 1: What do you think . . .

Dr. Gershaw: Mrs. Gill, when you talk to Alex, talk to him and say "you" instead of "he."

Patient 5: O.K.

Dr. Gershaw: Otherwise, it's kind of like he's not here.

Patient 1: Do you have any ideas of what kind of a job I should look for?

Patient 5: I don't know, 'cause I don't know what you like, Alex.

Patient 1: Well, I guess that's maybe part of the problem, too. I don't know, really.

Patient 5: What are you good at?

Patient 1: I like the courses I take, but I don't know how that helps me with a job.

Patient 5: How about teaching?

Patient 1: I don't know . . . I never did anything like that before.

Patient 3: Alex, I don't remember. Do you have any brothers or sisters at home?

Patient 1: No . . . no . . .

Patient 3: Oh, you're an only child.

Patient 1: Yeah.

Patient 2: You said you like the courses you're taking but you don't . . . you don't know if it'll help you get a job. Well, then, why do you want a job?

Patient 1: Well, right now, I'd like a job because I think I would like to maybe move into my own place. My parents are really kind of demanding about my time and, uh, things that I do. I would kind of like to live in my own place but I really can't afford to. There's no way I can. And they're willing to, you know, they're telling me that, uh, that I can stay there as long as I need to and they're interested in me finishing school sometime.

Dr. Gershaw: That's what they want you to do?

Patient 1: Yeah, I think so.

Dr. Gershaw: We got a lot of information from you, Alex, and I guess where we're at right now is to figure out what you want to do rather than what everyone else wants you to do.

Patient 1: Yeah, right.

Dr. Gershaw: And the skills we've got up on the board so far that people have mentioned all seem pretty relevant. There was Evaluating your Abilities, figuring out what you're good at, what you're capable of doing; Decision Making about, I guess about a specific . . . what you're going to do. Um . . . Assertiveness. And . . . I don't know, how do people see Assertiveness fitting into this? In what way do you see Mr. Kovack needing more Assertiveness?

Patient 2: His parents. He's got to go up against them and tell them what he wants.

Dr. Gershaw: Tell them what?

Patient 2: That he wants to go out on his own. He wants to get a job, um, that he won't be able to go on the vacation, or um . . .

Dr. Goldstein: Yeah. Does that make sense to you, Alex?

Patient 1: Yeah, I think Assertiveness is a real problem. Not just with my parents, but I had trouble with that in keeping a job. I even have trouble at the employment office.

Dr. Goldstein: Yeah . . . the other skill on the board is Setting a Goal and, you know, I wonder if that might not — if we could start arranging these in some order — be the right place to start. Because we're talking now about the goal of getting a job. And, then, maybe, since we've just talked about the obstacle that in some ways your relationship with your parents is to doing that, that the second skill we might ask you to role play here is Assertiveness.

Dr. Gershaw: While we're talking about this, can you all get out the learning points for each of these skills? And we can talk about some of the specifics that . . . um . . . of the learning points if we need to discuss them with Mr. Kovack before he role plays.

Patient 1: May I ask you a question now about it? I've already got out the card on Setting a Goal.

Dr. Gershaw: Mmh, mmh.

Patient 1: The first thing says: Decide what you would like to accomplish. and the second one says: Decide what you would need to do to reach this goal. And, I'm a little mixed up on whether the #1 would be getting a job or moving out of the house? Because like . . .

Patient 3: Alex, I think what you . . . the first thing you want to do is decide that you want to be on your own, maybe?

Patient 1: That's what I don't know. Should I do that? Or decide to get a job?

Patient 3: Well, I . . . the reason why you're going to get a job is because you want to be on your own. Right?

Patient 1: Think that should be my goal?

Dr. Gershaw: You're saying the biggest goal that Alex seems to have mentioned today is being on his own?

Patient 3: Yeah . . .

Dr. Gershaw: The job would be a way to do that?

Patient 3: Right. And then that would be . . . when he gets down to learning point #5, that his realistic goal, in light of his circumstances, is money and he needs a job for that.

Dr. Goldstein: Hmm, hmm. O.K. That make sense to you?

Dr. Gershaw: Get what Mrs. Wolf's telling you?

Patient 1: Yeah, I think that's right. That's really what I want to do . . . what I really want to do is move out.

Dr. Goldstein: O.K. So, let's hold that for the role playing itself. But, let's say now, in continuing to arrange these skills, that you're through Setting a Goal and that through Assertiveness, a discussion with your parents, we have up on the board, Evaluating Your Abilities and that might be a logical third step, um, in preparation for actually going out and trying to get a job?

Patient 1: Yeah, huh, if I have any . . .

Dr. Gershaw: Can we all look at the learning points for Evaluating Your Abilities. 'Cause that seems to be a real problem.

Patient 4: Can I share with you, Mrs. Nelson?

Patient 3: Yeah.

Patient 4: Thank you.

Dr. Gershaw: Do you want to look at those and see what you think about those learning points, Alex, and see whether any of those will give you any trouble in terms of the role playing?

Patient 1: I think they all give me trouble. Um, just #1 − decide what ability you want to evaluate and, um . . . well, that's the whole problem, I don't know what abilities I have. I just don't know how to really get into this one.

Patient 3: Well, the first one is your ability to get a job, isn't that it?

Patient 1: Maybe. Is it?

Dr. Gershaw: What you're saying is that he's trying to evaluate his vocational ability?

Patient 3: Yeah . . . yeah . . . I mean . . .

Patient 2: O.K. Number two says: "Think about how you have done in the past when you've tried to use this ability."

Patient 1: Well, if that's it, like, I did get a job before . . . when I tried to . . . are we just talking about being able to get a job as an ability?

Patient 4: Yeah.

Dr. Gershaw: So, #2 would consist of what happened when you tried to get a job in the past and what's happened on those jobs − what the problems have been?

Dr. Goldstein: Right. We know that the learning points for this skill cause some difficulty for you and that's really why we selected it a few minutes ago. I think the question is: Is this the skill it would be good for you to have? We'll try to help you do it. If this is the skill it would be good for you to have, then we should include it in the role playing. What do you think about that? Do you think this is a skill that it would be good for you to have?

Patient 1: That's what I'd like to have.

Dr. Goldstein: O.K., then, let's do that. What we have now is a sequence of Setting a Goal, followed by Assertiveness, and then this one here, Evaluating Your Ability. O.K. I see Decision Making is also on the board. Let's hold on that one. Let's see if at the point we get through Evaluating Your Ability, it makes sense to go on to that or something else. What I'm suggesting is that we get started now with role playing this and that we start with the skill of Setting a Goal. Do you all have your learning points out?

All: Mmh.

Dr. Goldstein: And, uh, why don't we get to it?

After selecting and ordering the basic skills, Alex begins with the role playing. Remember that the emphasis is on helping the person solve a real-life problem. Alex has selected the skills but as you will see in what follows, he is not equipped to role play the entire sequence. Thus, he is helped by the trainers and the group to shift in mid-role play to a different skill which seems more appropriate to solving his real-life problem. The sequence ends with discussion, feedback, social reinforcement, and homework for transfer training. As you will hear, the skills thus covered are, beginning with Setting a Goal, then Assertiveness, then Evaluating Your Abilities. However, it's with this skill, that the main actor, Alex, has some difficulties. So he is urged to shift to a more appropriate skill, that of Asking for Help. Listen now as the role playing begins.

Patient 1: Um, let's see, I gotta figure out really what I want to do. Yeah, I think the thing that I want to do most of all is just to move out of my parents' house.

Dr. Goldstein: So that's the goal.

Patient 1: Yeah.

Dr. Goldstein: O.K.

Patient 1: I really want to do that. Now, let's see. In order to do that I would really have to have some kind of income. I'd have to have a job because they're supporting me now and I gotta . . . I really got to get a job before I can do anything else. Um, yeah, that's right. I have to get a job before I can do anything else. Um, yeah, that's right. I have to get a job first and then I could . . . I could think about moving out of the house. So this sounds like a good plan — if I can look for a job and then I can start thinking about moving out, but really I'd have to talk to my parents about this before I do anything. I guess that's the goal I really have to set right now — I'd have to have a conversation with my parents about the whole thing.

Dr. Gershaw: O.K. Well, we'll hold our comments on that for now, until you're all finished with the three skills, Alex. Uh, right now let's move on to the Assertiveness, which was the second one, and for that I guess you'll need a mother and father to talk to or do you need just a mother or? . . . who's the one that you really have to . . .

Patient 1: It would really have to be both of my parents, I think, but where . . . where in this thing do I talk to them? 'Cause it sounds like most of it I'm making my own. . .

Patient 2: # 4 . . .

Dr. Goldstein: The last . . . the last learning point.

Patient 2: . . . taking a stand in a direct, reasonable manner.

Dr. Goldstein: The first three are sort of getting ready steps and the fourth one would be tell them what you were getting ready to say.

Patient 1: O.K.

Dr. Gershaw: And we could even have your parents talking a little bit before you get into the Assertiveness steps — kind of them doing their usual thing about you and working — making some comments which I think will help you to get into that role, feeling kind of put down. O.K.?

Dr. Goldstein: You know, in here we try to pick people who are most like the people in your real life. Uh, who might take the role of your mother and father here?

Patient 1: Well, I think it would sort of have to be Dave here for my father.

Dr. Goldstein: O.K.

Patient 1: And, uh, I don't know either . . . I think it could be either Mrs. Nelson or Miss . . . or Sally Wolf could probably . . . either one of them could be my mother . . .

Dr. Goldstein: What characteristic of your mother, what feature of your mother are you thinking about as you decide who should play it?

Patient 1: Oh, I don't know. She's very positive; she always sort of knows what she wants to do and, you know, just says things the way she . . .

Dr. Goldstein: Comes out straight with her opinions?

Patient 1: Yeah, yeah, real . . .

Dr. Goldstein: Well, which of the two do you think fits that role best?

Patient 1: I don't know . . . what do you think?

Dr. Goldstein: Well, I'd really be interested in your opinion. I really want you to feel like it's your mother that you're talking to.

Patient 1: I think it would be Mrs. Nelson.

Patient 3: Yeah.

Dr. Goldstein: Fine.

Dr. Gershaw: Could you give us your parents' names?

Patient 1: Well, let's see, my Father's name is James. He prefers being called James; and my Mother's name is Margaret. She doesn't use a nickname, either . . . just Margaret.

Dr. Gershaw: Uh, huh. And what do you call them?

Patient 1: Oh, I call them Mom and Dad.

Dr. Gershaw: Why don't you give us a little bit more about your Father. I think we have some feeling for what your Mom is like — that she's kind of open and she says what she has to say and . . .

Dr. Goldstein: And strong opinions.

Dr. Gershaw: Yeah. And what about your Dad?

Patient 1: My Dad is an attorney. He has his own law practice. He's very active in the community. He's usually very . . . he's really busy most of the time, very businesslike and, my Mother, also — she doesn't work, but she's really busy, too. She's active in community groups and things like that.

Dr. Gershaw: Hmm, hmm. Who seems to make most of the decisions in the house?

Patient 1: Well, in the house, with things really affecting me, I guess my Mother does — I guess she makes the decisions.

Dr. Gershaw: O.K. Do we have enough of a picture of your . . . of James and Margaret — James over there, do you know who you are?

Patient 2: Yeah, I've got it now.

Dr. Gershaw: You've got a good picture of it? and Margaret?

Patient 3: Yeah, hmm, hmm.

Dr. Goldstein: O.K. Fine. Let's just catch us back up then. You've set your goal. The long-range goal may have to do with a job, but your goal now is to talk to Mom and Dad because you want to what? What's your goal?

Patient 1: Well, eventually my goal is to live out — to move out of the house — but I guess right now I've just got to tell them I want to do that eventually — I want to get a job, I don't want to finish school.

Dr. Goldstein: O.K. so here we are then. His Mom — his Dad . . .

Dr. Gershaw: O.K. To get you in the mood, Alex, what I'm going to ask Margaret over here to do is to start talking about why you should go back to school and, uh, is that something that she will typically be discussing with you if you spend much time around the house?

Patient 1: Yes, yet it is.

Dr. Gershaw: O.K. Well, what kind of words would she use? What would she say?

Patient 1: Well, um, she's usually talking about me finishing my degree and, um, that it really doesn't matter how long it takes me and that, well, they can afford to take care of me.

Dr. Gershaw: O.K.

Dr. Goldstein: O.K., let's get started. Mrs. Nelson.

Patient 3: James, I think you should talk to Alex. He's . . . I'm getting worried because he doesn't seem to be interested in finishing school. I think it's important the way things are nowadays that he finish school.

Patient 2: Yeah, I think so. I think your Mother's right. You do need a good education.

Patient 1: Boy, this whole thing is making me nervous — it's the same old routine — they're always trying to push school and like they're trying to decide what I should do and I . . . I just . . . I don't know — I'm kind of tired of being home all the time now. I just want to, you know, I have friends and they all have their own places and they don't have their parents around constantly, to make decisions for them, um, I don't know. It seems to me it would be so nice to have a job and be able to support myself and I really don't want to go to school right now. I don't know how I'm going to tell them all that without making it sound like I'm angry. I mean, I don't know . . . I'm not really angry. I just want them to understand that I want to look for a job now and not finish school. Maybe it would sound better if I told them that, you know, we've talked about this in group and everybody sort of feels the same way. But that's not . . . that's not really something I should tell them. That's my decision. Um . . . Mom.

Patient 3: Yes.

Patient 1: You know, you were just talking about me continuing school, right? And I've really been thinking about this a lot. And I think that maybe at some point I would like to finish school. I mean, I've really enjoyed the courses I've . . . I mean I like Liberal Arts and things, but I've been thinking a lot about maybe . . . maybe moving out to my own place and in order to do that, I've got to get a job first. So, I really think I would like to postpone maybe finishing school now, and I really want to look for a job now, so that I can move out on my own.

Patient 2: I don't know, son. You know, you've got to have a degree to get somewhere in this world. What are you gonna take, some kind of a dumpy job?

Patient 1: No, but really . . .

Patient 3: It's cheaper here . . .

Patient 1: Oh, I mean I really, you know, I appreciate what you're doing, you know, like supporting me and everything, but I really want to just be on my own for a while and that means just getting a job right now. And, uh, you know, I'd like to consider going to school later on.

Patient 2: Well, what do you think? Maybe he should be out on his own, Margaret?

Patient 3: Well, I don't know. I . . . I really would like to see him finish school. I think this is important.

Patient 1: Well, it's really important to me, though, to just maybe find a job now.

Patient 2: You won't get stuck in a rut and not go back to school?

Patient 1: I . . . I don't know about that.

Patient 2: I don't know. You know, Margaret, if he gets out on his own, we're here if he really needs us, you know, and wants to come back. Maybe he should give it a try.

Patient 3: Well . . . I like having you at home here and we'll miss you if you're not at home.

Patient 1: Well . . . I'll probably miss you too, uh, like I've really made the decision though to look for a job so that I can move out. I can still see you. I really do want to move out and that means getting a job.

Patient 3: Well, O.K.

Dr. Goldstein: O.K. That was the Assertiveness learning points. Let's move right along. The next skill is Evaluating Your Abilities.

Patient 1: O.K. Let's see. I'm sort of sitting in a mess right now, 'cause I'm not working and I want to find a job and I want to move out of the house, but I don't really know . . . I guess I've got to decide what kind of work I can do — what I could do for a living. I know like, in the past I've really only had two jobs and, um, I was able to get a job, but not for anything I really wanted and, um, I really didn't keep either one of them for very long. They just weren't things that I liked — they weren't jobs that I thought I could do well. And, um, let's see. I don't know if I can do this third one — "Get any outside information you can about your ability" — like, I don't know, I haven't really gotten any, you know, I've had the jobs, a couple of jobs, but I don't know anything about, I've never had any . . .

Patient 2: You've never had any vocational testing?

Patient 1: No, nothing like that. When I got out of high school, I started in college full time. And, uh, the only jobs I did have were just — well, they were both just jobs that the man at the employment office told me were available and I really didn't find out anything about my skills or abilities — I just applied for the job and I got it. I really — I've never — did anything to find out what abilities I do have.

Patient 2: Well, they do have — don't they — for — opened up these areas where you can go — places where you can go and get the testing done?

Patient 3: Sure they do.

Patient 2: For anybody?

Dr. Gershaw: It seems like what's happened here is we can't really move on in this Evaluating Your Abilities because you haven't really done step three like David suggested — you haven't really taken any tests or gotten any — or done any — gotten any assessment of what your capabilities are.

Patient 1: That's right. I haven't gotten any outside information.

Dr. Gershaw: So, we can't move on to # 4, because that says to use the information from step #3 to figure out what you can do.

Patient 1: Right. That's why I don't understand what I can do . . .

Dr. Goldstein: Maybe there's a . . . maybe you can move on in a little different way. You know how interested we are in this role playing becoming real practice for solving real-life problems. In this role playing you've set the goal, you asserted yourself and now you're getting ready to go find a job so you can move out. O.K. You don't have the information you need. What might you do at this point, then, in real life? What would be the direction you might take? Is there some other skill, for example, that fits in here?

Patient 1: Well . . . well, like Dave mentioned, there are places where you can get testing or . . .

Patient 2: Well, I'm not sure, but I . . . I . . . how would you find out? I had mine done in school — high school. You didn't have it?

Patient 1: I think I may . . . it seems to me they had services like that at the employment office . . . at the State Office Building. No one ever told me about it . . .

Dr. Goldstein: O.K.

Patient 1: . . . so I didn't ask.

Dr. Goldstein: This is sounding very much to me like one of the skills . . . one of the Basic Skills we practiced in the past — Asking for Help. Would that fit in there? Would that be the logical thing for you . . . to really do at this point?

Patient 1: Well . . . I guess maybe it would, but I . . .

Dr. Goldstein: Take a look at the learning points.

Patient 1: Well, "Define the problem that troubles you" . . . and . . . well, that's what we just said . . . I don't know what abilities I have and . . .

Dr. Gershaw: Right.

Patient 1: O.K. Then the second one says, "Decide if you want to seek help with your problem," which I do, I guess. Then, "Identify the people who might help you"; "Make a choice of helper"; "Tell the helper about your problem." Yeah, that sounds like it. That would be . . .

Dr. Goldstein: O.K., then why don't we just continue the role playing and why don't you do those learning points.

Patient 1: Right back to one?

Dr. Goldstein: Yes, please.

Dr. Gershaw: Can we figure out who's going to be your helper? Who in the room might play a good helper for you?

Patient 1: Well, let's see. I don't know . . . Colleen, maybe?

Patient 4: O.K.

Dr. Gershaw: So, when he gets to the last step, he will ask you for some help.

Patient 1: O.K. Let's see. The problem is that I was trying to evaluate my abilities, but I never really got outside information about . . . or I've never had testing or anything like that. Let's see, and then . . . but I do want to find out about it because I am serious about looking for a job. I don't know . . . people to ask . . . could possibly there be somebody at the employment office where I went before? Maybe even high school, I don't know, sometimes they . . . I think they might give counseling there, where I went to school. I don't know . . . do they have anybody here at the Clinic, that does that kind of thing?

Dr. Gershaw: Well, part time . . .

Patient 1: Well, let's see. I think probably I'm going to try the employment office again because I was there before and I know the woman who helped me out before when I went in. I could ask her about it. Let's see. Miss Jones.

Patient 4: Yes.

Patient 1: I don't know if you remember me or not, but my name is Mr. Kovack. And I was in here a few years ago, and I spoke to you once before and at the time, although I have the same problem now I had then, I don't . . . I don't know what my abilities are — at the time you told me about some available jobs and it helped me out in a way, because I got a job but it didn't work out very well. And I'm sort of at the point now where I'm trying to — seriously looking for a job — but I want to have some more idea of what maybe I could do well, and, um, it was suggested to me that maybe if I talked to someone here at the office you might be able to refer me to someone who could do like aptitude testing or counseling or something — just to get some better ideas of what I would be good at.

Patient 4: Yes, we have that service here. In fact, probably this afternoon we could probably do something for you.

Patient 1: I could be back this afternoon. About what time?

Patient 4: About one o'clock.

Patient 1: O.K. Who do I ask for?

Patient 4: Ask for me again.

Patient 1: O.K. Thank you.

Patient 4: Hmm, hmm.

Dr. Goldstein: O.K. Well, we've gone through now, three skills — part of the fourth and our goal is to help with this real problem of job seeking. What's your reaction to the way this role playing went? You've all role played with Alex.

Patient 1: Mine? or . . .

Dr. Goldstein: Well, let's hold yours for a moment and get the reactions from the group.

Patient 4: Well, I think if he could act the way he did just now, it would be a big improvement and I think it would help.

Patient 2: I think he has to keep in mind, like the card for Assertiveness, he did follow all the learning points.

Dr. Gershaw: Talk to Alex.

Patient 2: I think you're going to have to keep in mind that your parents might not give in as easily as perhaps we did and . . .

Patient 1: That's right . . .

Patient 2: . . . and not to give up. You know, you've made the decision, you've taken the stand and everyone . . . nobody's going to answer or respond exactly as we did.

Dr. Goldstein: When he was being assertive with you as the Father and you as the Mother, did you feel he was being assertive — did you feel he was taking a stand?

Patient 3: I did, yeah . . .

Patient 2: Yeah, I felt he was — a lot more than he was in the other discussions we've had just in this group.

Patient 3: But he needs a lot of practice in it, though. He needs to be really tough to make it in this world the way things are now.

Patient 4: It may not be so easy, you know, with your parents.

Patient 1: That's the part that I was kinda worried about. I feel good about this . . .

Dr. Gershaw: Do you think your Mom would give you a tougher time than Mrs. Nelson did?

Patient 1: Maybe not. She might not have said anything differently but she would probably get to me with her . . . I don't know . . .

Patient 2: You know, Alex, when you . . . excuse me . . . when you said something about being afraid . . .

Patient 1: Yeah, I really didn't sound angry, no. . . .

Patient 2: . . . of hurting them. . . . No, you didn't sound angry.

Patient 1: Well, that's . . . you know, I feel good about doing it — seems nice — but, like, that's the only part that I would worry about.

Dr. Gershaw: With the feedback that you've gotten from Dave and Mrs. Nelson, we'd say that you really have that ability to confront them that way — that you really have shown a whole lot of progress in asserting yourself in the months that we've been working on these skills here and that, uh, you were really able to convince them.

Dr. Goldstein: Do you think that this is something that you would actually want to try in the near future?

Patient 1: Yeah, definitely. I don't know, um, the whole thing sounds good — it seems a little clearer —

Dr. Goldstein: Huh, huh.

Patient 1: . . . where to start . . . 'cause I'm sort of in a bind right now.

Dr. Gershaw: You sort of finished the whole first step here today. You finished the step of setting your goal and the next step would be, I guess in the form of a homework assignment for you which would be to talk with your folks.

Dr. Goldstein: Yeah, it's tough, huh? But if that works O.K., if the outcome of it is pretty close to what happens here, then you'd be in a position to move on to the next skill you practiced, which is, taking further steps toward getting the job which would help you function alone outside.

Patient 1: Yeah, I think if I can get through to my parents anway, the rest of it won't be too bad.

Patient 2: Dr. Gershaw, do you think he should come back and do the evaluating of his abilities here with the group after he's gone for the vocational counseling?

Dr. Gershaw: Why don't you ask Alex what he thinks? Whether that would be useful to him?

Patient 2: What do you think, Alex? Think you should come back and do that here or . . .?

Patient 1: Maybe . . . uh, if I get to that point.

Dr. Gershaw: How far in this kind of big homework assignment of finding yourself a job, how far do you think you can get in this next week? What would you like to have for your specific homework assignment . . . to have ready for us next week?

Patient 1: I don't know if I'd like it or not, but I think maybe if I could get the conversation with my parents out of the way . . .

Dr. Gershaw: O.K. That seems like a reasonable thing to accomplish within the next week.

Dr. Goldstein: We'd be very interested in how it works out and we hope it works out well.

Dr. Gershaw: O.K. We've been working hard here for about an hour, why don't we take a break for about ten minutes.

Patient 3: Good idea.

You have just heard the role playing of an application series. It was proceeded by discussion, selection, and ordering of basic skills and even shifting of skills during the role playing. The main actor also required some coaching and stage setting by the trainers during the role play sequence. In contrast, in the sequence that follows, the trainee has thought through her problem ahead of time and has selected appropriate skills. Therefore, there is less discussion at the beginning. The skills however, are put in the proper order with the help of the trainees and the trainers. Most of the stage setting for the role playing is done before the role playing begins. There is a minimum of interrupting or coaching during the role play sequence. As with the previous sequence, the role playing is followed by discussion, feedback or social reinforcement, and a homework assignment or transfer training.

Patient 3: You know, over the break I was thinking about what Alex was talking about. I think I've got a problem with jobs, too, but, uh, I mean, I've had a lot of jobs, but I seem to ... I really hate going to the interviews and such. I seem to make a bad impression. I know that, in this group, we've talked about the way sometimes I come on in a kind of angry style or something. So maybe this is what it is, but I don't know, but ...

Patient 1: You don't seem to me like you'd have trouble. I mean, you seem like you'd be able to handle it ... you know, you seem like you know what you want, what you like, and that sort of stuff ...

Patient 2: Yeah, but don't you think — she does get a little bit offensive though.

Dr. Goldstein: You're not saying your problem is Evaluating Your Abilities, are you? You're saying something else goes on in looking for a job, and that's the problem.

Patient 3: Yeah. I know my abilities. It's just when I go for the interviews, and I have to go for a lot of them usually before I get a job. Anyhow, during the break, I picked out some of the skills I thought I would need to work on here and, um ...

Dr. Goldstein: For help in the job interview?

Patient 3: Yeah. And ...

Dr. Gershaw: Why don't you read them to us and I'll put them on the blackboard. O.K.?

Patient 3: O.K., yeah. Well, one is Self-control and another one is Persuading Others, 'cause I could persuade the interviewer and, of course, Preparation for a Stressful Conversation.

Dr. Goldstein: Mmh. Mmh.

Dr. Gershaw: You see those as the three main skills that you would need?

Patient 3: Yeah, I think so. I couldn't see how any of the others would ...

Patient 1: What do you mean by Self-control? I mean, do you get angry at the interview?

Patient 3: Well, sometimes they ask you nasty questions, you know, and I get mad or I tell them where to go, you know. ...

Patient 4: They're just testing your stability that way.

Patient 1: I don't think you should be telling me this before I go for my interview!

Patient 2: Keep up your sense of humor when you fill out those forms, you know. Like I always put down when they ask for sex, put down occasionally!

Patient 3: Oh! I'd die. I wouldn't do anything like that.

Patient 4: I can't see me doing that either.

Patient 2: Why not?

Dr. Goldstein: Well, listen, what do you think about those three skills that Mrs. Nelson is suggesting? Do you think that that combination would be a real help to her in having a successful outcome from a job interview? Self-control and, what were the other two now? Preparing for a Stressful Conversation and . . .

Dr. Gershaw: And Persuading Others.

Dr. Goldstein: . . . Persuading Others.

Dr. Gershaw: What order do you think those should go in?

Patient 1: I think maybe Preparing . . . that long one there — Preparing for a Stressful Conversation. That seems like the biggest. . . .

Patient 2: Well, that's the first thing that happens. She says she worries before the interview, so I think the first thing she's got to do is take care of the worry part. Then she's got to have some Self-control, so that would have to be second. The last one — Persuading Others. She's got to convince the guy that she's good.

Patient 1: Yeah, I agree. I guess that makes sense.

Dr. Goldstein: That make sense to you?

Patient 3: Yeah, that makes sense to me, too. At least we can try it that way.

Dr. Goldstein: O.K. Shall we do that? Would you care to indicate who in the group might serve as the interviewer when you get to that point?

Patient 3: Well, I think Mr. Richmond should be the interviewer.

Patient 2: Oh, you can call me Dave, you don't have to be so formal.

Dr. Goldstein: O.K. That won't be until the third skill, but fine. . . .

Patient 3: Do you want to get into what kind of a role you want the interviewer to play at this point . . . to set that up?

Dr. Goldstein: Fine. . . .

Dr. Gershaw: Can you tell us what seems to happen Mrs. Nelson, during the interview, that you start getting upset and angry?

Patient 3: You know, they just keep asking a lot of questions and sometimes my answers aren't very good ones and I start feeling like I'm looking bad and I get mad.

Dr. Goldstein: What do you get mad at?

Patient 3: Well, I get mad at me and I get mad at the interviewer.

Dr. Gershaw: Can you give Dave an idea of the kinds of questions that get you upset?

Patient 3: Well, one of them they always ask is why you left your other job and, um, then they ask you about times when you weren't working — like when I was in the hospital. And, um, well, they sometimes it's just their manner — they just seem real suspicious about you.

Dr. Gershaw: O.K. You kind of got the picture, Dave?

Patient 2: Well, I was writing it down and I didn't hear that last one.

Patient 3: They just act suspicious of you.

Patient 2: Suspicious . . . I know what you mean by suspicious but I don't know how a person would act in an interview.

Patient 3: Oh, you know, they would ask you if you're married and my husband left me, so they ask me why he left and all kinds of things and that's none of their business.

Patient 2: Becoming very personal, then.

Patient 3: Yeah.

Patient 2: Yes. I think I have the idea now.

Dr. Gershaw: So those are the things that you're going to want to rehearse first in the Preparing for a Stressful Conversation of how to deal with those issues and then when we get into the actual interview, you'll be doing the Self-control and Dave will be asking a bunch of questions about those matters which, uh, which do tend to irritate you.

Dr. Goldstein: O.K.? Shall we go ahead with that now?

Patient 3: Alright. Now, let's see. So I'm going to start with Preparing for a Stressful Conversation. Um, well here I am in the interview office, um, looking for a job and I'm, uh, not feeling very good because I don't like to go for interviews and they make me very upset. Um . . . and, of course there's usually this man there who's . . . who has to decide if I'd be good for the job and he wants somebody who'll be good and who knows what they're doing and who'll be successful so he doesn't have to replace them in a hurry. And, of course, he never met me before so he has to decide on that one time whether or not he wants to hire me. So, I . . . at first I tell him that I want the job and some of my background and that I have the right skills and I think that . . . he'll think that's good. And then he'll be looking over my application and that's when the problem comes in because he looks over my application and then he'll start asking me questions, um . . . about why I've had so many jobs and . . . um . . . maybe personal questions — questions about my skills don't bother me, it's the other questions that I don't like.

Dr. Goldstein: O.K. You're doing fine. Let me just interrupt to say try to role play what you would say, what he would say, so you could really be preparing for doing this. Why don't you continue.

Patient 3: O.K. Um, well he would say "I see that you've had a lot of jobs, um, in the last few years" and then I'd have to say "Yes," and this is where I start getting mad and I don't know what to say. I would like to tell him, like, that's my business, you know, or just not answer or ask him a question or, something. I guess it would probably be better though if I said something about I've had a lot of personal problems and I've been moving around a lot and that's why I've had a lot of jobs. And then he might ask me what kind of personal problems and I can just say, well, like they're all O.K. now. I got some help for them, and I just don't think I should go on and tell him what my problems were. 'Cause we talked about this in group. And I think that would be the best way to handle it.

Dr. Goldstein: O.K. Fine. Do you want to gon to the next skill now, Self-control. I think this is where you're going to come in, uh, Dave.

Patient 2: Right, yeah.

Dr. Gershaw: Let's give you a name, Dave. You could be Mr. . . .

Patient 1: Mr. Rotunda . . . .

Dr. Gershaw: Mr. Rotunda?

Patient 2: Mr. Rotunda. O.K.

Patient 4: . . . from Washington.

Dr. Goldstein: O.K.

Patient 2: Um, when I play this role do you want me to ask all these questions that get you upset or just one?

Patient 3: Oh, probably just that one about why I've had all the jobs would be a good one.

Patient 4: Personal . . . ask her some personal . . .

Dr. Goldstein: Let's start with that one and see how it goes.

Patient 2: O.K. And you can cut if off and go into the card − into the second skill, anytime.

Dr. Goldstein: Right.

Patient 2: Oh, Mrs. Nelson, good morning. You've come here for a job?

Patient 3: Mmh, mmh.

Patient 2: Let's see. I see by your application that you've had a lot of other jobs in . . . quite a few jobs in the last few years.

Patient 3: Yes, I have.

Patient 2: Why is it that you left your last job?

Patient 3: Well, see, this is when . . . when I start feeling angry and I . . .

Dr. Goldstein: Why don't you go into the role playing of the Self-control points now?

Patient 3: I feel as if I'm going to lose control of myself because I'm feeling angry because he asked me that question and I wish he wouldn't ask me that question. It's very upsetting and it makes me feel very, very frustrated and I just don't know what to do. I think what I have to do — I have to answer him, but I think I have to figure out a way to answer him that I . . . I . . . will make me feel more in control of the situation, so that I don't think he's put me on the spot. So, I think I have to practice answers to these kinds of questions. So when he asks me a question like that I can give him the right kind of answer. What I'll do when he asks this question is . . . I . . . I will say to myself I've practiced the answer to this and I'm prepared for this and it shouldn't upset me.

Dr. Gershaw: O.K. That was very good. Those were the learning points for Self-control and now you can get back to the interview and, you know, pull out the learning points for Persuading Others, which is really what you want to do there.

Patient 3: O.K. Well, Mr. Richmond should start. . . .

Dr. Gershaw: Right. Why don't you ask her that question again and then we can go on from there. Ask her the question about all of her jobs. And then Mrs. Nelson, you can get right into the learning points for Persuading Others and tell him about why you think you're the one for the job. O.K.?

Patient 3: Yeah.

Patient 2: I see by your application that you've had several jobs in the last year. Why did you leave the last job?

Patient 3: O.K. I really wanted this job but I don't want to tell him too much that's personal and . . . so I'm going to have to put myself out, though, some so he'll like me. But if he's going to be worried at this point that I've had a lot of jobs, and a . . . I think a lot depends on how I answer this to whether he'll consider me anymore. Um, so he's not going to be interested in someone who's had a lot of jobs because they haven't gotten along with people or seem to have a problem. But I do have the skills, so maybe I can convince him. Mr. Rotunda, I am really interested in this job and I do have the skills that are needed for the job. I know that, um . . . that I . . . that you are concerned about the number of jobs I have held in the past, but this was because I was moving around a lot and I had some very personal problems which have been taken care of and I am settled down now and I don't think I'll be moving around any more. I am very, very interested in this job and I have the skills and I think you'd find that I would be a good employee. I wish you would consider me and look at my application — would consider what's on there before you make your decision.

Patient 2: I think we could do that. You know, there's a lot of good people that are affected by personal problems and, um, we'll take that into consideration.

Patient 3: Thank you.

Dr. Goldstein: O.K. Fine, fine. Let's get some reactions or impressions of that. You were role playing the employer, what about this applicant?

Patient 2: Well, I thought that she . . . let's see, you want me to talk about all three points that she . . .

Dr. Goldstein: Yeah, why don't you.

Patient 2: O.K. Well, I thought that she did spend time in Preparing for the Stressful Conversation, dealing with her feelings of worry and tension before the interview, and she did discuss her . . . how she would handle her anger — her feelings of irritability. When she got into Self-control, she was very controlled. She considered why she felt that way — what was causing it and acted in a very pleasant manner. Um . . .

Dr. Gershaw: As the employer, you felt that she was pleasant?

Patient 2: Um, yeah, I thought that she was and, of course, hearing her go through the skills I could see that she was deliberately taking time to think about her feelings, explain them to herself, and more or less slowing down, which we talked about — or counting to ten. So that she was ready to persuade . . .

Dr. Gershaw: Talk to Mrs. Nelson and tell her what she did.

Patient 2: O.K. So that when you were trying to persuade me I thought you were very pleasant and you . . . you stated your position.

Dr. Goldstein: There was a key . . . a key step here that had to do with her answer to that question about the number of jobs. How did you as the employer feel when she gave you the answer?

Patient 2: Well, in the beginning I think I was almost a little bit ready to be a little defensive just to try and throw her off a little bit, but she . . . about these personal problems — but I thought that she, um, came across quite relaxed and I didn't think that I wanted to be defensive to you at all. And so I accepted that, you know, you gave me the feeling that I better think that other people have problems too and they do affect people's jobs.

Patient 3: Well, that's good to hear.

Patient 2: I liked it . . .

Dr. Goldstein: Does that give you some added feeling that you may want to actually go out and do this — do what you practiced today?

Patient 3: Oh, yeah, I'll have to. I have to look for another job.

Patient 2: Another comment, I think, on that personal thing — when I asked the question about the... when it was getting very personal — when you responded to me, you didn't make it the big issue of the discussion, so I think that by not responding in a flustered way that may have been what did it with me.

Dr. Gershaw: So you're saying by underplaying it that that really kind of got you off onto the . . . a different track which was . . .

Patient 2: That's what I wanted to say, right.

Dr. Goldstein: How about some of the rest of you. Any other reactions to how this went?

Patient 1: I think the whole thing went well. It just amazes me that like you were able to figure out what the problem really was — pick out the skills yourself. 'Cause I had trouble getting to that point. You know, I think everything came out really good. I don't have anything else to say about it.

Dr. Goldstein: O.K. That's fine. Uh, just as we ended Alex's role playing by urging him to try this by next week, would the same be possible for you? Do you have job-seeking plans, for example, coming up?

Patient 3: Yeah. I was planning to go down this Friday, so . . .

Dr. Goldstein: Well, our time is about up for today, but we'd be very interested at the beginning of our meeting next week in hearing how that went and we hope it goes well.

Patient 3: O.K. Thank you.

You have just heard two demonstrations of role playing following Application Series modeling tapes with trainees who had been meeting for some time. In both instances, the purpose of the role playing was the rehearsal of selected skills for real-life applications. The two examples differed somewhat in the amount of discussion, support, and coaching that was required, but both embodied the same basic elements of Structured Learning Therapy.

Supplement D
Resistance and Resistance Reduction in Structured Learning Therapy*

My name is Dr. Robert Sprafkin. Dr. Arnold Goldstein, Dr. Jane Gershaw, and I have developed a series of Modeling and Trainer Preparation Tapes for use with Structured Learning Therapy. The trainer preparation tape which you will hear involves Dr. Goldstein and Dr. Gershaw demonstrating a variety of techniques for reducing or eliminating a wide range of resistance behaviors which can occur in Structured Learning Therapy groups. The categories of techniques for reducing trainee resistance which you will hear include empathic encouragement, simplification, threat reduction, elicitation of responses, termination of responses, and instruction. With empathic encouragement, the trainer follows six steps: first, he offers the resistant trainee the opportunity to explain in greater detail his reluctance to participate and listens nondefensively. Second, he clearly expresses his understanding of the resistant trainee's feelings; third, if appropriate, he responds that the trainee's view is a viable alternative; fourth, he presents his own view in greater detail with both supporting reasons and probably outcomes. Fifth, he expresses the appropriateness of delaying a resolution of the trainer-trainee differences, and sixth, he urges the trainee to tentatively try to participate as instructed. With simplification, the trainer employs one or more of the following techniques: reinforcing minimal trainee accomplishment; shortening the role play; having the trainee read a script portraying the learning points; having the trainee play a passive role, such as a responder or even a nonspeaking part in the role playing; having the trainee follow one learning point at a time, or having the trainer feed sentences to the trainee. With threat reduction, the trainer uses one or more of the following techniques: he may use live modeling by the trainers; reassurance of the trainee; clarification of any aspect of the trainee's task which is still unclear.

With elicitation of responses, the following techniques may be employed: calling for volunteers; introducing topics for discussion; or asking specific trainees to participate, preferably choosing someone who has made eye contact with the leader or other indication of interest. With termination of responses, one or more of the following methods may be used: interruption of the ongroing behavior; extinction through inattention to trainee behavior; backing off contact and

*Transcript of Trainer Preparation Tape #3

getting others to participate, or urging the trainee to get back on the correct track. And with instruction, coaching and prompting may be used or instructing in specific procedures or applications may be used.

What you have just heard are the recommended procedures for reducing or eliminating training resistance. Now we can turn to the various categories or types of resistance which we will be demonstrating.

The first category of trainee resistance you will hear is called active resistance to participation. There are five types of active resistance to participation demonstrated. These include: first, participation, but not as instructed; second, refusal to role play; third, lateness; fourth, walking out; and fifth, cutting or absences. The recommended methods for reducing resistance in this category are: empathic encouragement, threat reduction, and instruction. In the first vignette that you will hear, the trainee demonstrates participation but not as instructed, which the trainer deals with by offering instruction in specific procedures and applications.

Dr. Gershaw: O.K. We're just about ready to role play. Mr. Fuller, we're going to be ... you're going to be the actor in this and you're going to be thanking Pam on your ward for buying you a package of cigarettes down at the canteen. Or, you said it was a carton of cigarettes that she had picked up for you.

Patient 1: Yeah.

Dr. Gershaw: ... and you were going to Express Appreciation to Pam for picking up that package of cigarettes. Let me just go over the learning points once more before we start the role playing. The first learning point: Clearly describe to the other person what he did for you which deserves appreciation. Tell the other person — # 2 is: Tell the other person why you appreciate what he did; and 3: Ask the other person if there is anything you can do for him. O.K.? You understand that you're supposed to now, the first thing that you're supposed to do is describe to Pam over there — Mrs. Krause is playing Pam — what she did which deserves appreciation. So that's the first thing you should do — tell Pam what she did that was nice. O.K.?

Patient 1: O.K. She, uh, got me, uh ... she got me a carton of cigarettes.

Dr. Gershaw: Right. Now you tell Pam — see Pam over there; Mrs. Krause is Pam. Tell Pam what she did that deserves appreciation. Talk to her.

Patient 1: You . . . you got me some cigarettes. Can't I . . . can't I just thank her?

Dr. Gershaw: Yeah, well that's what the learning points are. If you follow the learning points; you did learning point 1. And if you follow all the learning points they will add up to a thank you. That's what we had talked about after we listened to the tape. That all of those things together are what the title is: Expressing Appreciation.

Dr. Goldstein: You just said to Pam, "You got me cigarettes." See the first learning point. Describe to the other person what he did and so on. Well, you've done that. Now let's move on to the second learning point.

Patient 1: Um, well, she got them for me 'cause I couldn't leave the ward, so, uh, she got them.

Dr. Gershaw: Right, O.K., now why don't you tell Pam over here learning point 2. Say, "Pam, I couldn't . . .".

Dr. Goldstein: Yes, you just described to us why you want to thank her and that's fine but what we're doing is sort of play acting, trying it out, practicing it. We want you not to tell Dr. Gershaw and myself but we want you to tell the person who's playing that role of Pam why you appreciate it. So, would you actually look at her and tell her why, you know?

Patient 1: Um, I couldn't leave the ward so you got me the cigarettes.

Dr. Goldstein: O.K. That was very good.

Dr. Gershaw: O.K., that was learning point # 2. And now can you go on to do the last one? Talking to Pam now, don't talk to us. Talk to Pam.

Patient 1: Is there something . . . something she wants me to do?

Dr. Gershaw: O.K. Don't ask . . . don't talk to us. Pretend we're not even here. Talk to Pam.

Patient 1: Um, do you want me to do something? I don't know . . . she . . . she's not saying anything.

Dr. Gershaw: O.K. I think maybe that has to do with the fact that we were kind of breaking it up a little bit. Let's see if you can do the whole thing now, pretending that nobody's here but Pam. O.K.? So don't say "she," say "you," and say "Pam you did this for me," instead of "she did that." O.K.? So you just talk to Pam and Dr. Goldstein and I will pretend that we're not here and you just talk to her. Start with learning point 1, describing what she did and go through all of the together. O.K.? ·

Patient 1: Pam, you got me cigarettes at the store, um, because I couldn't go get them. Do you want me to do something for you?

Dr. Goldstein: Terrific. That's really very good.

Dr. Gershaw: Very good.

In the next vignette, the trainee refuses to role play. The trainer deals with this by expressing empathic encouragement.

Dr. Goldstein: O.K., so those are the learning points for Expressing Affection and, um, based on things we discussed before, in terms of some trouble getting close to people, that's a feeling I've gotten somewhat about you. I was wondering – Mr. Jordan, would you come up and try this one?

Patient 1: No, I don't think I need that one. I don't have any problem with Expressing Affection.

Dr. Goldstein: You don't think you need it? You want to tell us a little bit more about why you feel that way?

Patient 1: Well, I guess . . . who do I want to express affection to here? . . . you know they're all crazy.

Dr. Goldstein: I see. So it's your feeling that there's no one in the group that you want to express affection to. Is that it?

Patient 1: No. Not here or back on the ward or any place here.

Dr. Goldstein: Do you feel that there's also no one in other places that you want to say something warm or . . .

Patient 1: Well, I . . . I got a friend outside . . . but . . . but, uh . . . we're not affectionate.

Dr. Goldstein: O.K. We've included this as one of the skills because, uh, just about everybody, there are people – maybe there's no one in your life right now, that's certainly a possibility, but there are times and people in most people's lives when it is worthwhile and important – it is something worth doing to express affection and it is something we'd like you to do – to have in your collection of skills. It may not be something that you feel you want to use right now either in the group or back on the ward, but it's something that it might be very worthwhile for you to have and know how to do for such time as you do want to express affection to somebody.

Patient 1: I know how to do it, but there's just nobody . . . I don't feel like being affectionate. You know, when they're affectionate to me and they're nice to me, then I'll worry about it. I . . . I don't need it now.

Dr. Goldstein: Well, what would you think of the idea anyhow of coming up and trying these skills because even though it's not something you want to use right now, the time may come when it may be something very handy to know. And, you may be less familiar with it then than you'd want to be. Why don't you just give it a try? See how it goes? And, uh, maybe it'll be rewarding for you? O.K.?

Patient 1: Well ... I think it's foolish, 'cause I don't need it. But, O.K., I'll go along with it. I'll give it a try.

Dr. Goldstein: Let's see how it works out.

Dr. Gershaw: O.K. Real good.

Next you will hear the trainer deal with the problem of lateness. The trainer instructs the trainee in specific procedures and applications.

Dr. Gershaw: O.K., we're just about ready to role play. We're going to be doing the Giving Instructions learning points and Miss Barr, you were going to be giving instructions to one of the other people on your ward about keeping the room cleaner. O.K.? Miss Krause, I noticed that you came in kind of late. This is about ... well, I guess it's the second or third time that's happened. I wonder ... we were just about getting ready to role play. I wonder how it is that you're coming in 20 minutes late?

Patient 1: It's ... it's a long walk for me.

Dr. Gershaw: Yeah.

Patient 1: I ... I didn't know what time it was.

Dr. Gershaw: O.K. Well, let me say to you something that we've talked about before. Um, and that's that these sessions are really important and it's important for you to be here on time for them. Um, the reason is that you've missed a good deal of the meeting already, and I think these skills are very important ones for you to learn.

Dr. Goldstein: We said we can understand it can be tough if it's a long distance and you don't have a wristwatch and so on, but maybe you want to leave a little earlier? Maybe you can check with the nurse on your ward about the time? Because Dr. Gershaw is right, it really would be to your advantage if you could be here for the entire session.

Patient 1: Yeah. I ... I'll try.

Dr. Gershaw: O.K. That would be a help. Now I guess we can get back to ... let's see, we were just about set for the role playing. Can we get back to that?

Next you will hear a trainee begin to walk out of his session, which is dealt with with reassurance and with empathic encouragement.

Dr. Goldstein: Well, we've had now, let's see, four role plays of Expressing Anger and I think we're getting much better at it. By the way, the feedback that you're giving is very good. Let's see now, who hasn't tried this role? Um . . . Mrs. Cappellini, would you . . . Mrs. Cappellini?

Patient 1: You know I don't like to hear all this . . . I think I'll go back to the ward. It's quiet there, you know, uh. . . . My husband might come to visit, you know, and uh . . . I have to listen to him and he's noisy and I don't like hearing people talk about getting mad at other people. I . . . I'd really like to leave.

Dr. Goldstein: I see . . . well, uh. . . .

Patient 1: They told me I could leave if I didn't like the group.

Dr. Goldstein: Yeah, well . . . would you hold on one second? You certainly are free to leave. That's true. Would you hold on a second? Um, we'd prefer it . . . we'd like it if you'd consider staying because we think that this is a skill that would be useful, not only to the people who have gone already, but in terms of what you just said to us, maybe it would be something that would be particularly useful to you. We're talking about anger – you've said that you don't like to hear it in a group and I can understand – it can be unpleasant, but you've also said you don't like to hear it from your husband and this whole area of anger might be something that would be useful for you to have some skills in. We . . . you know we here keep everything in the group.

Patient 1: You want me to learn to get mad, is that it? I . . . I don't . . . I'd just really rather just walk away from anger, you know.

Dr. Goldstein: Right, right. No, we don't want you to learn to get mad. We want you to learn how to express it when you are mad.

Patient 1: Well, I usually walk away, and it works.

Dr. Goldstein: O.K. And that is . . . that certainly is one way of expressing anger. But, you know, we've tended to find that people who have a variety of ways of handling their feelings do a better job of handling them. Sometimes you walk away – like I think maybe you are doing now because maybe you're a little angry and upset about what's going on here. That's O.K., but another way to handle anger is to follow these learning points and express the anger and we think that it might be a good idea if you tried it. We would try to give you the kind of feedback that would make this a helpful experience for you, not an upsetting one.

Patient 1: You mean you're not going to make it a fight?

Dr. Goldstein: Well, you're going to be doing the role playing, and uh, you can make it pretty much what you want. We're interested in your following the learning points and whether or not it turns into a fight is really mostly up to you.

Patient 1: I don't know how to do it though.

Dr. Goldstein: Well, why don't you come on back and sit down and we'll talk some more about the learning points and we'll give it a try.

Patient 1: I'll stay for a little while, but I wasn't listening last time. I was too nervous.

Dr. Goldstein: O.K. O.K. We'll go over them again then.

In the next vignette, the trainers deal with the problem of absence by offering reassurance and by clarifying aspects of the trainees' tasks which are still unclear.

Dr. Gershaw: Well, I'm glad to see that everybody's here today. Miss Barr, we haven't seen you in a couple of weeks. I'm glad to see you back.

Patient 1: Mmh, mmh.

Dr. Gershaw: Has there been some problem that you haven't been able to get to the meetings?

Patient 1: Well, I don't know if this is really doing me any good, you know, coming . . .

Dr. Gershaw: Yeah, well . . . I wonder what that's about. Was there something that happened the last time that you were here?

Patient 1: Well, you told us to . . . to kind of think of things to say and you gave us these cards and all . . . and I don't know if I really understand it all that well.

Dr. Goldstein: You mean the cards with the learning points or do you mean the homework?

Patient 1: Yeah . . . that homework . . . that homework . . . was kind of confusing.

Dr. Gershaw: Do you remember which homework that was?

Patient 1: Yeah . . . we were . . . we were supposed to be kind of thinking of things to say at the next session.

Dr. Gershaw: Huh, huh.

Patient 1: Only I don't . . . I took them and I did look at them, you know, I did spend time, but I really didn't understand it all that well.

Dr. Gershaw: And that had something to do with your not being here the last couple of weeks?

Patient 1: Yeah, I didn't want to come unprepared, you know, and look dumb.

Dr. Goldstein: Well, the skill we were working on a couple of weeks ago was Expressing a Complaint. And, according to my records, that was the homework and this is the first meeting back. Yeah, that was the homework the last time we were here — Expressing a Complaint.

Dr. Gershaw: You know, a number of people in the group have had problems getting the homework done . . .

Patient 1: Yeah, but they all seem to know what they're doing when they get here.

Dr. Gershaw: I wonder if anybody can comment on that? I know Mr. Fuller, Mr. Jordan, Mrs. Cappellini — at one time or another you've had problems doing the homework or coming here without your lesson prepared. . . .

Patient 2: Yeah, I can't always do it.

Patient 3: Well, I had to come today. They told me that I'd probably be dropped from the class if I didn't, so that's why I'm here today.

Dr. Gershaw: I wonder what else you might do besides not come to class if you can't do the homework? How else you might handle that?

Patient 2: Get someone else to do the homework for her.

Dr. Gershaw: I guess that's one way of doing it. Mrs. Cappellini, what did you do when you couldn't do the homework, do you remember?

Patient 3: Mr. Jordan helped me.

Dr. Gershaw: Uh, huh.

Patient 3: And Virginia there . . . they're very bright.

Dr. Gershaw: They helped you to do the homework? And Mr. Fuller, do you remember what you did?

Patient 2: Well, I just waited until I got here and asked questions.

Dr. Gershaw: So, what everybody is saying, Mrs. Barr, is that they kind of asked other people for some help in getting the homework done . . .

Patient 1: Well, I thought we were supposed to do it on our own.

Dr. Gershaw: . . . they couldn't always get it done by themselves. Well, I guess there's not so much agreement on that, that you have to do it all by yourself.

Patient 1: If I knew that, you know . . . I probably would have been here last time.

Patient 3: Well, we got together and did it. I went into the coffee shop and Virginia was there and we all got together and did it in a room on the ward.

Dr. Goldstein: Yeah, we'd like it if you could come to all group meetings. We think you get something out of the group. We think you're a good group member and we'd like you to be here. And I think if you follow Dr. Gershaw's suggestion — try to do the homework on your own. If it's tough, try to get help from someone else in the group or us — all of those things are fine. But, if possible, we'd like you to try to attend all the group meetings.

Dr. Gershaw: How about if we start today's session by going over your homework and we can figure it out together. Do you think that might help?

Patient 1: Yeah, it would make me feel a lot more comfortable.

Dr. Gershaw: O.K. Let's do that.

The next category of resistant behavior is inappropriate behavior due to pathology. The specific types included here include first, the person who can't remember; second, inattention; third, excessive restlessness; and fourth, bizarre behavior.

In the first vignette, you'll hear an example of a person in the group who cannot remember some of the material covered. The trainers help him with this by coaching and prompting.

Dr. Goldstein: O.K. Those were some good ideas, Mrs. Cappellini. I wonder now if we can get some feedback from the group for Mr. Jordan? Um, Miss Krause, can you give us your reactions in line with the kind of feedback we've talked . . . we'd like to have?

Patient 1: It was O.K., I guess. I was watching, but I can't remember what she said.

Dr. Goldstein: O.K. Now we've tried to set this up so that it's our task to see if the main role player followed the learning points. Can you tell us if you felt Mr. Jordan followed the learning points in his role playing?

Patient 1: I can't remember.

Dr. Goldstein: Well, you know, it is sometimes difficult to follow what's happening, Miss Krause, but it would really be useful to whoever's role playing and to yourself if you could try as best you can to follow the role plays so you can remember. Let me . . . let me just repeat, uh, what you might want to try to do. When role plays are going on, keep the card that has the learning points for that role play in front of you; listen and follow what's on the card and you might even want to take notes. You see those pads in front of you? When someone follows the learning point well, note that down; when they depart or don't follow the learning point well, note that down and write how they did it wrong. So that when we get to this part of giving feedback, you'll have it all written down and you'll be able to give people like Mr. Jordan the kind of feedback that will be helpful to them. Do you think you can do that?

Patient 1: Yeah.

Dr. Gershaw: I think that's kind of a good idea for everybody to start writing down your reactions to the role play — writing down whether the people are following the learning points. You do have pads and pencils in front of you.

Next you will hear an example of inattention on the part of one of the trainees. The trainers deal with this by simplifying the procedures for the trainee; by having the trainee follow one learning point at a time and by feeding him sentences during the role play.

Dr. Gershaw: O.K. Mr. Fuller we were going to work on the role playing for Setting a Goal and you were saying that the social worker's kind of given you the word that you aren't going to be in the hospital much longer and she told you that you have to start making some plans to get out and that was what we were going to work on. So the goal that we're talking about is plans to leave the hospital. O.K. Do you want to get started with learning point # 1? All of this is sort of in your head out loud to the group.

Patient 1: What do . . . what do you . . . what do you want me to do?

Dr. Gershaw: O.K. Learing point #1 is "Decide what you would like to accomplish." And why don't you. . . .

Patient 1: I don't know . . . I keep talking about all kinds of things I gotta do . . . about a place to live and about money. I don't know what to do . . . I can't . . . I don't know, I can't seem to pay attention to this. I'm really . . . it's very confusing. . . .

Dr. Goldstein: You mean you're having trouble paying attention right now?

Patient 1: Yeah, there's so many things going on and I'm trying to think of a lot of things . . . I don't know . . . I can't . . . I don't even know what to do with one.

Dr. Gershaw: Well, that's exactly what this is about. It's to try to help you de-confuse things; to get yourself — your planning somewhat organized.

Patient 1: I just can't seem to pay attention today.

Dr. Gershaw: Let's start with just learning point #1. Do you want to read that out loud?

Patient 1: Decide what . . . decide what you would like to accomplish.

Dr. Gershaw: O.K. Can you answer that? What is it that you would like to accomplish?

Patient 1: I don't know. I want to go . . . I want to leave. . . .

Dr. Gershaw: You want to leave the hospital you think? O.K. Let's try this for learning point #1. You just repeat what I say. "I think I would like to leave the hospital."

Patient 1: I think I would like to leave the hospital.

Dr. Gershaw: O.K. That's learning point #1. Now let's move on to learning point #2.

In the following vignette you will hear an example of excessive restlessness on the part of one of the trainees. This is dealt with by shortening the role play for that trainee.

Dr. Goldstein: Well, let's see now, I think we're ready. We've gone over the learning points for Ending a Conversation and the stage is set, so Mrs. Barr do you want to get to it now? You and Mr. Jordan, right?

Patient 1: O.K. Then you feel that we should go to the movie tonight and I want to go shopping tonight. Well, I . . . I think that your idea was better. You got a cigarette?

Patient 2: Yeah, yeah, I got one.

Patient 1: Then we can finish this . . . I want a cigarette now.

Dr. Goldstein: You having a little difficulty staying in the role? I noticed you were getting kind of restless, during the last session. . . .

Patient 1: Yes . . . yeah . . . I really would like coffee too, to go with the cigarette.

Dr. Goldstein: Well, listen you did those first two learning points. . . .

Patient 1: Thank you.

Dr. Goldstein: You did those first two learning points well – you summarized the two positions and you drew a conclusion. Some of these can get a little tough to hang in there, but, uh, why don't you just go ahead; you've done a fine job so far and you don't have to make it very elaborate, you know or very long, but why don't you see if you can finish them up.

Dr. Gershaw: And as soon as you're done with that, we'll all take a coffee break, Mrs. Barr. O.K.?

Patient 1: O.K.

In the following example of bizarre behavior, the noisy, disruptive trainee is hallucinating. The person he accuses of speaking to him in a harsh way, in fact, is not speaking at all. The trainers deal with this by terminating his responses, by interrupting the ongoing behavior, and by urging him to get back on the correct track.

Dr. Gershaw: O.K. That was really very good, Mrs. Daley . . .

Patient 1: Thank you.

Dr. Gershaw: Um . . . Mrs. Barr, you were doing the role playing with Mrs. Daley, I wonder if . . .

Patient 2: Wait, wait, just a minute. You know, Mr. Fuller, if you want to say that, you know, say it out loud, 'cause you . . .

Patient 3: Say what?

Patient 4: Yeah, you know she was talking to me . . .

Patient 2: Say what you just said! You know, talking about me like that, 'cause I'm getting a little bit pissed off and I'm going to hit you right in the fucking mouth. . . .

Dr. Gershaw: Mr. Jordan . . . Mr. Jordan . . .

Patient 2: Yeah, what?

Dr. Gershaw: We had just finished up the role playing with Mrs. Daley. . . .

Patient 2: Yeah, but did you hear what he said to me?

Dr. Gershaw: Yeah, but I wonder if you'd listen for a minute?

Patient 2: I was trying to listen but he keeps talking about me.

Dr. Gershaw: We had just finished up the role playing with Mrs. Daley and we were asking Mrs. Barr how she reacted as the co-actor in the role playing.

Patient 2: Yeah, but . . . but I know that, but what he was saying was . . . was . . . had nothing to do with you. He was talking to me.

Dr. Gershaw: Yeah. I wonder if you could focus on what we're doing here and try not to pay attention to Mr. Fuller for a minute. O.K.?

Patient 2: I'm trying not to but did you hear what he said?

Dr. Gershaw: Did you listen to the role playing?

Patient 2: I couldn't hear it 'cause he was talking.

Patient 1: He's always interrupting. . . .

Dr. Gershaw: I wonder if you would read the learning points and then the rest of us can comment on whether Mrs. Daley followed the learning points. You have that in front of you, the learning points for Setting a Goal?

Patient 2: I'll do that if you'll tell him to shut up!

Dr. Gershaw: O.K. How about reading learning point #1 for us.

Patient 2: Decide what you would like to accomplish.

Dr. Gershaw: O.K. Real good. Thank you. Did Mrs. Daley follow those learning points?

The third category of resistant behaviors include those behaviors characterized by inactivity; specifically these would include apathy, falling asleep, minimal participation, and minimal ability to understand. In the first vignette what you will hear is an example of trainee apathy. This is dealt with by the trainers by various elicitation techniques, by calling for volunteers, by introducing topics for discussion, and by asking specific trainees to participate.

Dr. Goldstein: O.K. That was the modeling tape for Asking for Help. What did you folks think of that? What impression did you have of those learning points? The way the model on the tape went about asking for help? There are times when we've discussed it here. There's something you want from a nurse, a change in medicines you want from the doc, a pass, something about visitors. In other words, there have been times when you people have mentioned that you wanted to ask for help for something. Um . . . did the way you did it correspond to the way the model on the tape did it?

Dr. Gershaw: Did anybody ever find that they have had trouble asking for help?

Dr. Goldstein: Mrs. Cappellini, when Dr. Gershaw just said that, just by the look on your face, it seemed to . . . maybe it struck a bell with you? Is that something you've had problems doing?

Patient 1: Not in particular.

Dr. Gershaw: I seem to remember that you talked last week about getting your medicine changed and having a problem going down asking your doctor about that. Do you remember talking about that?

Patient 1: You talking to me?

Dr. Gershaw: Yeah.

Patient 1: Not especially. It was probably somebody else.

Dr. Gershaw: Does anybody remember Mrs. Cappellini talking about that?

Patient 2: Was it last week? I thought it was the week before.

Dr. Gershaw: It may have been. Do you remember what the problem was there?

Patient 2: Well . . . I don't know . . . well, wasn't it something about, um . . . just exactly how to go about it or . . . you didn't really want to take up his time, or something like that? I don't know . . . I don't remember. Patty, do you remember?

Patient 3: No, I don't remember.

Dr. Gershaw: Does it ring a bell for you, Mrs. Cappellini?

Patient 1: Ring a bell? Yeah. Yeah.

Dr. Gershaw: Do you remember what the problem was there?

Patient 1: Nope.

Dr. Goldstein: Was it in this area of some difficulty in asking for his help of adjusting the dosage of medicine you were taking? I'm pretty sure that's what we discussed.

Patient 3: Yeah, I remember what it was. You didn't want to ask him because you were afraid of him.

Patient 2: Yeah, I remember, that's right, that's it.

Patient 1: Could have been. . . .

Next, the trainers have to deal with a trainee who has fallen asleep. They do this by using various termination techniques, by first interrupting the ongoing behavior and second by urging the trainee to get back on the correct track.

Dr. Gershaw: Well, let's get to some discussion about the tape we just listened to, which was finding an apartment — Finding a Place to Live. Um, what did you people think of that tape? I noticed that Mr. Jordan seemed to be sleeping. Mrs. Barr, could you just poke him a little bit and tell him to wake up?

Patient 1: Mr. Jordan.

Patient 2: Mmh. . . .

Dr. Gershaw: Mr. Jordan, we're talking about the tape that we just listened to, which was Finding a Place to Live. I wonder if you could stay awake and participate in that discussion?

Patient 2: Well, I'll try . . . Um, I don't know . . . I'm tired.

Dr. Gershaw: I can understand that, but if you'd try to stay awake and listen to the discussion, I'd appreciate that.

Patient 2: O.K. I'll try.

In the following vignette, there is minimal participation on the part of the group. In this instance, it is dealt with by threat reduction, by live modeling by the trainers. Specifically, the trainers present the vignette and urge the trainees to follow the individual learning points.

Dr. Goldstein: It seems that most of you are having a little bit of a difficult time about this idea of Assertiveness and the idea of trying to role play. Maybe we ought to, Dr. Gershaw, do something in terms of some actual modeling by us, do you think? You know, as an example to the group?

Dr. Gershaw: Would that be helpful? If we had another example for you to listen to and watch? If Dr. Goldstein and I . . .

Patient 1: I think so.

Dr. Goldstein: Fine. We're going to try to enact the learning points with different content, but the same learning points you heard enacted on the modeling tape. And then we'll get you involved, at that point.

Dr. Gershaw: I remember you were talking, Mr. Fuller, a little bit about going out of the hospital on a pass one day and having trouble at the clothing store where you tried to buy yourself a shirt. Remember. . . .

Patient 2: Yeah. . . .

Dr. Gershaw: Remember talking about that? About how the salesman wouldn't pay any attention to you?

Patient 2: Yeah . . . he was trying to sell me something I didn't want.

Dr. Gershaw: I see. So, I had it a little bit wrong. He was trying to sell you a different shirt than you wanted? How about if Dr. Goldstein and I portray that? O.K.? And I will . . . I'll be the customer. O.K.?

Dr. Goldstein: Fine. I'll be the salesman. And I'll try to sell something that you really can't use.

Dr. Gershaw: O.K.

Dr. Goldstein: Let's say I've done that and you have to respond to that.

Dr. Gershaw: O.K. Well, what kind of store could we be in, where that would happen? Um . . .

Dr. Goldstein: How about shoes? A shoe store?

Dr. Gershaw: O.K. That's a good place. I'm sure people have encountered that. Has anybody here ever encountered that where you . . . don't want the shoes and the salesman keeps trying to sell them to you?

Patient 3: It's happened to me.

Dr. Gershaw: O.K., then, let's give that a try. It could be either shoes or a shirt or anything where you get kind of a hard sell from the salesman. So I'm . . . you're behind the counter . . .

Dr. Goldstein: O.K.

Dr. Gershaw: . . . and you showed me a number of pairs of shoes and I decided that I only want one pair and you're trying to sell me both pairs that I tried on.

Dr. Goldstein: O.K. Look, now those shoes you bought are nice but these shoes are really very nice, also. I really think you should take both pairs. Why don't you do that? The prices are good.

Dr. Gershaw: *Now, now wait a minute. I'm getting all upset here. I only want the one pair of shoes and he keeps telling me to buy two pairs of shoes. I really only want one pair. I don't have enough money for two pairs and I don't want two pairs. I think that's what's getting me so upset. He keeps trying to sell me something I don't want. I'm going to have to figure out what to do. I think maybe I just have to tell him that I just want one pair of shoes and that he should leave me alone and that if he doesn't get off my back, that I . . . that I won't take any shoes. He's really been bugging me for about 15 minutes here.*

Sir, I want this pair of shoes. I don't want the other pair of shoes. And if you don't want to sell me just the one pair of shoes, I'm just going to have to leave the store or talk to the manager.

Dr. Goldstein: O.K. That won't be necessary. I'll wrap them up for you.

Dr. Gershaw: O.K. Thank you. How did that sound to people? Were the learning points followed? Were you . . . did you . . .

Patient 1: It sounded alright.

Patient 2: Yeah, it sounded good.

In this vignette, one of the trainees is having a great deal of difficulty in understanding what is going on. In this instance, the trainers terminate contact by backing off and letting others participate.

Dr. Goldstein: Well, that was really a good role playing of this learning skill and your feedback, your discussion of it, very fine. Let's try another role play now. Mrs. Cappellini, would you come up now and role play these steps for Listening?

Patient 1: Listening? Huh? How . . . how can you role play listening?

Dr. Goldstein: Well, now, what we just did in the last role play . . .

Patient 1: I was listening.

Dr. Goldstein: You were listening? O.K. Now what we want to have you role play now is these learning points. Look at the other person. Show your interest by doing things, like nodding. Ask questions on the same topic.

Patient 1: I don't know anything about listening to ask questions.

Dr. Goldstein: The steps on the card in front of you?

Patient 1: It says Listening.

Dr. Goldstein: Right. Those four steps that are under the word Listening are the steps that make up what listening is. We want you to come up and try to go through those steps right here. Think you can do that?

Patient 1: What steps?

Dr. Goldstein: Let's do this. Why don't you observe — let someone else role play now. Why don't you watch what we do and you'll see again what steps I mean. And then we'll have you come up here a little later.

Patient 1: And then I'll listen.

Dr. Goldstein: O.K. Yeah. Mrs. Barr, would you care to come up now and try it.

Patient 2: O.K.

The last category of resistant behavior is hyperactivity. This includes the trainee who interrupts, who monopolizes, the one who acts as the trainer's helper, the trainee who jumps out of role frequently, and the trainee who digresses frequently.

In the first vignette, you will hear a trainee who interrupts frequently. This is dealt with by the trainers by extinction through inattention to trainee behavior.

Dr. Gershaw: O.K. We just finished the tape and let's see if we can get some discussion going about following instructions. How did people react to the tape?

Patient 1: Kevin, Kevin, sit down. Kevin, sit down. You're very distracting. I wish you'd sit down.

Dr. Gershaw: Mr. Jordan just got up and I guess he's doing some pacing, which has happened in the past in the group, and I think we kind of learned that if we pay attention to it that he paces for longer. So why don't we just not pay any attention to it, and have our discussion and when he's ready to come back he'll come back and sit down.

Patient 1: O.K. What was the question? I didn't even hear it because of him.

Dr. Gershaw: O.K. We were talking about the tape that we just listened to.

The trainers deal with the monopolizer in the following vignette by interrupting his ongoing behavior, by backing off contact and attempting to get others to participate, and by urging the trainee to get back on the correct track.

Dr. Goldstein: O.K. So we've just seen Mr. Jordan role play the skill that would help us ... this application tape — Positive Marital Interaction, that's what we've seen now. Let's get some comments now, from first you, Mrs. Barr, who he role played it with, and then the rest of you. How did that seem as he went through this?

Patient 1: Well, now wait. The reason I did it that way, you know, was because my wife and I ...

Dr. Goldstein: Mr. Jordan ... Mr. Jordan, why don't you hold on a sec. Let's get comments first from, you know, the person who role played your wife and then we'll get back to you a little later.

Patient 1: Well, I've got another one we can do, you know, on this ... using these same learning points.

Dr. Goldstein: Well, fine. We might want to get to that later, but let's follow our usual procedure and let's first get the comments from the people that observed. . . .

Patient 1: If we get two incidences right there, then maybe they can ...

Dr. Goldstein: Well, let's not right now. Why don't you just hold and we'll get back to you later. O.K.?

Patient 1: O.K.

Dr. Goldstein: Well, now, Mrs. Barr, in the role playing Mr. Jordan seemed to get a little angry at you, as your husband. How did that make you feel?

Patient 2: Well, I really reacted to that. I felt like it was happening, you know.

Dr. Goldstein: How did you feel toward him though?

Patient 2: Well, he made me mad.

Patient 1: Wait a minute. You know ... excuse me a minute. You know, I think that if we get into another one ...

Dr. Gershaw: Mr. Jordan, one of the rules of the group is for the person who role played with you to start to explain how they felt first. Then the group will talk and then you will get a chance to talk again. Right now, I'd like you to listen. O.K.? You've had your chance to role play and then you'll be able to talk. O.K.?

Patient 1: Alright.

The trainer's helper in the following vignette is dealt with by interrupting her ongoing behavior and by offering empathic encouragement.

Dr. Gershaw: O.K. Mrs. Cappellini, you were going to do the first role playing in Responding to Persuasion and what you said you'd like to do would be talk with your son who always tries to get you to baby sit.

Patient 1: Excuse me, don't you think that this would be something that would be more appropriate for Patty?

Dr. Gershaw: Well, why don't we try with Mrs. Cappellini first and if Patty would like to role play second, we can do that. Mrs. Cappellini did give us an example of a problem she has in always getting talked into baby sitting when she really doesn't want to and I think that that would be a real good one for us to role play.

Patient 2: I probably would anyway. I probably would baby sit. Maybe she's right.

Patient 1: Well, I'm only trying to help, you understand, but . . . I don't know, it just seems that it isn't something that's very difficult for her anyway.

Dr. Gershaw: I kind of think that we have to reserve judgment on that until after we see the role playing to see how Mrs. Cappellini does when her son tries to persuade her.

Patient 1: I see . . .

Dr. Gershaw: I appreciate your comments. Why don't we give Mrs. Cappellini a try with the role playing, if that's alright with you, Mrs. Cappellini. And then we can discuss how you do at it. O.K.?

Patient 2: Well, I'll give it a try.

Dr. Gershaw: Mrs. Cappellini, who in the group do you think should play your son?

Patient 2: Um, the man next to me.

Dr. Gershaw: And what's his name?

Patient 2: I don't know.

Dr. Gershaw: How about asking him?

Patient 2: What's your name?

Patient 3: Mr. Jordan.

Patient 1: Don't you think Steve would be better — a better choice?

Dr. Gershaw: Well, Mrs. Cappellini, what made you pick Mr. Jordan?

Patient 2: He's direct.

Dr. Gershaw: Uh, huh. And your son is like that? O.K. Why, Mr. Jordan, don't you come and sit over here and Mrs. Cappellini come and sit over here and . . .

Patient 1: I still think Steve would be better.

Dr. Goldstein: We, uh . . . we appreciate your suggestions, Mrs. Daley. I know you want to be helpful and that's nice, but the way Dr. Gershaw is setting it up with . . . arranging the role playing with Mrs. Cappellini, seems like it might be useful to Mrs. Cappellini in her actual interaction, getting along, and so on . . . so, why don't you hold off with your comments about this and then later if you'd like to make comments about how the role playing went and how well the learning points were followed, we can get to that later. Would that be O.K.?

Patient 1: Oh, sure, sure.

Dr. Gershaw: And, in addition to that, if you think there might be other ways that you think Mrs. Cappellini could approach these problems, we can talk about it then.

The trainee in the following vignette who continually jumps out of role is helped by the trainer's offering coaching and prompting.

Dr. Gershaw: O.K. I think we're ready to role play. Mrs. Barr, you were going to Prepare for a Stressful Conversation with Dr. Marshall about your pass. Are you . . . do you feel like you're ready to get started?

Patient 1: Yeah, I think so.

Dr. Gershaw: O.K. Why don't you start with learning point #1 — imagine yourself in a stressful situation.

Patient 1: O.K. *Well, tomorrow I'm going to ask Dr. Marshall for a town pass and, really, I know I'm going to be awfull nervous and I . . . I'm just a little afaid of him. I think I know why I feel that way too.* Wait a minute, uh, is that how I'm supposed to be doing this?

Dr. Gershaw: You're doing really fine. You just finished learning point #2 and now you can go on to learning point #3. And try to stay in role. Try to finish all of the learning points before stopping. O.K.?

Patient 1: O.K. *Oh, you know, he's awfully busy and that's probably why he always acts like he doesn't have time, you know, when I want to ask him these things.* Is that right? Am I doing it right now?

Dr. Gershaw: Yes. But stay in role and now move on to learning point # 4.

Patient 1: *I . . . I'm going to say to him, uh, I'm doing real well and everybody on the ward thinks so, and I think I really deserve a* *pass. I've been abiding by the rules and I'm going to O.V.R. and I think I've been doing everything right lately. Oh ... I'll just go in there and I'll say to him, "Doctor, I think I deserve a town pass. I really do."* Uh, is that right so far? You know, I'm not really sure.

Dr. Gershaw: Yeah, that's fine. Now keep going on to learning point #5 — what he'll say.

Patient 1: *Well, I just have a feeling he's going to say no. And then I'll just ... I'll just try to reason with him. And maybe I can persuade him.* Is that right so far?

Dr. Gershaw: Yeah. Now, you got through learning point #5 and you can now go back. Learning point # 6 say "repeat the above steps, using as many approaches as you can think of." So, would you like to try doing it another way? Approaching him in a different way?

Patient 1: O.K. *If he definitely tells me no, I'll just say, "O.K., then maybe I'll ask you next week. Maybe you'll be more confident in me then." Maybe he'll go along with that.*

In the following vignette, the trainee who digresses continually is urged by the trainers to get back on the correct track.

Dr. Gershaw: Well, how did Mr. Fuller do on the role playing? Did he follow the learning points?

Patient 1: Well, you know, it wasn't bad, but I noticed that it's very similar to the situation I have on the ward. I've got a complaint about something to somebody and they just don't want to listen. You try to talk to them about it and they just get irritable and, uh ...

Dr. Gershaw: Yeah. Mr. Jordan, maybe that will be one that you will want to role play later. How did Mr. Fuller do on the learning points?

Patient 1: Well, he ... he did good, but let me tell you about what happened to me, on ... on my ward, about when I was sitting down and I was trying to talk with this employee. It really made me angry and he really wouldn't listen and, oh, that reminds me of a situation ... when I was home ...

Dr. Goldstein: Mr. Jordan, excuse me. I think what you just started to talk about at home, is important to you and we're going to want to get involved in talking to you about that, and role playing that, but not right now. Let's stick with the business at hand. Mr. Fuller has role played this situation as it applies to him and we really want reactions from the group, including yourself, as to how well he followed the learning points. So, could we stay on that topic now?

Patient 1: I thought he was real good, but you know, it did remind me of the situation that happened at home. It really got hot, and, uh . . .

Dr. Gershaw: One of the rules of our group, Mr. Jordan, is to try to stick with the one thing that we're talking about until we're finished with it and then we can get on to something else. If we get on to your subject right now, I think we're all going to forget about the role playing that just happened. So, let's try to stick with that and go through how he followed the learning points and any comments we might have about how Mr. Fuller did with the role playing he just did.

Patient 1: Alright. O.K.

You have heard a variety of examples of the ways in which trainees can be resistive in Structured Learning Therapy groups. You have also heard demonstrated a number of techniques for dealing with these resistant behaviors. Effective use of these resistance-reducing techniques has been shown to result in more rapid and more effective trainee skill learning in Structured Learning Therapy.

Supplement E
Skill Surveys

FORM S   *SKILL SURVEY*   Patient: _____
                                                      Age: _____

   We are planning to run a series of classes at the hospital which are
geared toward teaching patients a variety of interpersonal and planning skills. These skills have been shown to be important for both
in-hospital adjustment and in determining whether a patient "makes
it" in the community following his discharge from the hospital.
   In order to get the classes started, we need to know what skills
your patients are good at and what skills they need work on. As a
staff person working closely with patients, we believe that your
assessment of their strengths and weaknesses will be most accurate
and up to date.
   Please rate the patient whose name appears at the top of the page
by circling one number for each skill.
   Circle 1, if the patient is *never* good at using the skill.
   Circle 2, if the patient is *seldom* good at using the skill.
   Circle 3, if the patient is *sometimes* good at using the skill.
   Circle 4, if the patient is *often* good at using the skill.
   Circle 5, if the patient is *always* good at using the skill.
   Do not mark those skills for which you have no information on
the patient's ability. Thank you for your cooperation.

SKILLS
   1. *Starting a Conversation:* Talking to someone
      about light topics and then leading into more
      serious topics.   1 2 3 4 5
   2. *Carrying on a Conversation:* Opening the main
      topic, elaborating on it, and responding to the
      reactions of the person you are talking to.   1 2 3 4 5
   3. *Ending a Conversation:* Letting the other per-
      son know that you have been paying attention,
      and then closing the conversation appropri-
      ately.   1 2 3 4 5
   4. *Listening:* Paying attention to people, trying to
      understand them, and letting them know you
      are trying.   1 2 3 4 5

5. *Expressing a Compliment:* Telling someone that you like something about him or about his actions.　　　　1 2 3 4 5

6. *Expressing Appreciation:* Letting another person know that you are grateful for something he has done for you.　　　　1 2 3 4 5

7. *Expressing Encouragement:* Telling someone that he should try to do something which he is not sure that he can do.　　　　1 2 3 4 5

8. *Asking for Help:* Requesting that someone who is qualified help you in handling a difficult situation which you have not been able to manage by yourself.　　　　1 2 3 4 5

9. *Giving Instructions:* Clearly explaining to someone how you would like a specific task done.　　　　1 2 3 4 5

10. *Expressing Affection:* Letting someone know that you care about him or her.　　　　1 2 3 4 5

11. *Expressing a Complaint:* Telling someone that he is responsible for creating a particular problem for you and attempting to find a solution for the problem.　　　　1 2 3 4 5

12. *Persuading Others:* Attempting to convince another person that your ideas are better and will be more useful than his.　　　　1 2 3 4 5

13. *Expressing Anger:* Presenting your angry feelings in a direct and honest manner.　　　　1 2 3 4 5

14. *Responding to Praise:* Letting a person know that you are pleased with his praise and that you appreciate it.　　　　1 2 3 4 5

15. *Responding to the Feelings of Others:* Trying to understand what the other person is feeling and communicating your understanding to him.　　　　1 2 3 4 5

16. *Apologizing:* Telling someone sincerely that you are sorry for something you have done to cause him discomfort.　　　　1 2 3 4 5

17. *Following Instructions:* Carrying out directions in a competent manner and giving your reactions.　　　　1 2 3 4 5

18. *Responding to Persuasion:* Carefully considering another person's ideas, weighing them against your own, and then deciding which course of action will be best for you in the long run.   1 2 3 4 5
19. *Responding to Failure:* Figuring out what went wrong and what you can do about it so that you can be more successful in the future.   1 2 3 4 5
20. *Responding to Contradictory Messages:* Recognizing and dealing with confusion that results when a person tells you one thing but says or does things which indicate that he means something else.   1 2 3 4 5
21. *Responding to a Complaint:* Dealing fairly with another person's dissatisfaction with a situation attributed to you.   1 2 3 4 5
22. *Responding to Anger:* Trying to understand another person's anger and letting him know that you are trying.   1 2 3 4 5
23. *Setting a Goal:* Deciding on what you would like to accomplish and judging whether your plan is realistic.   1 2 3 4 5
24. *Gathering Information:* Deciding what specific information you need and asking the appropriate people for that information.   1 2 3 4 5
25. *Concentrating on a Task:* Making those preparations that will enable you to get a job done efficiently.   1 2 3 4 5
26. *Evaluating Your Abilities:* Examining your accomplishment fairly and honestly in order to decide how competent you are in a particular skill.   1 2 3 4 5
27. *Preparing for a Stressful Conversation:* Planning ahead of time to present your point of view in a conversation which may be difficult.   1 2 3 4 5
28. *Setting Problem Priorities:* Deciding which of several problems is most urgent and should be worked on first.   1 2 3 4 5
29. *Decision Making:* Deciding on a realistic course of action which you believe will be in your best interest.   1 2 3 4 5

30. *Identifying and Labeling Your Emotions:* Recognizing which emotion you are feeling. 1 2 3 4 5
31. *Determining Responsibility:* Finding out whether your actions or the actions of others have caused an event to occur. 1 2 3 4 5
32. *Making Requests:* Asking the appropriate person for what you need or want. 1 2 3 4 5
33. *Relaxation:* Learning to calm down and relax when you are tense. 1 2 3 4 5
34. *Self-control:* Controlling your temper before things get out of hand. 1 2 3 4 5
35. *Negotiation:* Arriving at an agreement which is satisfactory to you and to another person who has taken a different position. 1 2 3 4 5
36. *Helping Others:* Aiding others who are having difficulty handling a situation by themselves. 1 2 3 4 5

FORM T   *SKILL SURVEY*   Sex: M ____ F ____
                                                Age: _____

There are several skills people need to make use of almost every day in order to get along with other people and feel good about themselves. These skills are important both in and out of the hospital. We would like to know which skills you feel you are good at and which skills you feel you are not good at.

Below you will find a list of skills. Read each skill carefully and then put a circle around the number which describes best how good you are at using the skill.

Circle 1, if you are *never* good at it.
Circle 2, if you are *seldom* good at it.
Circle 3, if you are *sometimes* good at it.
Circle 4, if you are *often* good at it.
Circle 5, if you are *always* good at it.

Try to rate yourself for every skill. If you do not understand a word or are unsure about what a skill description means, please ask the person who gave you this survey. There are no right or wrong answers, we are only interested in your feelings about your skills. Please do not skip any items. Thank you for your cooperation.

SKILLS

1. *Starting a Conversation:* Talking to someone about light topics and then leading into more serious topics.   1 2 3 4 5

2. *Carrying on a Conversation:* Opening the main topic, elaborating on it, and responding to the reactions of the person you are talking to.   1 2 3 4 5

3. *Ending a Conversation:* Letting the other person know that you have been paying attention, and then skillfully closing the conversation appropriately.   1 2 3 4 5

4. *Listening:* Paying attention to people, trying to understand them, and letting them know you are trying.   1 2 3 4 5

5. *Expressing a Compliment:* Telling someone that you like something about him or about his actions.   1 2 3 4 5

6. *Expressing Appreciation:* Letting another person know that you are grateful for something which he has done for you.   1 2 3 4 5

7. *Expressing Encouragement:* Telling someone that he should try to do something which he is not sure that he can do.   1 2 3 4 5

8. *Asking for Help:* Requesting that someone who is qualified help you in handling a difficult situation which you have not been able to manage by yourself.   1 2 3 4 5

9. *Giving Instructions:* Clearly explaining to someone how you would like a specific task done.   1 2 3 4 5

10. *Expressing Affection:* Letting someone know that you care about him or her.   1 2 3 4 5

11. *Expressing a Complaint:* Telling someone that he is responsible for creating a particular problem for you and attempting to find a solution for the problem.   1 2 3 4 5

12. *Persuading Others:* Attempting to convince another person that your ideas are better and will be more useful than his.   1 2 3 4 5

13. *Expressing Anger:* Presenting your angry feelings in a direct and honest manner.   1 2 3 4 5

14. *Responding to Praise:* Letting a person know that you are pleased with his praise and that you appreciate it.   1 2 3 4 5

15. *Responding to the Feelings of Others:* Trying to understand what the other person is feeling and communicating your understanding to him.   1 2 3 4 5

16. *Apologizing:* Telling someone sincerely that you are sorry for something you have done to cause him discomfort.   1 2 3 4 5

17. *Following Instructions:* Carrying out directions in a competent manner and giving your reactions.   1 2 3 4 5

18. *Responding to Persuasion:* Carefully considering another person's ideas, weighing them against your own, and then deciding which course of action will be best for you in the long run.   1 2 3 4 5

19. *Responding to Failure:* Figuring out what went wrong and what you can do about it so that you can be more successful in the future.   1 2 3 4 5

20. *Responding to Contradictory Messages:* Recognizing and dealing with the confusion that results when a person tells you one thing but says or does things which indicate that he means something else.   1 2 3 4 5

21. *Responding to a Complaint:* Dealing fairly with another person's dissatisfaction with a situation attributed to you.   1 2 3 4 5

22. *Responding to Anger:* Trying to understand another person's anger and letting him know that you are trying.   1 2 3 4 5

23. *Setting a Goal:* Deciding on what you want to accomplish and judging whether your plan is realistic.   1 2 3 4 5

24. *Gathering Information:* Deciding what specific information you need and asking the appropriate people for that information.   1 2 3 4 5

25. *Concentrating on a Task:* Making those preparations that will enable you to get a job done efficiently.   1 2 3 4 5

26. *Evaluating Your Abilities:* Examining your accomplishments fairly and honestly in order to decide how competent you are in a particular skill.   1 2 3 4 5

27. *Preparing for a Stressful Conversation:* Planning ahead of time to present your point of view in a conversation which may be difficult.   1 2 3 4 5

28. *Setting Problem Priorities:* Deciding which of several problems is most urgent and should be worked on first.   1 2 3 4 5

29. *Decision Making:* Deciding on a realistic course of action which you believe will be in your best interest.   1 2 3 4 5

30. *Identifying and Labeling Your Emotions:* Recognizing which emotion you are feeling.   1 2 3 4 5

31. *Determining Responsibility:* Finding out whether your actions or the actions of others have caused an event to occur.   1 2 3 4 5

32. *Making Requests:* Asking the appropriate person for what you need or want.   1 2 3 4 5

33. *Relaxation:* Learning to calm down and relax when you are tense.   1 2 3 4 5

34. *Self-control:* Controlling your temper before things get out of hand.   1 2 3 4 5

35. *Negotiation:* Arriving at an agreement which is satisfactory to you and to another person who has taken a different position.   1 2 3 4 5

36. *Helping Others:* Aiding other who are having difficulty handling a situation by themselves.   1 2 3 4 5

37. *Assertiveness:* Standing up for yourself by letting other people know what you want, how you feel, or what you think about something.   1 2 3 4 5